Rochelle Hudson

Suzan (Rochelle Hudson) is a sight for any convict's sore eyes in *Men Without Souls* (1940).

Rochelle Hudson
A Biography and Career Record

DAVID C. TUCKER

McFarland & Company, Inc., Publishers
Jefferson, North Carolina

ALSO BY DAVID C. TUCKER
AND FROM MCFARLAND

*S. Sylvan Simon, Moviemaker: Adventures
with Lucy, Red Skelton and Harry Cohn
in the Golden Age of Hollywood* (2021)

*Pine-Thomas Productions: A History
and Filmography* (2019)

Gale Storm: A Biography and Career Record (2018)

Martha Raye: Film and Television Clown (2016)

*Joan Davis: America's Queen of Film, Radio
and Television Comedy* (2014)

*Eve Arden: A Chronicle of All Film, Television,
Radio and Stage Performances* (2012)

*Lost Laughs of '50s and '60s Television: Thirty
Sitcoms That Faded Off Screen* (2010)

Shirley Booth: A Biography and Career Record (2008)

*The Women Who Made Television Funny:
Ten Stars of 1950s Sitcoms* (2007)

ISBN (print) 978-1-4766-8950-0
ISBN (ebook) 978-1-4766-4799-9

LIBRARY OF CONGRESS AND BRITISH LIBRARY
CATALOGUING DATA ARE AVAILABLE

Library of Congress Control Number 2023001706

© 2023 David C. Tucker. All rights reserved

*No part of this book may be reproduced or transmitted in any form
or by any means, electronic or mechanical, including photocopying
or recording, or by any information storage and retrieval system,
without permission in writing from the publisher.*

On the cover: Studio publicity photograph
of Rochelle Hudson (author's collection)

Printed in the United States of America

*McFarland & Company, Inc., Publishers
Box 611, Jefferson, North Carolina 28640*
www.mcfarlandpub.com

To the memory of my mother, Louise Curtis Tucker.

You are missed every day.

Acknowledgments

Once again, I sing the praises of Barbara Bogart Allen, a top-notch researcher who dug some real treasures out of the Rochelle Hudson Papers at the University of Wyoming's American Heritage Center. That institution's Vicki Glantz and Nora Plant made it completely painless to have several photographs from the collection duplicated for publication in this book.

Rochelle's mother, Leonora Mae Hudson, deserves much credit not only for enabling and supporting her daughter's Hollywood career, but also insuring that much of Rochelle's history was preserved. One of two Rochelle Hudson namesakes I met in researching this project was her great-niece, Rochelle Goddard McNear. I am tremendously grateful to her for sharing her first-hand memories of Miss Hudson, as well as of her mother and of her fourth husband Bob Mindell.

My thanks as well to Adriane Scheinost, whose parents were friendly with Rochelle in the last few years of her life, and to Rochelle Melchior Dupuie, whose father gave her a name commemorating one of his favorite stars, for sharing their recollections. Retired North Carolina police officer Luther Hathmore, a longtime collector of Golden Age of Hollywood memorabilia, kindly copied a few of his treasures for me, including a signed copy of Miss Hudson's real estate license.

On the home front, Ken McCullers is always a source of support. I am appreciative as well of my supportive colleagues James Robert Parish, Jacqueline T. Lynch, Hans Wollstein and Derek Sculthorpe. My nephew Timothy Sassone and his wife Kim also make my world fuller, and have my best wishes always.

Table of Contents

Acknowledgments	vi
Preface	1
Biography	
Rachael Elizabeth	5
Baby Star	11
"It Stinks"	17
The Men in Her Life	26
TV and Movie Mom	39
Final Act	47
Filmography	
Major Film Roles	51
Minor Film Roles and Short Films	183
Animation and Voice Work	185
Radio Performances	187
Television Performances	188
Guest Appearances	193
Chapter Notes	199
Bibliography	205
Index	207

Preface

With every passing year, it becomes more difficult to write a book about one of Hollywood's Golden Age stars. It is made even more so when the individual in question passed away more than 50 years ago, and has no known descendants. While Rochelle Hudson continued making films into the 1960s, her most important and enduring work belongs to the 1930s and 1940s, and those colleagues are no longer there to share stories.

Nonetheless, I took on the challenge of writing a book about the life and career of Miss Hudson (1916–1972), one of the most beautiful and charming stars of her day, largely because she deserved one. Researching and writing nine previous books, as well as a previous career as a professional librarian, sharpened my skills in the areas of archival research and genealogy, but it would have been nearly impossible to tell Miss Hudson's story to my satisfaction without the six boxes of material that make up the Rochelle Hudson Papers at the University of Wyoming's American Heritage Center.

Six boxes may not sound like much to represent a person's life of more than 50 years. But Mae Hudson, Rochelle's mother and biggest fan, saved an array of memorabilia that went a long way toward allowing this book to happen, and wisely entrusted it to skilled archivists who have kept careful watch over it for the past 45 years. "Papers" is a slight misnomer where Rochelle's boxes are concerned, as it is truly a multimedia collection. Along with records dating back to Rochelle's school report cards, and photographs covering much of her life from babyhood to middle age, Mrs. Hudson even saved her daughter's baby books, childhood dresses and shoes. Also preserved were several issues of Rochelle's 1930s fan club newsletters, which featured occasional notes to the members written by either Mae or Rochelle.

When writing a book about a Hollywood figure, I make every effort to see as much of that person's work as possible. With Rochelle Hudson, somewhat to my surprise, this task was more challenging than with previous subjects Gale Storm, Eve Arden and producer-director S. Sylvan Simon. I was able to see all of Miss Storm's films, and all but one of Martha Raye's. But several of Rochelle's films of the 1930s remained frustratingly out of reach. Though we may think of lost films being primarily those of the silent era, circumstances have resulted in the unavailability of even some of Fox and 20th Century–Fox's releases of less than a hundred years ago, often attributed in part to a fire that destroyed some of the studio's storage prints of its films.

Trained by her mother for a performing career from her childhood, Rochelle moved with her family from Oklahoma to California in the late 1920s. Within two years she had her first studio contract, though she wasn't yet a high school graduate. Named a WAMPAS Baby Star in 1931, she went on to work with some of the most important actors of her day, among them W.C. Fields, Henry Fonda, Fredric March, Claudette Colbert and Wallace Beery. Among her most noteworthy films are the original *Imitation of Life* (1934) and *Les Misérables* (1935), as well as three with Will Rogers. She was under contract during the 1930s to RKO, Fox and ultimately Columbia, the latter finding her useful primarily for playing leads in B movies.

Later, she freelanced, going where the work was, even making one surprisingly decent picture at the Poverty Row studio Producers Releasing Corporation (PRC). From that point forward, there were sometimes gaps in her career; she made no films between *Queen of Broadway* (1942) and *Bush Pilot* (1947). As her movie work slowed, she made a belated stage debut, touring with comedian Bert Lahr in his show *Burlesque*. Her role encompassed singing and dancing as well as her acting skills. She went on to play Natalie Wood's mother in one of the most iconic American films of the 1950s, *Rebel Without a Cause*. She also made occasional television guest appearances, and was the female lead in the situation comedy series *That's My Boy* (CBS, 1954–55).

By the 1960s, she was telling interviewers that while she still enjoyed working as an actress occasionally, as when she supported Joan Crawford in *Strait-Jacket* (1964), she neither needed to do so as a source of income, nor felt unfulfilled without a script in her hand. In 1967, a brief engagement in a bottom-of-the-barrel horror film brought her performing career to a close shortly after the age of 50. Away from Hollywood, she had skills that went beyond acting, singing and dancing: At various times in her life, she worked in public relations and real estate, and helped run a cattle ranch she owned. During World War II, while married to first husband Hal Thompson, she even engaged in a bit of espionage on behalf of the U.S. government.

Rochelle not only played female leads in numerous films, but was the object of desire for many men away from the camera as well. Her marital track record does not represent the ideal to which many aspire. She was married four times and divorced four times, the last time shortly before her death in 1972. None of her marriages produced children, and none lasted as long as ten years. It may or may not be significant that, of all the material her mother preserved for archival researchers, the Hudson Papers have little to say about the four men she married.

Newspaper and magazine interviews with stars from the Golden Age often have to be taken with a grain of salt, and I have endeavored to do so here, being selective in what I chose to excerpt. Like any other attractive young actress being given the benefit of a studio publicity buildup, she was occasionally reported to be romantically involved with men who were really no more than colleagues, friends or acquaintances. (Had she enjoyed all the dates attributed to her in print, it's hard to imagine she could have found the time to star in as many films as she did.)

Despite becoming a movie star while still in her teens, and having a sweetly demure face that often saw her cast as innocent young women, Rochelle's true personality could not be obscured by fan magazine fluff. She often spoke her mind freely, even when it came to journalists. She horrified her Fox bosses in 1935, when asked her impressions of Claremore, Oklahoma, the town where publicists falsely reported she was born. She replied that her primary recollection was that it smelled bad, a comment that brought her publicity tour to a screeching halt. A few years later, when Fox began casting her in second-tier, action-oriented films that displeased her, she complained about them openly, which may have been a factor in her contract being dropped when it expired in 1938. One journalist said admiringly of her, "When she opens her mouth, you're confronted with honesty—in healthy doses. There's no shyness or offensive false modesty."[1]

Another factor that may have limited her climb to stardom was her seeming unwillingness to play games with lecherous studio bosses. She spent time as a contract player at two studios whose chief executives were known to expect favors of actresses in their employ. One of her leading men recalled that she rebuffed entreaties to meet with the studio head after hours. That decision to maintain her integrity may have come at a price, where career advancement was concerned. Undaunted, Rochelle starred in the B movies she was handed, and began making plans for her life beyond Hollywood.

A truly beautiful woman in her young adulthood, she maintained her looks and trim figure into middle age. One magazine writer, attempting to convey her appeal, wrote, "Rochelle is small. Her dark hair sweeps back from a wide, intelligent forehead. Her face is round and her features regular. She photographs well from almost any angle. Her eyes are gray [others said blue], which in measure explains them. They contribute a great deal to her smile—and what a smile! ... Rochelle's smile has a happiness complex—and it is contagious."[2]

More than a pretty ingénue, Rochelle demonstrated early in her career that she could play characters with sharper edges. The women she enacted in *Such Women Are Dangerous* (1934) and *Queen of Broadway* (1942) have agendas of their own, and aren't inclined to let men dissuade them. Sometimes her characters strayed over to the wrong side of the law—and usually paid for it.

On the fiftieth anniversary of her passing, Rochelle Hudson has not been forgotten. This book will shine a bit more light on her achievements. Even during her lifetime, however, there was a sense that she had been underappreciated. By the mid-1940s, when her career was past its peak, columnist Ed Sullivan (June 25, 1944) lamented, "Rochelle Hudson should have won a much huger success. She had everything." Indeed she did.

Biography

Rachael Elizabeth

Rochelle Hudson's career as a performer was in the planning stages even before she was born. She was born Rachael Elizabeth Hudson on March 16, 1916, in Oklahoma City, Oklahoma, at 1212 N.W. 32nd Street, the only child of Ollie Lee Hudson (1872–1971) and Leonora Mae Goddard (1882–1976). Ollie Lee grew up on a farm in Missouri, son of James and Nancy Hudson. He had an older sister, Annie, an older brother, James, and a younger sister, Elizabeth. Hailing from Nortonville, Kansas, Leonora Mae Goddard was born April 21, 1882, to the former Rachel Elizabeth Coppinger (1846–1897) and her husband, George Newton Goddard (1841–1923). Rachel, a Missouri native, died in 1897, when Leonora was a teenager. The following year, George took a second wife, Eva. He did so after breaking his engagement to schoolteacher Louie Conkey, which cost him $6000 when she successfully filed a lawsuit against him for breach of promise.

Rochelle's parents were married on January 12, 1910. "Ollie L. Hudson and Miss Lenora [*sic*] M. Goddard were married at 4:30 p.m. yesterday at the residence of J.J. Cunningham at No. 710 West Maine Street by Rev. Simmons," read one account. "The ceremony was simple and only intimate friends were present. The happy couple left immediately for Oklahoma City where they will make their home."[1]

Initially, the newlyweds were boarders at a home on West Fourth Street, where he told a census taker he was employed in the clothing industry. Much later, mention was made of Mr. Hudson's job at "the Overstreet Bros. store in Shawnee, for which mercantile company ... O.L. Hudson [Rochelle's father] worked."[2]

A few years later, he went to work for the Labor Department, where he built a solid career helping other men finding gainful employment. In the summer of 1916, shortly after he became a father, an article appearing in multiple Oklahoma newspapers reported, "The free employment branch of the state department of labor is to be enlarged with the opening of a department devoted exclusively to professional and clerical workers. The office will be opened and will be in charge of O.L. Hudson, at present statistician for the department of labor."[3] Hudson set about organizing his new department, devising forms to gather information from applicants so that "employers who obtain their stenographers, bookkeepers and other clerical help through the state free employment bureau will have a better record of their qualifications, habits, tastes and experience than if they secured them in the usual way."[4] He served in that capacity into the 1920s.

Arriving six years into their marriage, Rachael (as she was christened) would be their only child. She was named after her maternal grandmother, Rachel Elizabeth Coppinger Goddard, though she also had an Aunt Elizabeth on her father's side of the family. She was a later-in-life child for her father, a few weeks short of his 43rd birthday, and to a lesser extent for her mother, who was soon due to turn 33. That summer, Mrs. Hudson took her new baby to Kansas City, where they visited her sisters.

Rochelle maintained close contact with her mother her entire life. Leonora said that her own strict religious parents wouldn't allow her to develop her artistic skills. Because she came of a large family (13 children), Mae (as she was usually called) felt that not enough attention had been paid to helping her make plans for her adult life. She settled into the life of a wife and mother, but she hadn't forgotten her aspirations. When her daughter came along, Mae seized upon the opportunity to find a new outlet for her thwarted dreams.

"These wasted talents made me very determined that when my own child came to me, to give her something no one could ever take away from her," Mae wrote some years later. "[I] just felt it right to give the child every advantage and develop every talent.... Each talent developed so beautifully that it was hard to choose any particular one to concentrate on so the work grew and required strict discipline and timing to be able to get it all in and still preserve the little body and not overdo."[5]

Her daughter began taking part in recitals at the age of four. "She took lessons three times a week as she, and her mother, dreamed of the day when her dancing would bowl audiences out of their seats," wrote one

Baby Rachael, later to become Rochelle, greets the world (University of Wyoming, American Heritage Center, Rochelle Hudson Papers, Box 4).

scribe.[6] On this subject, Rochelle's parents were not in accord. "Her father objected to this early training so it was very necessary to prove I was right," Mae noted.[7]

Along with performance training, Mae also sought to train her daughter in proper behavior and manners. At the age of three, Mae found an overturned bottle of ink. The little girl denied having played with it, so was spanked and punished with work. Finally she gave in and admitted what she had done. "I promised her then that I would never punish her no matter how bad the crime if she would tell me the truth. And I can truthfully say after seventeen years I have kept that promise." Mae recalled her as "a happy laughing baby." Of her disciplinary methods, Mae wrote, "I had seen too many children raised with 'sparing the rod.' I firmly believe that ones [sic] whole life can be controled [sic] by the very early training as Rochelle is still [at 20] so impressed by the lessons she learned before she was six years old that she remembers them and finds them governing her life today."[8]

Ollie Lee Hudson was not the only one worried that too much pressure was being put on his daughter at a tender age. Some years later, a studio publicist wrote, "The family doctor predicted a nervous breakdown for Rochelle Hudson before she would be 6 years old. That was because the blue-eyed Oklahoma beauty … was such a precocious youngster. Despite the physician's dire foreboding, Miss Hudson has never suffered the breakdown and remains among the healthiest of the Hollywood stars."[9]

As the Roaring Twenties got underway, Mr. and Mrs. Hudson were living with their daughter on West 32nd Street in Oklahoma City. Mr. Hudson's government job left them sufficiently well-fixed to have household help. The family employed "a devoted faithful little Negro girl [named Fairy Kirkland] in Oklahoma City when Rochelle was a tot." Years later, Mae would describe to a reporter "days when Rochelle was naughty at the table and her mother would send her out to

Young Miss Hudson, a beauty from an early age (University of Wyoming, American Heritage Center, Rochelle Hudson Papers, Box 4).

the kitchen to have her dinner with Fairy. Mae says she can still hear the giggles of delight during those kitchen dinners. She was certain that many times Rochelle forgot her table manners just so she could go to the kitchen with her friend."[10]

The little girl also began her schooling, attending Jefferson Grade School and then Harding Junior High School. Report cards from fourth and fifth grade showed her to be an average student, earning mostly As and Bs with an occasional C. Her conduct was usually rated A; her effort, sometimes a notch lower at B.

Through his work with the Labor Department, O.L. Hudson wanted to help people find the work they needed to survive and prosper, but he understood that their need left them vulnerable to being exploited by unscrupulous employers. At that time, it was not uncommon for farm laborers to be expected to work two daily eight-hour shifts. A reporter explained, "Hudson urges the men he sends out to insist on an agreement as to how many hours constitute a day before they begin work."[11]

In the fall of 1921, O.L. Hudson gave a newspaper interview in which he came out strongly in support of a city bond referendum about to go before voters, saying it would be "the salvation of Oklahoma City." In particular, he welcomed the anticipated help it would give citizens who were unemployed. He stated,

> There are approximately 3,000 people out of employment here now. The situation is somewhat relieved by the call for cotton pickers in some parts of the state. But when the harvest is over, all these men come back, and winter is on, the situation will be worse. The employment of thousands of men in the big civic improvement program would give impetus to all kinds of business activity, and I feel sure, would go far toward bringing a return to prosperity.... It would enable hundreds of families to get through what probably will be a hard winter.[12]

Meanwhile, little Rachael began to show the results of her dance training, appearing in local recitals and live entertainment venues:

> "Mrs. Gertrude Cox Simms has completed the program for her dance festival to be presented ... Saturday evening.... Those taking part will include.... Rachael Hudson...."[13]
>
> "The opening autumn dance festival given by pupils of Mrs. Gertrude Cox Simms was an enjoyable affair.... Misses Rachael Elizabeth Hudson, Octavia Overby, and Zoda Bentley presented the French Babies dance which was beautiful."[14]
>
> "The feature of the evening was the solo dance by little Rachael Elizabeth Hudson."[15]

As early as 1924, the Hudson family made occasional trips to the West Coast. That fall, they returned from a visit that was recounted in the local newspaper: "The trip used 71 gallons of gasoline and 21 quarts of oil." Mr. Hudson said they were "back home and glad."[16] Little Rachael was by then studying piano, with teacher Josephine Wissman advertising in local newspapers that she offered "private and class instruction" in the "Dunning System of Improved Music Study for Beginners." In the summer of 1924, the child took center stage in "a musical recital to be given Friday night at the home of Mr. and Mrs. O.L. Hudson ... by their little daughter Miss Rachel Hudson who is a talented reader and dancer."[17]

After Rochelle Hudson began to achieve Hollywood success, an Oklahoma feature writer looked back on her childhood and remarked, "It cannot have been an easy task for Rochelle. Hours of running the scales of a piano; more hours of doing one-two-three-four over polished floors; hours of learning pitch, diction, expression, dramatics; and then hours of recitals."[18] She also studied French and became a good swimmer. But when the subject was raised by a reporter, Rochelle never copped to any feelings of resentment; she said firmly that she had loved it.

Little Rachael wasn't the only family member pursuing a show business career. Mae's younger brother Homer Clinton Goddard (1889–1961) found his lifelong calling when he became a clown with the Ringling Brothers Circus. He spent nearly 30 years in that line of work, before his retirement in 1954. According to his granddaughter Rochelle McNear, Goddard can be seen clowning and juggling in the Academy Award–winning 1952 film *The Greatest Show on Earth*.

Five-year-old Rachael Elizabeth Hudson, not yet known as Rochelle, played Cupid in an Oklahoma City pageant.

In 1927, Rochelle's father narrowly escaped death when he was a passenger in a car that became trapped in a flood. Driver W.C. Ballard of Oklahoma City was passing through New Mexico, "on [the] way to California with O.L. Hudson, head of the Federal-State labor bureau, when their car was caught in an onrush of water and carried downstream. Hudson managed to save himself." Ballard, not so fortunate, drowned.[19]

Though it was usually assumed that the family's ultimate relocation to the West Coast arose from Mae's desire to further her daughter's career, Rochelle, in one interview, gave a different explanation. "When I was eleven, my father had a nervous breakdown and we came to California for his health. Like most Middle-Westerners, he had a farm 'hang-over,' so we settled on a ranch in the San Fernando Valley, across the hills from Hollywood. I went to public school in Van Nuys for a couple of years."[20] Given that there was a significant stigma attached to any hint of mental illness in that era, this was another example of Rochelle's tendency to speak the truth, which would become increasingly evident during her Hollywood years.

Between 1928 and 1930, the soon-to-be Rochelle continued her education at Van Nuys High School. Alongside traditional academic studies, she took advantage of

This family snapshot from 1953 shows Mae alongside her brother Homer Clinton Goddard, who enjoyed a lengthy career with the Ringling Brothers circus (courtesy Rochelle E. McNear).

classes that might further her career goals. Her name underwent a slight modification when Rachael gave way to "Rachelle," as she was called on her school documents and report cards. In high school, she proved to be a good if not outstanding student. For the semester ending June 29, 1928, she earned an A in her studies of music, English and physical education. For cooking, she received a B. Her weakest subject appeared to be history, in which she was given a C. The following year, she received As in drama and algebra, along with Bs in English, Spanish and beginning voice.

While working toward a high school diploma, Rachelle did not neglect any opportunities to perform, or undergo further training. For a time, she studied dance with Ernest Belcher, father of Marge Champion. In 1927, a social note in the Van Nuys newspaper stated, "Members of the Junior Auxiliary of the Van Nuys Womans [sic] Club were entertained with a charming program.... The French folk play, *The Three Wishes*, given by Miss Rachelle Hudson, was very much appreciated. Her second number, an impersonation of an Italian speaking broken English, amply proved her versatility. Miss Hudson is a pupil of Mrs. Hazel Penny."[21] Another such item noted that she appeared at an event sponsored by the Ladies Aid Society of Cahuenga, "charming all with her exquisite toe dancing, poise and stage presence."[22]

Though the Van Nuys location was chosen to help improve her father's health, he did not immediately give up his work in Oklahoma. As late as the spring of 1929, he was interviewed for an article there, describing his work as manager of the federal-state employment bureau: "Hudson daily sits at a small file desk that represents the 'hub' of the city's unemployed. Along a partition are gathered daily hundreds of men who overflow out to the sidewalk." Hudson told a young man who had been offered a chance to work as a baker's helper, "Go out with the resolve to make good, son. It's a good trade and just make up your mind to stay with it. Here's your chance." Commenting on his work, O.L. said, "I often talk to these boys and advise them to go take a bath and get cleaned up and then come back. After they rest, they usually can win the job I give them."[23] Later that year, the appointment of his replacement was announced: John R. McCarty, superintendent of the federal-state employment service. According to one newspaper, O.L. Hudson then went back to California.[24]

The Hudsons returned to Oklahoma City in the summer of 1929, during Rochelle's school vacation: "Mrs. Luther H. Patton entertained with an informal afternoon honoring Miss Rachel [sic] Elizabeth Hudson. Miss Hudson is the daughter of Mr. and Mrs. O.L. Hudson of Los Angeles, formerly of Oklahoma City, who have been spending the summer here. The Hudsons will leave Friday for California and the party was given to bid goodby [sic] to the little guest."[25] But as the 1920s wound down, the minds of Mae Hudson and her daughter were set firmly on the West Coast. It was time for Rochelle, just entering her teens, to find a foothold in the entertainment industry.

Baby Star

"We moved out to Hollywood in 1930," Mae later stated (their time in Van Nuys notwithstanding). "I did not go out there to commercialize Rochelle. Her success came a little sooner than I expected. Since she was a baby I have steered her and given her music and dancing lessons. I wanted to bring out in her the things I missed." Still smarting at her own lost chances, Mrs. Hudson added, "I know I was prettier than she is when I was her age. All my friends say so."[26]

In April 1930, a census taker found the Hudsons living on Dickens Street in Los Angeles, where they reportedly owned a house valued at $12,500 (equivalent to about $200,000 in modern terms). Mr. Hudson was then 56, his wife 45. He reported that he still performed work in the federal and state employment field. No job was listed for Rochelle (her legal name Rachael was recorded on the document), recently turned 14. But in fact, she had just a few weeks earlier taken a major step forward in attaining her career goals.

A friend of Mae's, Jessie Lee, who worked at the Fox studios, suggested that Rochelle be tested and helped make the arrangements. The focus of the test was intended to be Rochelle's lovely singing voice, but the friend noted, "Her voice records perfectly, but what is more, she photographs beautifully."[27] Fox executives were sufficiently impressed to offer a beginner's film contract, which was signed on

March 27, 1930. Her starting pay would be $75 a week, with her salary to increase to $100 if her option was picked up after six months. Further step increases were built in should she have a lengthy stay. Because she was still a minor, both parents affixed their signatures to the paperwork.

The contract included most of the Fox Film Corporation's standard clauses. She was to be given 15 days' notice each time her option came up. There was a typical "moral turpitude" clause, stipulating that she could not act in such a way as to offend public sensibilities, as well as one saying she could be dismissed in the case of a facial or other physical injury that altered her appearance. Fox would have the right to loan her out for assignments at other studios. She would continue her education at the studio school.

In what had become a commonplace Hollywood practice, Rochelle was signed in part to send a message to one of the studio's current stars. Per author Richard Lamparski, "At the time production head Winfield Sheehan was squabbling with Janet Gaynor and Rochelle was hired as a threat to the star."[28] As fate would have it, Rochelle later inherited one of Miss Gaynor's roles, thanks to the star's illness.

Mae lost no time alerting the media as to her daughter's good fortune. The *Van Nuys News* reported, "Rachelle Hudson, daughter of Mr. and Mrs. O.L. Hudson of Cahuenga Park, and former Van Nuys high school student, has been awarded a five year contract with Fox Productions, and for the past three months has been at the studios in Hollywood where juvenile classes in dancing and voice culture are conducted to prepare the young people for talking pictures." The article went on to say, "Gaining wide popularity in Valley musical and dance circles through her distinctive terpsichorean presentations in local stage renditions Miss Hudson's reputation as a stellar artist has spread rapidly, and predictions for her theatrical career are rapidly being realized."[29]

Rochelle seemed to suddenly be on the fast track to success, but the reality was a bit different. One scribe noted, "For the six months that she was under contract she did nothing but go to school and take various lessons."[30] Rochelle later recalled, "That first year at Fox, they didn't do one darn thing with me except pay me to attend the studio school. I never even saw a camera. As a matter of fact I couldn't have directed a soul to any office on the lot because I'd never been to any of them myself. No one seemed to know I was around except the cashier who handed me my check every week, and I don't think he cared particularly."[31]

Little wonder that, within a few months, her option was in danger of being dropped. Director Frank Borzage (1894–1962) gave her a screen test, in hopes of interesting Fox bigwigs in her potential. The test, as she later admitted, "failed to startle the executives and my contract was allowed to lapse. However, Frank took it to [RKO] Radio and they signed me immediately. I was so naïve I didn't even know what Radio was, much less where their studio was!"[32]

The advent of sound pictures had led many studio executives to pursue actors with stage experience, but her new studio had other criteria. As the *Los Angeles Times* reported,

R.-K.-O. and William LeBaron are keeping right along with their policy of engaging fresh and unknown talent, believing that such talent is most easily molded to screen requirements.... Miss Hudson is but 17 years of age [sic]—too young for the stage in Oklahoma, where minors are not permitted to act on the stage for money until they are 18. ...She has been playing small bits and parts, but yesterday was accepted by R.-K.-O. officials as having the qualifications of a feature player, and as such received a long-term contract.[33]

The studio did not immediately announce a first assignment for its new player.

One doubting Thomas, apparently unaware of Rochelle's brief stint at Fox, wrote in *Motion Picture News* (November 14, 1930), "Radio is up to its old tricks of signing unknown girls with no professional experience. Rochelle Hudson is the latest 'discovery' with William LeBaron listed as 'discoverer.' The youngster is 17 [sic] and hails from Oklahoma. Only previous experience is in amateur shows." Rochelle's new duties didn't prevent her from continuing to work toward a high school diploma, as she had done at Fox: "A high school with only one pupil is now functioning on the RKO lot, where Rochelle Hudson ... is continuing her education. She's only 17 [sic], which is within the legal school age."[34]

Like many Golden Age actresses (and some actors), Rochelle's age was falsified by studio publicists. Unlike the vast majority of them, however, she was said

Rochelle (left) gathered contributions to a fund for disabled veterans from her colleagues on the RKO lot, including director Melville Brown.

to be older than she actually was. RKO didn't think that audiences would be comfortable with a leading lady who was 14, so her official birthdate was reported to be 1914 rather than 1916. Her hometown newspaper, in 1934, knew better: "Rochelle tells everybody she is 20, a two-year overstatement.... Her father, O.L. Hudson, used to be head of the federal employment agency here."[35]

At first it seemed that her experience at RKO was likely to be another disappointment. She posed for plenty of publicity photos showing off her face and legs. But, as she later complained good-naturedly, "I should have been on the publicity payroll. Occasionally I got some acting to do!"[36]

Rochelle soon began getting camera experience, playing bit parts in *The Public Defender* and *Laugh and Get Rich* (both 1931). Before the year was out, she was judged ready to take on supporting roles. Rochelle had essayed the minor role of Joan in *Laugh and Get Rich*, a vehicle for Edna May Oliver; in the fall of 1931, moviegoers saw Rochelle in a larger role as Oliver's daughter in *Fanny Foley Herself*.

Her studio bosses began to recognize her potential. *Variety* proclaimed, "At no time since pictures became big business have there been so many young players groomed for stardom as at present," and noted that the majority were female. After listing the young hopefuls of other studios, the article added, "[RKO] Radio is pushing Rochelle Hudson, Arline Judge, Roberta Gale, Lita Chevret, Eric Linden, John Darrow, Morgan Galloway, Jill Esmond and Laurence Olivier."[37] It was the first time Rochelle's name appeared in the pages of the show business bible. A few weeks later, *Are These Our Children* cast her as the beautiful, loyal girlfriend of leading man Eric Linden. Dramatically, the role was no stretch—she would play many virtuous ingénues during this period—but she did get enough footage to catch the attention of audiences.

She won a break in 1931 when she was named one of that year's 13 WAMPAS Baby Stars. The organization, per a fan magazine, "presented its thirteen Baby Stars of 1931 to a radio audience of 50,000,000 over an 82-station radio broadcast and to an audience of 115,000 at the Olympic stadium."[38] The stadium event presented the actresses on a "float ... equipped with a great mechanical stork which reached its neck into a little adobe house on the float, lifting out one by one of the thirteen stars." After the event, "the homegoing traffic jam was so terrific that many actresses and actors did not get home until 3 and 4 o'clock in the morning and no work could be done at any of the studios that day."[39]

A few months later, WAMPAS members and their wives threw a Christmas-themed party for the starlets: "Three of the starlets—Anita Louise, Barbara Weeks and Rochelle Hudson—found notices in their stockings from their respective studios stating that their contract options had been exercised and that nice salary raises would be theirs as Christmas presents."[40]

Selection as a WAMPAS baby star in no way guaranteed an easy path to stardom. Certainly Joan Crawford, Joan Blondell, and many others went to great success. By 1938, one article noted that, of 145 actresses chosen during the contest's history, 40 were still active on movie screens. The 1931 group was lauded as having "presented films with a group of permanent headliners [who had] reached stardom,"[41] Rochelle among them. Ironically, by the time that article appeared, her career prospects were becoming less certain.

But in 1932, she was on her way upward, and began to be featured in newspaper and magazine profiles. As one article put it,

> A little over a year ago Rochelle persuaded her mother to give her a trip to Hollywood. A girl with those powers of persuasion was bound to get on and it was not long before she persuaded someone at Fox to give her a screen test. The result of that test persuaded the chiefs of Radio Pictures to give her a screen contract, and two pictures persuaded the Wampas that their list would be hopelessly inadequate without the name Rochelle Hudson. Rochelle, who is one of filmland's prettiest girls, still lives with her mother but ... cannot persuade her to relax the home by-laws regarding those Hollywood parties... [T]hough Rochelle may be a big star in the studio, she must be home by midnight.[42]

After being featured in *Are These Our Children*, she was handed the role of Western star Tom Keene's leading lady in the low-budget drama *Beyond the Rockies* (1932). If not a memorable role, it was good solid experience for an actress who was still somewhat green.

Studios always wanted to keep their contract actors earning their weekly paychecks, so for Hudson, the walk-on parts didn't end right away. She did an amusing minor role in *Penguin Pool Murder* (1932), playing a lackluster telephone operator in a scene with Edna May Oliver. Describing her career ambitions in 1932, Hudson said, "I'm no Katharine Cornell. I know that. But I love to act. I don't want to be starred. There is too much responsibility connected to it. I want to do character after character and no two alike."[43]

While Mae Hudson was thrilled to see her daughter's acting career progressing, it contributed to a rift between Rochelle's parents. At some point in the early 1930s, Mr. and Mrs. Hudson went their separate ways (with Mae staying at her daughter's side) and ultimately divorced. By 1934, Rochelle was telling a Hollywood columnist, "My father has an eight thousand acre ranch in Kansas, and he just found gold on it, so I'm going back home to help him dig."[44] Several years later, the U.S. census found 68-year-old Ollie living with his nephew in Kansas. He classed himself as widowed, and perhaps that's how he felt. He stated that he worked as a tool dresser, but had no income.

Though still not of legal age, Rochelle found time for a social life after hours, under Mae's cautious eye, with a curfew strictly in place. Columnists paired her, truthfully or not, with a few men, as when syndicated columnist Harrison Carroll (February 25, 1932) wrote, "Pretty Rochelle Hudson is dividing her time these days between John Arledge and young Von Brecht, of the candy Von Brechts."

Though Rochelle got experience and steady paychecks at RKO, her stint there didn't lead to the kind of opportunities a young leading lady needed. In addition, though she remained on the studio payroll, the U.S. economy was hurting, and more than once she was obliged to accept a lower rate of pay than she had originally been promised. As early as June 1931, she agreed in writing to earning $75 per week rather than $100; in November, she was given a $25 weekly raise, but she was still one step behind. In May 1932, RKO picked up her option for six more months, raising her pay to $150 per week.

On loan-out, she starred as a lady Tarzan in a low-budget jungle adventure, *The Savage Girl*. She was dispatched to Paramount in late 1932 to play a featured role in *She Done Him Wrong*, starring Mae West. The following year, she made two films for the Poverty Row studio Chesterfield. "I just feel like taking up stenography or something," she complained of her typical assignments. "I want to play parts that will stir people. Ever since I've been a kid, I've been standing in front of my mirror at home, playing Juliet and Camille."[45]

A few years later, she ruefully recalled some of the hard lessons she learned during her leaner days. "When I signed my first contract, I immediately started getting all sorts of publicity.... By the end of the year I had begun to believe what I read about myself in the papers.... That's when I stumbled—went for nearly a year without working. It was a good lesson for me. It made me realize that I wasn't so important."[46] That publicity, as she acknowledged, had been misleading. "My first advice would be to steel yourself against your press agent," she said. "Once you start believing your press agent, whose job it is to boost you to the skies, you're sunk. Take all flattery and bowing and scraping with a shaker full of salt.... Cultivate friends outside the business who will keep you on your toes with fresh viewpoints."[47]

At times, her private life provided more excitement than her soundstage stints. During that fallow period, multiple newspapers reported that Rochelle had narrowly avoided being involved in a small plane crash near Yuma, Arizona: "When the oil pump of his airplane broke, [pilot John] Nagel turned off the motor and glided 10 miles, landing safely at the Yuma airport." Her reaction, according to the published account: "It was the thrill of a lifetime."[48]

Finally, after a discouraging lull that lasted nearly a year, Rochelle signed for the second time with the Fox Film Corporation. Her contract, finalized August 7, 1933, stipulated that her Fox assignments would begin once she had completed the second picture for Chesterfield, *Walls of Gold*. Her starting salary would be $125 a week. Provided the studio continued to pick up her options, she would receive pay increases every six months. If she worked out the entire life of the contract, she could rise to a weekly salary of $800.

One newspaperman wrote of the move to Fox, "Rochelle Hudson ... was known as Hollywood's 'Queen of Stills. She was under contract to RKO nearly three years, and scarcely had a bit to play. She got plenty of publicity, though, because her face and figure were constantly being photographed. The studio finally let her contract lapse, and she stepped right over to Fox and stardom."[49] Columnist Sidney Skolsky (November 9, 1933) agreed that posing for multitudes of stills, and staying in the public eye, had actually worked to Rochelle's benefit: "Every time the studio needs a dame to sit on a rocket and pose for a Fourth of July picture for a fan magazine they summon her.... She posed for every kind of a picture imaginable while she was on the Radio pictures payroll. This saved her job for her." With her signature on a new Fox contract, he said, "Now she is really on her way to becoming a name in pictures."

Her opportunity came more quickly than it otherwise might have when the illness of another actress interrupted the making of *Doctor Bull,* starring Will Rogers: "The director was ahead of schedule when a terrible calamity occurred. Boots Mallory, who was playing the ingénue lead, was taken ill with a serious case of the flu. After holding up the company for four days, necessarily of course, Boots returned to work, but the rushes proved that she obviously was not strong enough to do justice to the role."[50] With no time to be lost, executives didn't try to borrow an actress from another studio; instead they scanned the contract list and handed the role to Rochelle. She acquitted herself well enough that her option was picked up and she was given a raise. With the studio envisioning additional pictures teaming Rogers and Hudson, publicists built up a largely phony account that called her a native of his home town, which she wasn't, and a protégée of his. Though they got along well, his role in promoting her career was exaggerated.

She did like Rogers, though she sometimes found his penchant for ad-libbing disconcerting. Audiences loved the homespun homilies he dispensed in character, but she recalled "listening for cues that never came... [He] had me adlibbing to myself in my sleep long before my first picture with Bill was finished."[51]

On loan-out to First National, she played a minor role in a memorable film, William Wellman's *Wild Boys of the Road.* Warners' studio teacher, Lois Horne, later recalled Rochelle as "one of the most serious, moody girls who ever came to her."[52]

Back with Rogers for a second time in *Mr. Skitch,* she was cast this time as his teenage daughter. For those who might envy her life of glamor, she later told a few truths: "Remember when the Skitch family was traveling along the road in the car? Well, that was not made on location; it was on a stage, and it took about six weeks to make it. The dust storms we encountered were blown fresh on us daily, and was it filthy! And that dog in the picture; no dog ever had so many fleas."[53]

"It Stinks"

One year after signing with Fox, Rochelle was released by court decree from Mrs. Hudson's guardianship of her, as she had attained the age of 18 and was legally an adult. It was time for her to give up playing the loyal girlfriends of teenage characters and enact more adult roles. Still, she wasn't yet leaving ingénue roles behind altogether.

One observer opined that the implementation of the Production Code benefited Rochelle's career progress, as the ladies known for playing shadier characters found fewer such roles being written in the new effort to sanitize movies. Previously, she "went into a slump, pulling herself out only by the strongest perseverance during the last year. Now she's going strong again and fortunately for her she doesn't look the least bit worldly on the screen."[54]

She made a charming love interest for Stuart Erwin in a highly enjoyable comedy, *Bachelor Bait*, back on her old RKO stomping grounds. But the assignment didn't greatly impress her. "That's one of my pictures I'd just as soon forget," she said in 1964.[55] She said she was a longtime friend of George Stevens, who helmed *Bachelor Bait* (his one time directing her).

On a visit back home to Oklahoma in 1934, Rochelle was asked to advise other young women who wanted acting careers. She told aspiring actors to go to Hollywood and make the rounds of casting offices: "It's a long hard pull by that route, but if the applicant has any ability they'll soon recognize it."[56] At the same time, the ups and downs she had experienced had left her with a slightly jaded view of Hollywood. "I'm not foolish," she said. "I intend to make as much money as I can, and then quit and marry."[57]

In the meantime, it was full steam ahead. "Rochelle Hudson will continue on as a star with Fox," reported one journalist in 1934. "Her contract is being continued, and it is likely that she will appear in *The County Chairman* with Will Rogers."[58] A letter to the editor from a male fan in *Hollywood* (April 1934) attested, "I have just seen Will Rogers' *Mr. Skitch*. With the exception of Will, I think Rochelle Hudson displayed the best acting ability of the cast. Why don't producers build up this dark haired girl and make her a star? She is the prettiest brunette on the Fox lot."

"I don't know whether you would say I'm a star or not," she said in a fan magazine interview. "But what does it matter, after all, whose name is on the top? Starring doesn't mean a thing to me. I might be just as bad a star as I was good as an ingénue."[59]

Some of Rochelle's best opportunities during this period came away from her home lot Fox, as when Universal borrowed her to play Claudette Colbert's daughter in *Imitation of Life*. She acquitted herself well amidst a cast that also included Warren William and Louise Beavers. In a 1970 interview, she said, "They kept me sweet and innocent for years. When I finally convinced them I was no longer a teenager I was immediately cast as a chippy, which I remained until I quit."[60]

Columnist Louella O. Parsons wrote (December 22, 1934), "I prophesy that at the end of 1935 Rochelle Hudson will be a big name in the movies. Miss Hudson has been in several important pictures [and] surprised even those who always had faith in her ability with the excellence of her performance." In an August 24, 1935, column, Parsons added, "None of your younger players knows the value of patience in fighting for a picture career better than Rochelle Hudson. For several years the little Oklahoma gal was one of the many who posed only for studio stills…. Darryl Zanuck, who borrowed her for *Les Misérables* last season, evidently shares Winfield Sheenan's enthusiasm for the dark-eyed Hudson." In *Les Misérables*, her strong supporting turn opposite Fredric March added substantially to that film's appeal, a rare opportunity for Rochelle to play a costume role. If career advancement had to take priority over other aspects of her life for a while, Rochelle insisted she didn't mind. "You can't mix romance with hard work that is necessary for a young player to carve out a niche in the film world…. I have just about all I can do to build a career for myself, without wasting time listening to sweet nothings, which so often are just that."[61]

She received an unexpected opportunity in early 1935, when another actress' illness left a vacancy in the cast of a film then in production. One reporter noted, "Janet Gaynor collapsed on the set during the filming of *Way Down East*… The petite star had collided with Henry Fonda several days before her breakdown and spent a week in bed…. She returned apparently in good condition but suffered a relapse during a scene and was taken home where it was found that she had a concussion."[62] A skeptic, however, noted, "There are a lot of speculating meanies around who said that in reality she didn't even have a teensie-weensie headache," pointing out that she had departed for vacation after clearing out her dressing room.[63] Whatever the reason, Rochelle took over from Gaynor, the actress for whom she had been hired by Fox as a possible replacement five years earlier.

Rochelle received good notices for *Way Down East*, and suddenly it appeared that Fox executives valued her services more than they might previously had done. Said Louella O. Parsons (February 15, 1935), "Requests for Rochelle Hudson from all the studios are being frowned upon by the Fox Company. Rochelle, from now on,

Edward Norris (right) was Rochelle's leading man in *Show Them No Mercy!* (1935).

will be kept busy at Fox and with plans being made to build her into a star, why not? She certainly has served her apprenticeship and she is a delightful young actress." She gave a more than capable performance in *Show Them No Mercy!,* released in late 1935.

Just as things were looking bright, however, Rochelle's outspokenness created a tempest in a teapot. The young actress was asked while on a publicity tour what she recalled of Claremore, Oklahoma, the town that studio publicists had erroneously called her birthplace. As she later told it, "I said that my memory of [Claremore] was somewhat prejudiced by the odor of the mineral water there."[64] Reporters put it more succinctly—and bluntly: She had supposedly said that the town "stinks." Columnist Ed Sullivan (March 19, 1935) clutched his pearls and wrote, "Miss Hudson's statement will not only cost her the fan population of Claremore, which numbers 3,720 persons.... Every small town in the country will feel equally offended."

"You'd think that I had uttered blasphemy," she recalled nearly 30 years later. "The studio was on the phone for me to come home before I said anything else. I received a mountain of mail, half of it condemning me and half of it patting me on the back for saying what I thought."[65] Newspaper accounts mostly sided with her critics. "Well, it came out in the papers," she explained, "and I was suddenly a quite notorious lady. Will Rogers went to bat for me. 'Don't you mind, honey,' he said, and he put something in his column to kid about it.[66]

Still, both Rochelle and her mother realized some damage control was needed. Mae explained, "Rochelle was talking about the radium water in Claremore. We were all chatting about it and explaining the wells and the odor. Imagine our surprise when we read that headline."[67] Rochelle said, "I told my publicity man at the beginning that I was from Oklahoma. He didn't wait to hear any more and walked out. Subsequently he had me coming from Claremore as a protégé of Will Rogers.... I'm retracting nothing I said, but I want to make it clear that the radium water was obnoxious but that the people were always nice to me."[68]

The ensuing publicity busted the phony stories about her upbringing. Rochelle's uncle (Mae's brother John) said flatly, "Rochelle never lived in Claremore."[69] She also laid to rest—or tried to—the exaggerated accounts of Will Rogers' mentoring role in her career: "To be accurate, he's been kind to me, but not extraordinarily so. I've only seen him on the sets and I've never met any of his family. Mother had known him years ago, but I never met him until I was cast in *Doctor Bull.*"[70]

Little wonder that she was given a few hasty lessons in diplomacy from her studio bosses. A fan magazine writer stated that Rochelle had "grown-up ideas. It is a delight to encounter such intelligence in an ingénue… [However,] the ideal star is a master diplomat, tempering inherent independence to a discreet front. They are trying to pound this into the lovely Rochelle's head."[71]

She had the last word nearly 30 years later when syndicated columnist Bob Thomas recalled the brouhaha. Having visited Claremore a few years earlier, she told him in 1963, "Yes, it still stinks."

Soon, though, her career, having survived the nine days' wonder of a publicity gaffe, seemed to be taking her to a new level. She signed a new multi-year contract with Fox in the spring of 1935, with the studio announcing five new projects for her, including the Shirley Temple vehicle *Curly Top*. "I still can't believe it is true—that this is I, Rochelle Hudson. It doesn't seem to me that I am any different or that I have done any better work, but everyone seems to be 'discovering' me. They discovered I screened well, and then that I could sing. Now, next, I suppose they'll suddenly find out I can dance."[72]

Changes were underway at the studio in the spring and summer of 1935, as Fox Films executives pursued a merger with 20th Century Pictures. It seemed a natural marriage, as Fox had the physical assets and distribution channels, but 20th Century was making more successful pictures. By the end of the year, the result was 20th Century–Fox, under which name the company flourished. The merger brought into Rochelle's work life the dynamic filmmaker Darryl F. Zanuck (1902–1979), who had a reputation for turning out profitable pictures. Zanuck apparently admired the young actress' on-screen work, so for the time being all seemed rosy. Within a year, however, producer Winfield Sheehan, Rochelle's champion at Fox, was shown the door, as Zanuck's power grew.

With her career enjoying an uptick, columnists worked harder to publicize the alleged details of her love life. "The mysterious gold bracelet on Rochelle Hudson's left arm has been explained," dished Louella O. Parsons (March 1, 1935). "It was placed on her wrist by Buddy Eichelberger, wealthy young Los Angeles socialite, before he took the boat for New York several weeks ago. Saturday Rochelle will take the train east, ostensibly on a vacation, but her friends say really to see Buddy…. Well, Mr. Eichelberger has good taste for they don't come any prettier or sweeter than Rochelle." Harrison Carroll (February 9, 1935) reported that as Eichelberger left by boat for his round-the-world trip, "Rochelle was on the dock waving…." But on May 1, Carroll wrote that the Hudson – Eichelberger romance "seems definitely to have cooled off." Louella (August 16, 1935) concurred that the "romance [is] apparently dead; Rochelle has been going places with Harry Peale of the R.K.O. studios."

Asked about the men in her life, she said, "I love to go out and I love attention. But I believe in thinking of only one thing at a time. Just now, I seem to be started on some rather important phase in my career. And there wouldn't be any time to fall in love even if I wanted to."[73] She claimed that the demands of her work often left her too busy or too tired for socializing. "You know, I like to dress up like this. It's such a relief after weeks of wearing old clothes in *Way Down East*. Day after day I would have to get into a ragged coat, and simply wallow in grime. I'd come home and dress for dinner just for pure relief, and then take off my finery and plump into bed, worn out."[74]

As for other leisure time activities, an item in her November 1935 fan club newsletter said, "She is an accomplished dancer, singer and painter, and she can speak French fluently. She is keen on the radio, does not care about reading and loves the

Rochelle (right) and Mae, circa 1936 (University of Wyoming, American Heritage Center, Rochelle Hudson Papers, Box 6).

rumba. She loves to spend as much time on the beach as possible, in order to get a thick coating of tan."

Though it took her colleagues a while to discover it, her vocal talent was finally being noticed. "They are all agog at the Fox studio over Rochelle Hudson's singing voice," wrote Louella (July 11, 1935). "Winfield Sheehan, who is responsible for giving Rochelle Janet Gaynor's role in *Way Down East*, is so excited over the Hudson singing that he is planning to co-star her with John Boles in *The Song and Dance Man*." Another columnist claimed that Sheehan learned of his contract player's voice when she started whistling in his office one day. Annoyed, he asked her sarcastically if she had any other musical abilities, to which she replied, "Yes, I play the piano and I sing a little. Like to hear me?"[75] Her ambitions going strong, she was ready to achieve her full potential. She commented, "I've worked like the devil to get where I am—nobody has given me a single push. And as long as I'm in the game, I'm not going to let anything stop me from going clear to the top."[76]

As always, she pursued her goals with her mother at her side, though Mae told an interviewer she did not consider herself a "Hollywood mother." As Mae explained it, "Of course I watch over Rochelle, but I do not rush out in front of the camera when she is on the set to comb her hair. In fact, I do not go to the studio with her unless she's working all night." She noted that some stage mothers hurt their daughters' careers. Rochelle said she and her mother made an effective team: "We call ourselves 'Hudson, Limited.' I'm the executive, and Mother is the brain trust."[77] Mae was an active member of Motion Picture Mothers, Inc., a group formed by Marie Brown, whose son Tom Brown was Rochelle's co-star in two films, as well as her off-screen beau for a time.

Her Fox contract gave the studio the right to feature Rochelle's image in commercial endorsements. In 1936, a full-page Max Factor makeup ad in *Photoplay* depicted her advising other young ladies, "Everyday [sic], I see girls who are only half as lovely as they could be if they would harmonize their powder, rouge, lipstick to their type, the way screen stars do." A handy coupon allowed these unfortunates to describe their complexion, eye and hair color, and skin type to send away for a sampler of Factor cosmetics.

The death of Will Rogers, known to Rochelle as "Uncle Bill," in an August 1935 plane crash brought to an end their successful movie collaboration. Her 1936 release *Everybody's Old Man* found humorist Irvin S. Cobb stepping into the lead role originally earmarked for Rogers. Four years later, she and actor Leo Carrillo traveled to Fort Worth, Texas, where they represented the motion picture industry at the grand opening of a $2 million coliseum and auditorium bearing Rogers' name.

In the fall of 1935, another opportunity to fill in for a sidelined star was dangled in front of her. The *Los Angeles Times* reported,

> Rochelle Hudson will gain celebrity as a pinch-hitting star before long. First it happened with *Way Down East*, when she took the place of Janet Gaynor, and is again being repeated with *Ramona*. Owing to Loretta Young's illness, which may last another month, Miss Hudson

has been elected for the title role in the Helen Hunt Jackson story. Being selected means a new blooming for her career, which has prospered very much since ... *Curly Top*.... Darryl Zanuck, it seems, decided that Miss Hudson should be the star.[78]

Rochelle's fan newsletter quotes her letter of October 19, 1935: "I'm so awfully busy preparing for *Ramona*. We begin shooting November the fourth. I'll probably be on it at least two months as it's the big picture of the year for 20th Century. It seems as though I'm the very best replacer in the business." She also noted, "I hope the club members all like me in *Way Down East* and don't compare me too much with Gish because she was too marvelous."

Loretta Young's replacement in *Ramona* was occasioned by an out-of-wedlock pregnancy that she concealed from the world. The shooting of *Ramona* was delayed and the baby was born, enabling Young to play the role after all.

Interviewed for her fan club newsletter (December 21, 1935), Rochelle described the types of roles she most enjoyed: "Bright and happy parts—comedy and music. I suppose I like those kind because I so seldom do anything but drama." Responding to an inquiry about her fan mail, she answered, "My mail averages about a thousand letters a week. A lot of it from England, Canada, Australia and South America." In a later newsletter (February 14, 1936), she was asked if she welcomed comments from fans. "Yes, if it is constructive criticism. Fanatics on subjects like using no lipstick only annoy me. However, I always welcome any useful ideas anyone might have concerning my actions or looks on the screen."

She penned a short letter to members of her fan club (November 5, 1935): "Oooooooh, am I a bad girl! But truthfully I just haven't had a minute. This week I started on a new picture. I'm loaned to Columbia for *Rollin' Along* with Harry Richman. It's a very cute story and I do a little singing.... For once I get some good looking clothes so I'm very happy."

She suffered a mishap during a location shoot for her film *The Country Beyond*. As published accounts told it, "Miss Rochelle was buried beneath several feet of snow yesterday when a man-made avalanche roared down a 300-foot slope.... Miss Hudson was rescued in three minutes by a frantic crew of camera men and others on location. She was unconscious when rescued, and suffered from shock and cold."[79] Though the story reeked of a publicity stunt, her mother wrote to fan club members (February 8, 1936), "Rochelle is quite recovered from the snow slide experience but very tired from constant work.... She is giving all her time to her work and hopes to please each [fan], but we can't expect her to please everyone as we all have our own ideas. So, she will do the best she can and leave for you to decide."

That summer, Hudson sailed to Hawaii for a much-needed vacation. "Honolulu has meant a delightful rest for me," she commented. "When I left Hollywood a month ago I was tired from overwork, nervous, tense.... Now I am rested. The belief that work in pictures is easy is wrong. It's work—hard work. It's not easy to get away from the studio for a rest."[80] She and Mae traveled on the S.S. *Lurline*, returning to the mainland on June 13.

She admitted that movie stardom had its downside, saying that an actress was apt to be "virtually a prisoner for four or five years, but it is worth it, because you make enough money in those years to last a life-time." As for the public recognition that came along with her growing success, she admitted, "I don't like crowds."[81]

Leisure time activities helped her relax in her hours away from the studio. "My tennis is very indifferent," she admitted. "I used to ride horseback quite a lot on my grandfather's ranch in Oklahoma, but one day the cinch strap on the saddle broke and I got quite a nasty spill, and that sort of cured me of riding." She also tried her hand at painting. "It's lots of fun, and I dabble with it whenever I can find time."[82]

In 1935, Rochelle was getting good roles and enjoying the feeling that her career was on the upswing. But the next year or two saw her assigned to projects that made her feel that her moment in the spotlight might be short-lived. Edward Norris, her *Show Them No Mercy!* leading man, suggested one reason her favored status might have dimmed: She had caught the roving eye of vice-president of production Darryl F. Zanuck.

"She was being chased around by Zanuck," Norris told film historian Dan Van Neste. "One day, Zanuck's messenger came to tell her he wanted to see her after work. She said, 'Tell him no, I'm going home.' She was fighting that all during the production."[83] (For his part, Zanuck later denied ever having a liaison with an actress under contract, saying, "It was too big a gamble, and a payoff meant a contract or exercising an option. I never touched a soul."[84]) By 1937, rather than playing lead roles in important Fox films, she was becoming familiar with the studio's B unit.

During this period, columnists often found it more interesting to chronicle Rochelle's dating life—or dream one up for her—than to talk about her average-quality movies. Harrison Carroll (March 21, 1936) reported, "She poo-pooed [sic] the rumors that she will marry Fred de Cordova, of the Schubert staff in New York. Rochelle has a chance to go on a personal appearance tour at five times her movie salary and is crazy to take it." Of de Cordova, she said frankly, "He's too far away. I find that absence makes the heart grow more forgetful." Her erstwhile beau, who escorted quite a few beautiful women around Hollywood in his bachelor days, went on to become the longtime producer of *The Tonight Show*.

Cowboy actor Allan Lane was another of her reported beaux, with Louella O. Parsons (May 26, 1937) noting, "Rochelle Hudson stepping out with Allan Lane at the polo game and later at a night spot." A few days later, Ed Sullivan (May 31, 1937) chimed in: "Rochelle Hudson and Allan Lane are having fun." Another columnist reported, "Rochelle Hudson and Allan Lane are romancing at the Tropics night after night."[85] (After Lane's Western fame faded, he became known for providing the voice of the title character in TV's *Mister Ed*.) A few weeks later, her name was attached to a different movie player: "Rochelle Hudson's new happiness is named Billy Bakewell."[86]

New York–based columnist Louis Sobol (September 30, 1937) went so far as to make a list of Rochelle's dates that was entertaining, if not entirely convincing. "If

I am to believe my fairly authentic source," he wrote, "Miss Rochelle's escorts for the week were as follows: Monday, Sidney Burnap; Tuesday, Lee Bowman; Wednesday, Ivan Lebedef [sic]; Thursday, Sidney Burnap; Friday, Jimmy Flood (of the San Francisco Flood millions); Saturday, Count Theo Rossi (Italian speedboat sportsman and heir to the liquor fortunes); Sunday, Bill Caldwell." Burnap, a Hollywood surgeon whose patients included Jean Harlow, continued to have his name linked with Rochelle's into the following year.

Occasionally, too, the studio sent Rochelle on an arranged date with another contract player in need of publicity, as when she was escorted to an event at the Biltmore Hotel by Tyrone Power (1914–1958). Power claimed that her picture *Show Them No Mercy!* had made a great impression on him before his own Hollywood career began.

Another potential gossip item was axed before it saw print. Columnist Sidney Skolsky (April 21, 1936), observing that screenwriter Norman Krasna was a frequent visitor to the set of *Poppy*, concluded that its pretty leading lady was the attraction. Skolsky's bubble was burst when he spoke admiringly of Rochelle to Krasna, but then noted, "He walks about the set touching, I should say caressing, antiques. 'They're real ... they're genuine, and they belong to the property department. They won't sell. I'm trying to buy antiques like these for my new house.'" Scotched his romantic "scoop," the columnist wrote stingingly the next day, "Krasna is really queer for antiques. As for me, I still believe Rochelle Hudson is more appealing, and when Krasna gets over his schoolboy crush on antique furniture, I'm certain he'll agree."

Responding to published gossip about her romantic life, Rochelle said, "Tom Brown was the only actor I ever really went out with. And that was a long time ago. Since then ... I have gone out mainly with men outside the profession. Army men interest me, especially those in the aviation end. They lead more exciting lives, and aren't forever talking shop.... Besides, they don't take such a possessive attitude, and when you turn them down, whenever you'd rather spend an evening at home, they aren't offended."[87]

It was, in fact, a military man who was soon to bring about a major change in Rochelle's life: her first marriage.

The Men in Her Life

By the mid– to late '30s, Rochelle, though still in her twenties, was thinking seriously about her life beyond the motion picture industry. In 1937, she took a short leave of absence from Fox, for which she had to reimburse the studio by slightly extending her contract. That same year, one journalist reported, "Rochelle Hudson is the only actress who'll name a date for her departure from the screen, and that's 1943. She expects to be married by then, although now there's nobody definitely in sight."[88]

Her increasing restlessness was amplified by dissatisfaction with the roles she was being assigned, and eventually she began to talk about it in interviews. "I'm the Queen of the B's!" she complained. "Honestly, I've played Cops and Robbers so much that every time a car backfires I rush for my make-up kit!" She voiced frustration, saying, "I don't understand why I've suddenly been demoted to the underworld! It isn't as though I'd made a smash hit as a moll! I haven't! And there are so many other types of roles I could do and be of real value!"[89] Instead, she had become a staple of Sol Wurtzel's B unit at Fox. Columnist Ed Sullivan, with more candor than tact, wrote (April 3, 1938), "Funny how Rochelle Hudson slipped down the scale in flickers.... At one time she looked like a lead-pipe cinch for stardom."

When she wasn't needed at the studio, she tried to keep busy with other activities, even signing up for flying lessons in 1938. Her instructor, pilot Marion McKeen, said, "Movie people learn flying much quicker than any other class to whom I give instruction.... Miss Hudson, for instance, could, in a year or so, become an ace flyer. She's what we call a natural."[90]

That spring, Louella O. Parsons (March 9, 1938) reported, "Rochelle Hudson and Dixie Dunbar, who have been so widely publicized for their numerous beaux, are parting company with 20th Century–Fox after several years on that lot." Rochelle signed a document acknowledging that her employment with the studio would come to a close on March 24, 1938. Her publicity sought to cast Rochelle's departure from Fox in the best possible light:

> She's been under contract eight years. Now she's free—and glad to have an apartment in New York. She doesn't know just what she'll do next—maybe a play.... She's not married but she's had almost as many beaus as pictures, including Allan Lane, Bud Eichelberger, Billy Bakewell, Sidney Burnap, Ivan Lebedeff and Norman Krasna. But she's glad to be free—contractually and matrimonially speaking.[91]

The lady herself explained, "For the first time since I was 15 I don't have to eat, sleep and breathe according to contract.... It's all been hard work. Now I want to sleep and play ping pong."[92]

Within a few months, however, Rochelle was back in Hollywood, where she made two films for Republic and one for Universal in late 1938. A promise of steadier work came at Christmastime, when *Variety* (December 28, 1938) reported, "Rochelle Hudson Inked Player Pact at Columbia." She surely knew going in that signing with Harry Cohn's studio wasn't necessarily going to result in the higher caliber pictures she craved. Columbia thrived on quantity more than quality, releasing a new movie to theaters every week, many of them average-quality B pictures. Her first Columbia release, *Missing Daughters*, was yet another gangster quickie, this time opposite one of the all-time B movie stalwarts, Richard Arlen.

If her movie activity was in the doldrums, her romantic life was not. She fell in love with Harold Edward Mexia Thompson, employed in an editorial capacity at the Disney Studios. Born in Denver on June 9, 1907, Thompson had previously been married to Kathryn Cornell—not the actress, but a Tulsa oil heiress. Mae disapproved of her daughter's new relationship; Erskine Johnson (November 14, 1938) wrote, "Rochelle Hudson still can't get Hal Thompson at Walt Disney's staff off her mind and she and her mother aren't speaking." Whether Mae had a specific reason to dislike Hal, or simply wasn't ready to see her daughter possibly headed for matrimony, wasn't disclosed.

The romance kicked into high gear nonetheless, but one obstacle—aside from Mae—slowed things down. Columnist Jimmie Fidler (April 22, 1939) stated, "Wedding bells will peal for Rochelle Hudson and Hal Thompson, Walt Disney studio executive. The date's set for August when his divorce from a former wife will become final." Fidler's predication proved correct; a wire service story said, "Rochelle Hudson, brunette film actress, and her writer-husband, Hal Thompson of Hollywood, are honeymooning at a ranch in Lower California after their surprise marriage here last night [August 16, 1939]."[93]

According to another account, "[Thompson] and Miss Hudson went to Ensenada to be married by a Mexican judge, one of his old friends. Thompson told the judge that the marriage was 'secreto.' It was. When newsmen tried to get details of the ceremony, the judge insisted he didn't even know the newlyweds."[94] An irritated Walter Winchell, feeling entitled to know everything about stars' private lives,

Rochelle and Hal Thompson on an evening out at the Hollywood Brown Derby, 1939, just prior to their wedding.

wrote (August 19, 1939): "The thing that makes me mad is the Rochelle Hudson–Hal Thompson matter. What a big fuss they made—'How untrue it is'—last year."

Syndicated columnist Louella O. Parsons (August 18, 1939) reported that Rochelle and Thompson "spent their wedding night at the Rosarita Beach Country Club near Ensenada." By November, the couple was in New Mexico, where they toured the Carlsbad Caverns in the last days of their three-week honeymoon. Expected back at the studio, Rochelle confessed with a laugh that she didn't know the name of the next film she'd be making. "The last name I heard about was *Daughters of Today*," she explained, "but that was three weeks ago, and they've probably changed it several times since then." As for her leading man, "I don't know that either. They just wired me to report on location the twenty-fourth—and that's about all I know about it."[95] (The film in question was ultimately released as *Convicted Woman*.)

Rochelle's mother denied reports that she was upset by the marriage, telling Louella (August 23, 1939), "I think those stories must have started when we sold our home in Beverly Hills and during the moving melee Rochelle moved into an apartment." Mae said that she had been aware of her daughter's plans all along. About two weeks after the wedding, Jimmie Fidler (September 2, 1939) commented, "That reputed family feud over Rochelle Hudson's marriage ... has evidently been settled by appeasement—Mrs. Hudson has invited the happy couple to dinner." Another source noted, "Columnists reported that Rochelle and her mother parted over Hal Thomas [sic]. Rochelle married the man. Mother and daughter were reconciled and the three of them are now in Mexico." But Rochelle's new marital status didn't change Mae's ultimate goal: "Rochelle Hudson's jolly, gray-haired mother was ... determined that her daughter should be famous."[96]

After several months of marriage, Rochelle and Hal took a vacation trip to Honolulu in April 1940, sailing on the S.S. *Matsonia*. On board, they became friendly with Mrs. Edgar Rice Burroughs, wife of the "Tarzan" creator, and his family. Mr. Burroughs himself arrived via a different vessel a few days later. As author David Lemmo explained, "Edgar and Florence were very social by nature, and though they were a couple drifting apart, they made friends with film editor Hal Thompson and his actress wife Rochelle Hudson."[97]

Hudson told an interviewer that her marriage seemed to have brought about an overdue change in the type of roles she was offered. "Producers ... got into the habit of thinking of me as a 14-year-old kid who could emote at the drop of a remark. Then, about a year ago, I got married, and all of a sudden ... I get glamorous parts." She insisted that she was not solely a career girl: "I want to settle down and do some of the things I've wanted to do for years. I want to paint, and compose a little on the piano, and study some voice and dancing." Though she still enjoyed acting, she said that she would take a break: "As soon as this *Babies for Sale* picture is finished, my husband and I are going clear out of the country for three months."[98]

That fall, she returned from another Hawaiian vacation and, according to

Rochelle and husband Hal Thompson pay a visit to the circus, where they chat with her uncle Homer (far right). The clown in the background is unidentified (courtesy Rochelle E. McNear).

columnist Harrison Carroll (September 3, 1940), she received a memento: three bottles of perfume, with a note reading, "To Rochelle Hudson, from some island boys who have voted her the girl they would most like to be stranded with on the mainland."

Away from the cameras, she signed up for another project, a touring vaudeville show called "Hollywood Starlit," with George Jessel overseeing the proceedings. A party at Toots Shor's (in New York) was comprised of "Jessel and the members of his company which opens today at Loew's State.... Present were Jessel and his company of seven starlets, including Jean Parker, Rochelle Hudson, Isabel Jewell, Lya Lys, Steffi Duna, Betty Jane Cooper and Jean Gary."[99]

Reviews were generally positive when the show opened a few days later. *Variety* (October 16, 1940) caught the revue at the State Theatre in New York and reported,

> Right at home in the midst of a flock of young beauts, George Jessel manages to contrive an interesting hour's entertainment out of the troupe of seven Hollywood femmes with whom he has been traveling as a unit.... Rochelle Hudson gets a bit of production buildup. She chirps "Too Marvelous for Words." Her voice falters, but she also gets by on appearance.... For the finale, all the femmes are brought on stage and Jessel appears in the [Clark] Gable getup from *Gone with the Wind*.

The show embarked on an East Coast tour, opening in St. Louis. In Indianapolis, Rochelle explained that touring with a show took some getting used to. "My luggage was scarcely full when I left Hollywood two weeks ago," she said, "but now I have a hard time getting everything in. I've acquired such things as a paddle from a fraternity in St. Louis where the boys made me an honorary sweetheart. But the worst part of this whole thing is that when I'm at the theater and I need something, I'll remember that it's at the hotel."[100] Going from the heat of St. Louis to the chill of Chicago, she soon had a cold. In Philadelphia, a journalist learned in a brief backstage interview that Rochelle "is more interested in her marriage than movies, that she doesn't think there will ever be any pictures to take the place of the Will Rogers films, in which she often played Rogers' daughter, and that she can't imagine why audiences should be surprised at her singing voice because she has sung many times on the screen, if never in out-and-out musicals."[101]

Rochelle dropped out of the show after a few weeks, as it continued its East Coast tour. "Jessel show was minus Rochelle Hudson and Jean Parker when it left here last Thursday (14) for Syracuse and a three-day stand," said *Variety* (November 20, 1940). "Miss Parker flew back to Hollywood for a picture and Miss Hudson, accompanied by her husband, Hal Thompson, headed for Texas and will vacation in Mexico for couple of weeks before returning to coast."

The Thompsons' familiarity with Mexico proved useful when Rochelle's husband was recruited to take part in a bit of espionage on behalf of the U.S. government. Many years later, the *Los Angeles Times* reported,

> After the Japanese attacked Pearl Harbor, Thompson was in line for a Navy commission. First, however, the Office of Naval Intelligence asked him to undertake an intelligence mission in Mexico. Japanese submarines had been sighted off the coast of California and several

of them had fired shells onto the mainland. There was a real fear that the Japanese might follow up their crippling blow at Pearl Harbor with a full-scale invasion of the West Coast.... ONI believed that the Japanese had built secret landing strips in Mexico and had cached supplies of fuel. Thompson's assignment was to go to Mexico, accompanied by Rochelle, and try to locate them.

According to Rochelle,

We went to La Paz and boarded a yacht owned by the Singer Sewing Machine Co. George Vanderbilt was aboard. We were three people trying to find whether submarine or aviation fuel had been hidden in Baja California.... Subsequently a geological expert with the Army Air Force found terrain in the middle of Baja that was very perturbing. G-2 verified that an air strip had been built there and located a reserve of high-octane fuel.[102]

Rochelle hoped to one day write a book about their experiences, but never did.

Rochelle was seen in four Columbia programmers that reached theaters in 1941. But the following year found her freelancing again, and finding work primarily at Poverty Row studios. Nineteen forty-two saw the release of *Queen of Broadway*, in which she starred for PRC. It was in fact a better-than-average release from that company, which had been promising exhibitors an upgrade in the quality of its pictures. It would also be Rochelle's last film assignment for five years.

With Rochelle's marriage now two years old, her mother Mae quietly undertook a second matrimonial adventure of her own. She married Henry William Baly, a lumberman, at her Westwood, California, home on December 14, 1941. Only a handful of guests were in attendance, including the couple's children. On this occasion, no mention was made in newspaper accounts that Mae Hudson was the mother of a Hollywood actress, just that Mr. and Mrs. Hal Thompson were present for the ceremony. Both Mrs. Hudson and her new groom were 59 years old. Baly, who had a son and daughter of his own, had been widowed the previous year. By the time Baly died in 1974, he had been living in San Mateo, California, for the past ten years. He was described as "at one time one of California's more prominent lumbermen." He and Mae had long since parted ways; she went unmentioned in his *San Mateo Times* obituary (July 12, 1974).

While Mae once again settled into wedded life, the state of Rochelle's marriage was uncertain. Thompson was still in the Navy, and his wife made the newspapers with a story that was open to innuendo. In early 1942, she was called as a witness in the divorce case of Quentin Smith and Lucile Rawleigh Smith, the latter said to be a well-to-do Bel Air heiress. Smith was attempting a movie career under the screen name Quen Ramsay. At issue was Mrs. Smith's contention that her husband had enjoyed the company of other women, including Rochelle, during their marriage. Rochelle had been spotted with Smith at the Trocadero, but claimed that it did not represent a threat to his marriage vows—or her own. "It was decided," Rochelle told the court, "that the best way for him to get along in pictures was to be seen in public with some movie personality."[103]

She had first met Smith several years earlier, when her onetime acting coach Josephine Dillon had introduced them. In the summer of 1936, three years before her

In 1936, several years before she became a witness in his divorce trial, Rochelle went out on the town with "wealthy socialite and sportsman" Quentin Smith.

marriage to Thompson, a newspaper photo of Hudson and Smith described Smith as a "wealthy Chicago sportsman," captioned with her comment saying they were merely friends. Likewise, columnist Ed Sullivan (August 3, 1936) included Rochelle and Smith in a list of "Hands-Across-the-Table" dating couples.

Rochelle testified in court that, before her two evenings out with Smith, his wife Lucile okayed the plan. This was corroborated by testimony from Smith himself as well as Mrs. Dillon. After meeting with Smith and Mrs. Dillon, Rochelle said, "The next day I saw him again when we went to the Trocadero. I had told the management there that I was coming with Smith for publicity purposes and asked them to please see that the story was planted." With that in mind, they posed for photographers, but she clarified that the date had been innocuous, saying, "In the car he conducted himself with the utmost propriety."[104]

But another witness, Smith's chauffeur Charles Cartwright, claimed that his boss and the young movie star were "caressing." Cartwright testified that she told Smith she "had to go home, but might be able to sneak out later." Asked by Smith's attorney to respond, Rochelle said, "I might have said I had to go in. But I most certainly did not say that I intended to come out later."[105] A few days later, Superior

Court Judge William R. McKay granted Mrs. Smith's divorce, and in his summation stated that there appeared to have been no wrongdoing on Rochelle's part.

Still, as Louella O. Parsons (May 20, 1942) commented, "Rumor continues that Rochelle Hudson and Hal Thompson will soon call it a day." In response, Rochelle wrote to Parsons, who printed the letter in her May 27, 1942, column: "We have been living happily in Mexico for almost a year and now that Hal is a lieutenant in the United States Navy we are even happier. Our home is in San Diego and we expect to go on living in it together indefinitely. I hope to do some pictures again after my long vacation."

In early 1943, it looked as if Rochelle's career might take a new direction when it was reported that she was up for a role in a new Broadway-bound musical, *Dancing in the Streets*, starring Mary Martin (1913–1990). One of the first mentions came from columnist Sidney Skolsky (January 25, 1943): "[Producer] Vinton Freedley is trying to get Hugh Herbert and Rochelle Hudson for his show, *Dancing in the Street* [sic]." By early February, virtually every other New York–based show business columnist—Dorothy Kilgallen, Ed Sullivan, Leonard Lyons—offered the same news, with Sullivan (February 3, 1943) reporting that a contract was signed.

Dancing in the Streets opened out of town, in Boston, on March 23, 1943. Rochelle did not appear in the Boston company, which received mixed reviews, and *Variety* (March 31, 1943) reported that Freedley "realized that the show needed more fixing than usual." Martin biographer Ronald Davis wrote, "The show was not good, and Boston critics were merciless in pointing out its weaknesses."[106] According to another source, "Mary Martin, who quit Hollywood to return to the stage in the $180,000 musical, *Dancing in the Street* [sic], wept when the show closed in Boston without ever reaching Broadway, because script revisions were found to be necessary."[107]

While awaiting new projects, Rochelle kept busy with an occasional radio assignment, as well as efforts supporting the war. In July 1943, she was a guest on NBC's *Hollywood Open House*, emceed by Tobe Reed. A few weeks later, she took part in a benefit concert with the United States Coast Guard Band, 11th Naval District. Radio star Rudy Vallée led the concert, with proceeds benefitting the Naval Aid Auxiliary.[108]

Whether it represented mere patriotism, or an indication of the state of her marriage, another radio appearance found her being offered as a dream date for an enlisted man. "A prize well worth hours of 'cramming' … awaits the winning serviceman on the broadcast of *Noah Webster Says*, heard over KSO.… The lucky uniformed individual will win a date with one of Hollywood's best-known young leading ladies, Rochelle Hudson."[109] Haven McQuarrie hosted the show, heard on the national Blue Network.

By all appearances, however, she was still Mrs. Hal Thompson. Her hometown newspaper reported that fall that she was in Oklahoma City, "en route to Washington, D.C., where she will join her husband.…"[110] Be that as it may, Rochelle and he were separated as of December 9, 1943.

Word of her marital problems continued to leak out. Louella (April 3, 1944) told her readers a few months later, "Rochelle Hudson, prettier than ever, is back from South America. She was at the Clover Club with Roy Randolph and he told friends she is divorced from Hal Thompson." This Rochelle denied, forcing Parsons to print a follow-up item two days later: "Rochelle Hudson tells me she is only separated from her husband, Hal Thompson, by miles; Roy Randolph, she says, is a close friend of both her husband and herself and was with them when Hal left for South America for naval duty." Later that year (November 16, 1944), Sidney Skolsky wrote, "Rochelle Hudson says there will not be a divorce between her and her Navy husband, rumors to the contrary."

Rochelle began making public appearances near the end of the war, getting her name in the papers as she looked to the possibility of becoming a full-time actress again in her late twenties:

"The Perfect Legs Institute of America felt that the lovely gams of Rochelle Hudson, stage and screen star, belonged there, so Joseph S. Armand, the illustrator, ordered them cast in bronze to decorate the institute's art shelves."[111]

"She's Rochelle Hudson on the screen, but now the dark-haired star will be known as 'Princess Laughing Leaves' to the Kawias Indian tribesmen. Miss Hudson, who is said to bear a marked resemblance to the immortal Ramona, yesterday was given the Indian girl's name and adopted by the tribe."[112]

Not until the summer of 1945 was Rochelle's marriage resolved in court. Her blunt testimony depicted Thompson as a less-than-ideal spouse. "While he was stationed at El Toro," she testified, "we had a home in Balboa. I spent two or three days a week doing radio work in Hollywood, and when I returned I found all the evidence of parties and entertainment." She found dirty glasses stained with lipstick that wasn't hers. "When I asked him about the parties," she said, "he slapped me. He had a vicious temper." By her account, it was mostly Hal who no longer wanted to continue their marriage: "He said he had made his plans, and I wasn't included—he was not made for marriage."[113]

Despite the ensuing divorce, columnist Walter Winchell (October 10, 1945) once again seemed to be asleep at the switch where she was concerned, noting, "Rochelle Hudson is amused at the report she'll wed a Navy Lieut, since she's been happily sealed to a Lt. Comdr. For six years." What he didn't point out was that the flawed newsflash was in fact his own scoop from a few weeks earlier.

Once the divorce was granted, Hal moved on. On May 7, 1947, Navy Lieutenant Commander Harold (Hal) Thompson married Julia Asmussen, a native of Chile, in Guatemala. But, as time would tell, Rochelle and Hal weren't out of each other's lives for good.

That same year, Rochelle made her first film since 1942: She accepted the female lead in an independent production, *Bush Pilot*, shot in Canada. She also sought opportunities on stage. Though she had frequently entertained live audiences as a child, and been featured in George Jessel's vaudeville revue, she now took on the challenge of a professional stage show, signing to be comedian Bert Lahr's leading lady in the musical comedy *Burlesque*. The show had originally played on Broadway from December 1946 to January 1948, with Jean Parker as Lahr's leading lady. As one reviewer wrote of *Burlesque*, "The simple story was about Skid, a comedian who liked liquor and women too well, and periodically deserted his faithful wife, Bonny, who had all the family's ambition. She persuaded him to take a Broadway job, which he lost when he couldn't stand prosperity, and planned to wed a wealthy Westerner. A friend gave Skid a chance to come back, and Bonny left her cattle man for Skid and show business."[114]

Once it closed on the Great White Way, Lahr immediately made plans for a national tour. A company of 25 players would travel by baggage car, with bookings across the U.S. Lahr chose Fay McKenzie to assume the role of Bonny in the touring company, which successfully played numerous dates over the next few months. In August 1948, Lahr's group assembled in Princeton, New Jersey, to launch a fresh tour. Going into his third year as Skid, the star comedian had by then played around 700 performances, but was happy to continue. This time around, Rochelle was signed for the role of Bonny. In Indianapolis, Lahr explained, "Yeah, we're booked to the first of the year, and it will probably be longer. We do such places as Minneapolis and St. Paul and then hop all the way to Yakima, Washington. We fool around the North country and then move down the coast.... We now have Rochelle Hudson playing the heroine and she ought to be all right. I've found that these people from California work hard and take the theater very seriously."[115]

Rochelle accepted the gig at the suggestion of her agent, Louis Shurr. It required her to join the company with only one week's notice. "He felt that the play would give me the chance to do something utterly different and thus set up a new career," Rochelle explained.[116]

The company began work during a heat wave that saw the thermometer climb past 100 degrees. The dance and song routines were arduous, and early on she hurt her knee and strained her foot in a scene where she catches Lahr in a fall. "My knee is better now, but it was very painful for a while. I had to have treatments and dressings every day for a time." Undaunted, she soldiered on, saying she couldn't let Mr. and Mrs. Lahr, "such swell people," down. Retained in Rochelle's personal papers as a memento of the experience was a warmly inscribed photo from Lahr, who wrote, "It's been an extreme pleasure working with you. Affectionatly [sic], Bert."

"The play has more comedy, more songs and dances than when it was originally produced," Rochelle said. "Bert himself is largely responsible for these changes from the original and I think he has done a wonderful job."[117]

The tour's first date was in early September, in Madison, Wisconsin, after one final day of rehearsal at a local hotel. A dress rehearsal took place at the theater the following day, and that evening it was showtime, ready or not. Said one local reviewer, "It is funny, pleasantly sentimental and has a lot of hokum and, fortunately for the cause of merriment, its star, Bert Lahr.... Hollywood's Rochelle Hudson made her initial appearance as the attractive, impulsive and good-hearted Bonny.... Miss

Hudson has yet to fit naturally into the framework of plot and wasn't at her secure ease."[118] But another local publication viewed her contribution more positively: "She and Lahr gave a lively, fun-filled impersonation of an old-time song-and-dance team with gags worked into their stepping routine. This response carried over into the last act, when she went to work on the play's situation like an actress."[119]

Her accolades grew as she settled into the role. A few days later, in Minneapolis, a notice read, "The play is well mounted and cast, with Rochelle Hudson of Hollywood fame, new to the role, making a sympathetic Bonnie [sic]."[120] Sometimes it was her looks more than her technique that reviewers praised, but the reaction was positive just the same. One writer noted, "Rochelle Hudson, shapely and attractive, plays opposite Lahr."[121]

About two weeks later, they were in Vancouver, Canada. "Bert Lahr was excellently supported by Rochelle Hudson, who played the part of Bonny with exquisite charm and sincerity of approach," one journalist commented.[122] Another noted, "Rochelle Hudson—5 foot 2 and what is best described as a 'neat dish.' She has 'interesting' eyes and a figure to match...."[123] Soon it was Tacoma, Washington: "Miss Hudson's vivaciousness and pleasing voice, almost entirely absent from the screen since her starring days as Will Rogers' leading lady, added sparkle to the performance."[124]

The troupe traveled down the West Coast, hitting Medford, Oregon, in early October and Sacramento, California, soon afterwards. Then it was on to the big time, as the show opened in Los Angeles. The *Los Angeles Times*' Edwin Schallert wrote, "Rochelle Hudson acts very nicely indeed in the role of Bonnie [sic]. One would hardly sense that this was her first appearance on the stage. She gives an earnest sincerity to her very youngish (by contrast) portrayal of the heroine." Schallert described the format that had evolved: "The first act is a slight sketch of what goes on behind the scenes in show business, the second becomes practically a one-man marathon for Lahr himself, and the third is really the high spot of the performance."[125] Another reviewer chimed in, "Rochelle Hudson scores nicely and, in the second act, outstandingly in the song and dance numbers into which she throws herself avidly. She generously displays a shapely figure that we, nor apparently anyone else, didn't overlook."[126]

Once the tour came to an end, Rochelle was back in California, and free to resume her latest romance, with *Los Angeles Times* sportswriter Dick Hyland (1900–1981). His widely read column was known as "The Hyland Fling," and he had been called "one of the most highly-opinionated writers on any sports page." Hyland's expertise drew on personal experience: He played football at Stanford "back in the days when Pop Warner was holding forth at Palo Alto."[127] As his friend Frank J. Mackin, a retired judge, noted in later years, "Dick was a star of the U.S. rugby team that won the gold in the 1924 Olympics."[128] In 1932, four years after he began covering sports for the *Times*, he published a book, *The Diary of a Line Smasher: Adventures of a College Football Player* (A.C. McClurg, 1932). He later joined the Marine Corps, attaining the rank of lieutenant colonel.

Hyland took no prisoners when he wrote about teams and athletes in his column; his unfailing bluntness made him some enemies. He saved his greatest scorn for players who, in his opinion, had top-notch skills but weren't working up to their capacity. A *Saturday Evening Post* writer, profiling Hyland, commented, "He has been challenged to a fist fight on the Rose Bowl public address system, in hearing of 90,000 witnesses. He has been knocked down by a Stanford team which charged him *en masse*, and has knocked down a Northwestern player who charged him singly. Yale alumni have publicly burned his writings, and Alabamans have lynched him in effigy."[129]

He and Rochelle began seeing each other in 1947, columnist Harrison Carroll (June 3, 1947) calling the duo "a new romantic item." Jimmie Fidler (June 14, 1947) described them a few days later as "altar-bound." But things really heated up the following year; columnist Hedda Hopper (November 30, 1948) wrote, "What's this about sports writer Dick Hyland and Rochelle Hudson edging their way to the altar?" Hyland made a passing reference to his lady friend in his November 20, 1948, column: "Some wonderful things come out of Oklahoma. [Sports publicist] George Goodale, Rochelle Hudson, Will Rogers and [football player] Glenn Dobbs for instance...."

Asked a few days later if it were true that he and Rochelle had set a date, Hyland nonchalantly told Harrison Carroll (December 6, 1948), "You never know from day to day with Hudson." But on December 13, 1948, wire service reports indicated that Rochelle and Hyland had obtained a marriage license. It would be her second marriage, and his fourth. One of Hyland's previous matrimonial adventures was a marriage to the famed journalist Adela Rogers St. Johns. They married in 1928 and split in 1934.

Rochelle became Mrs. Hyland on December 18, 1948, at the home of friends Dr. and Mrs. Frank Nolan, with Mae the only other witness. One columnist noted, "Met an old friend, Rochelle Hudson who had just got herself married. That afternoon she and Dick Hyland ... went down to Dr. Frank Dyers [sic] and did some marrying.... I used to attend [Dyer's] church ... that beautiful Wilshire Congregational located at the corner of Wilshire and Plymouth."[130] The newlyweds honeymooned at the Palm Springs Racquet Club.

Even on their wedding day, Hyland filed a *Times* column, making no direct reference to Rochelle. However, that day's entry found him supposedly straining to think of a topic, noting, "I guess I've just got something else on my mind, for today."

Though busy with stage work and a new husband, Rochelle continued to act in occasional films, averaging one low-budget picture per year in the late 1940s. In later years, she explained that she had chosen to broaden her horizons after spending most of the 1930s and 1940s as a film actress. "You can only be an ingénue for so long. Besides, I wanted to climb down off this pedestal and be a normal person for awhile."[131] She told another interviewer, "I reached a point where my world had come to be bounded on the north by Malibu, on the south by Palm Springs. I wanted to do things that weren't in scripts, to see things besides sound stages, to go places besides location sites. So I took off."[132] She visited Europe and traveled extensively in the States.

In 1949, movie audiences could see Rochelle on-screen in a low-budget programmer, *Sky Liner*, and a few of them may have seen her in an industrial film, *Roots in the Soil*. Other than that, her movie career was winding down, at least for the time being. She wouldn't make another feature film for more than five years.

As the new decade got underway, Rochelle was once again a single woman, her marriage to Hyland having hit the skids before it was two years old. They separated in March 1950, and she filed for divorce shortly afterwards. Testifying in the Los Angeles courtroom of Superior Court Judge William R. McKay, Rochelle sarcastically called Hyland "the man who never came home to dinner." Wire service reports noted, "She testified that he would miss dinner about six nights a week and not come home until 4 o'clock of mornings."[133]

Her complaint was less severe than that of his previous wife, Adela, in 1934, though there was at least one problem on which both women agreed. The first Mrs. Hyland had stated, "He was very unkind and argued with me on almost everything. He told me that I was half-witted—that I ought to be ashamed to express any opinion.... He was in the habit of leaving me alone for days and weeks at a time."[134] Up for grabs in the Hudson-Hyland settlement was the couple's apartment at 1440 North Hayworth Street, as well as $250 he owed her in a property settlement. By the time the dust settled, one source reported, "Hyland, 48, also dropped a decision on who gets the family apartment.... Rochelle scored there."[135] The *Honolulu Star-Bulletin* (July 26, 1950) couldn't resist headlining its account, "Dick Hyland Muffs 4th Try at Marriage."

In July 1981, Hyland, 80, died in his sleep at a hotel at Yosemite National Park, where he had been attending a celebrity golf tournament.

TV and Movie Mom

In the late 1940s, with her movie career in the doldrums, Rochelle dipped her toes, work-wise, into the newly popular medium of television. By then, with movie production slowed, many longtime film stars were finding better prospects in TV. There was also a renaissance of interest in her work as her films of the 1930s and early 1940s began to appear on video screens. Their frequent late-show airings brought her new acclaim, but had a downside, as she soon discovered. Seeing her perform in movies nearly 20 years old, and not knowing how young she had been at the time, some viewers thought she was older than she really was. "It's terrible," Rochelle complained. "Showing all those old movies on TV is so unfair to the actors. After all, actors don't like to admit that time marches on. And, to make it tougher, they forget I started work when I was 13.... People see me on TV and think they have to bring out the wheel-chair."[136]

Syndicated columnist Erskine Johnson (June 13, 1951) reported that Rochelle, "whose old pictures have made her a TV star, has hired herself an agent for video stints." She had already been a celebrity panelist on a short-lived game show, but soon made her video dramatic debut in a 1951 episode of the crime drama *Racket Squad*. That appearance, and others that followed, made it clear that, in her mid-thirties, she was still a very attractive woman, as well as a competent, experienced actress.

When not at work, she spent time with family and friends, and volunteered her time with various charities. In the summer of 1953, Rochelle received a letter from two officers affiliated with the Sawtelle Veterans' Administration Hospital in Los Angeles, thanking her for her "excellent musical comedy readings presented in ward D each week during the month of June, 1953.... For these men who have had Polio, who have known the futility of long desperate lonely hours, the activity ... becomes a helpful and needed instrument that plays an important part in their social and psychological therapy."[137]

Mae wrote, "Rochelle Hudson entertained every Monday night in the Polio Ward of Sawtelle Hospital during the War. She was the only one permitted in the ward except perhaps some favorite of one of the boys. The studios let her use any of their music before it was released."[138]

Despite her good-natured laments about the televising of her old movies, the screenings, and her occasional TV guest appearances, paid off. Columnist Aline

Family portrait, 1953: Rochelle (second from left) and her mother Mae pose with Mae's brother Homer Clinton Goddard (left). His son Homer Deane Goddard holds the newest addition to the clan, his daughter Rochelle (courtesy Rochelle E. McNear).

Mosby wrote, "CBS called her in to audition for Ann Southern's [sic] *Private Secretary* show," after a dispute between Miss Sothern and her producer caused Sothern to walk away. Though Hudson wasn't chosen to play Susie McNamara, writer-producer Cy Howard saw her test, liked her, and hired her for a new comedy series, *That's My Boy*, which debuted in April 1954.

That's My Boy, adapted by Howard from a 1951 box-office hit starring Dean Martin and Jerry Lewis, featured Rochelle as Alice Jackson, a suburban mom whose husband, "Jarrin'" Jack Jackson, was a middle-aged businessman still reliving his glory days as a student athlete. Jack was frustrated that their teenage son, "Junior," was a bookish, nerdy type, utterly oblivious to the charms of a sporting life. Her character was described as "a former tennis star, who has a more realistic attitude toward life than her husband."[139]

The show's top-billed star was Broadway and movie comedian Eddie Mayehoff (1909–1992), with real-life sportscaster Gil Stratton, Jr., chosen to play the Jacksons' egghead son. Though Rochelle had frequently demonstrated her comedic skills in films, she understood that her function in the role of Alice was primarily to serve as a straight woman. She commented,

> It's not easy, in a company of laugh-makers like this, to keep my feet on the ground. And it is most important that I do play the mother role straight. If I start getting into the laugh end of the program, then we could have trouble.... Like every other dramatic actress or actor, I have an inner urge to do comedy. Fortunately, the years of experience have taught me to resist the urge, play things straight, and, as a result, I've been able to keep Mrs. Jackson a straight character.[140]

Happy to be back in the spotlight, Rochelle said, "I don't know of any other actress who voluntarily quit pictures and then had a new career dropped in her lap like this. They want veterans like me. TV is a tough medium and there's no substitute for experience."[141] Asked how she would react if fans began recognizing her not as herself but as her TV character, Rochelle said, "I'm going to love it. For years I've been playing different roles, and having to be different characters all the time. Now, I'm just going to be one person every week. And incidentally, I love television."[142]

That's My Boy played on CBS throughout the spring and summer of 1954, and was renewed for a second season to begin in September. That fall, Rochelle was included in a *TV Guide* feature spotlighting video moms who had previously toiled in film; also featured were Mary Brian (*Meet Corliss Archer*), Marjorie Reynolds (*The Life of Riley*) and Jane Wyatt (*Father Knows Best*). "Where the movies made Eternal Youth a fetish, TV has liberated the ingénues of yesteryear, and made them TV mothers," the article proclaimed. Of the changes that age brought to actresses, Rochelle said, "It's not easy. Agents, studios or audiences refuse to accept you. During the time I didn't work, I think I passed through this awkward 'no woman's land.' When I faced an audience over TV, the past was dead." According to the interviewer, she said her TV role "feels so natural to her that she considers TV the best psychiatrist in the business; it got her over the self-conscious years."[143]

Behind the scenes, there were some rocky moments working with a star who had a more-than-healthy ego. Years later, Stratton said, "I worked for six months with Eddie Mayehoff, and got an ulcer. It was not a happy experience.... He was crazy." (Stratton "had nicer memories of Rochelle Hudson."[144]) Gossip columnist Sheilah Graham, writing for *TV Guide* (December 11, 1954), was not a fan of the series star either, noting, "Eddie Mayehoff is a good actor, but he also acts up. The other day the photographer on the set wanted him to pose with Gil Stratton and Rochelle Hudson for some publicity shots, but That's My Eddie huffed, 'I'm the star of this show. I want pictures of me alone.'"

That's My Boy underwent some changes as the second season got underway, notably a switch from live broadcasts to film. Rochelle welcomed the switch. "At first, the show was live. Oooh, that's a challenge. That's opening night every week before 20,000,000 people. The jitters get you as early as Thursday for a Saturday show. Now we're on film. I like it better. I'm enough of a perfectionist to prefer film."[145]

All looked good for the CBS sitcom until the fall season brought a new comedian, George Gobel, to NBC. TV viewers were immediately taken with the rising star, and *That's My Boy* had the misfortune to be in the same time slot he rapidly began to dominate. Of the competition with Gobel's show, Stratton said, "We were

Rochelle and Eddie Mayehoff as Mr. and Mrs. Jackson on CBS-TV's *That's My Boy.*

doing fine for 26 weeks, and all of a sudden they went on, and we were like a balloon shot down."[146] Before the end of the year, the sitcom's sponsor pulled the plug. It aired for the last time in January 1955.

Just as her television commitment wound down, however, another opportunity presented itself, when she was offered a featured role in *Rebel Without a Cause*, starring James Dean. Louella O. Parsons (April 19, 1955) announced the casting, adding, "Jimmy McHugh Jr. put over the deal and he tells me she looks as pretty as ever." Rochelle was signed for the role of Natalie Wood's mother.

Though her screen time would be limited, she told a reporter she welcomed a return to making feature films after the hectic experience of a weekly television show. "Those stop watches in TV almost got me," she said. "In television, everything is split-second timing. For instance, I'd be doing a scene when the director would rush madly out of his little glass booth yelling, 'No good, no good, you're three seconds over. Speed it up, speed it up, pull-eese!'"[147] Columnist Erskine Johnson (October 26, 1955) reported that acting wasn't her only source of income from Hollywood: "Rochelle Hudson, once a big star at 20th Century–Fox, is back on the payroll. The studio is paying her royalties for oil under property she owns adjoining the studio's backlot oil field."

Rochelle's private life took an interesting turn with the revelation that she was once again seeing her ex-husband Hal Thompson: "The actress said that they revived their romance several months ago."[148] Both had married—and divorced—others in the interim. The rekindled flames were serious enough that they made plans. One report stated, "Friends of actress Rochelle Hudson and Cmdr. H.E.M. Thompson disclosed today that the pair were on the way to Ensenada, Mex., to be remarried."[149] Another journalist added, "Lately, friends reported she has been seeing the Navy officer on leaves from his recent assignments as an air-attaché in South America and the Caribbean area. One friend said the actress had planned to fly to Florida to spend Christmas with her ex-husband. Instead, according to current reports, he came to California and they plan to be honeymooning at Christmas time."[150] Whether or not the remarriage actually took place remains uncertain. Syndicated columnist Harrison Carroll (December 31, 1955) reported on it as a done deal, writing, "The honeymooners, Rochelle Hudson and Cmdr. H.E.M. Thompson, are back in town. They were married in Tijuana instead of Ensenada as originally planned. The commander ... is going on an inactive status. He tells me he and Rochelle will live in California." However, no record of the marriage has been located, and within a few months there was a new man in her life.

Born in Pittsburgh, Charles Kenneth Brust, Jr. (1916–1982), was vice-president and general manager of a Santa Ana firm called Armament Components. He and Rochelle were both 40 years old, with Charles just two months older than his bride-to-be. They were wed on September 29, 1956, near Kansas City, per published reports: "Actress Rochelle Hudson and Manufacturer Charles K. Brust of Santa Anna [sic], Calif., were married yesterday at nearby Unity Village ... headquarters of the Unity religious movement."[151]

Wedding plans had been altered at the last minute when Rochelle was notified that her father had been hospitalized: "Friends in Kansas City said the marriage took place there because Miss Hudson's father had been seriously ill and it was necessary for her to go there."[152]

"We had made other plans," Brust said. "Mr. Hudson was taken rather ill. We came on here to return him to California." Brust said the father has been ill since an accident several months ago.

After the ceremony, "she and her father, O.L. Hudson, flew here [L.A.] from Kansas City last night, but Brust had scheduled a trip to the east."[153] The 83-year-old Ollie Lee Hudson lived another 15 years.

Mostly out of the public eye since her appearance in *Rebel Without a Cause*, Rochelle was referenced in a musical comedy number, "The Rochelle Hudson Tango," which was featured in producer Ben Bagley's musical revue *Shoestring '57*. Performed by Dody Goodman and G. Wood, members of Bagley's ensemble cast, Ellie Sten's song was a comic tribute to performers who were well-known in an earlier era, but whose stars were perceived to have faded. Rochelle's name appeared only in the title, but the lyrics made mention of more than a dozen other notables— mostly women, though Butch Jenkins and James Dunn snuck in. One of them was actress Sally Eilers, with whom Rochelle had appeared in *Walls of Gold*.

In truth, having appeared in both a major motion picture and a television series as recently as 1955, Rochelle was hardly long gone and forgotten, but it was true that she put acting on the back burner after marrying Brust. Though she wasn't busy professionally, TV viewers saw her again throughout the summer of 1959, as CBS brought back her five-year-old sitcom *That's My Boy* in reruns. Away from Hollywood, her new occupation was a slightly unexpected one: She bought a 10,000-acre cattle ranch in Arizona, just north of Mexico. She commented, "Don't get the idea that I was saddling ol' Paint every sun-up and riding the range. But it was a working ranch, and I worked at it and ran it."[154]

As it had in the past, the dawning of a new decade meant a page had been turned in Hudson's life. She and Mae were traveling in the spring of 1960, visiting old friends in Oklahoma. Rochelle had recently completed a job serving as coach to the contestants in a beauty pageant. "Miss Hudson urges every one [sic] to mail a postcard or letter to the major studios and let them know what the public's likes and dislikes are, so that the industry can get a better idea of the class of pictures to turn out in the future," one journalist wrote.[155] The article made no mention of third husband Charles Brust, and that year's voter registration rolls in California showed her as "Miss Rochelle Hudson," a registered Republican, living at 1258 Devon Avenue. Brust, for his part, married Ingres Colleen Wilson in 1962.

With her poise, intelligence and charm. Hudson found other outlets as acting opportunities slowed. The *Los Angeles Times* mentioned the three years she spent running her cattle ranch, and added, "She was hired by a major petroleum company in Tulsa to tutor its executives in communications so they could express themselves better."[156] From the latter experience came a recording called "Communications," which she shared with influential businessmen and academics. One oil company executive wrote to her in the summer of 1960, saying, "You have presented an inspiring and practical message that is needed by anyone who is called upon in any capacity to express himself orally.... I hope that you will reproduce your tape in phonograph record form, and am confident that if you do, it would be used enthusiastically by businessmen and executives."[157]

But Hollywood wasn't quite through with her yet. When she turned up as a guest star on the popular television detective show *77 Sunset Strip* in the spring of 1961, a columnist stated, "She plans to continue her career, and her old studio, 20th Century–Fox, is talking a two-picture deal with the actress."[158] The guest appearance was a good showcase for her, reminding viewers and casting agents both what an accomplished actress she was.

It wasn't that she really needed to work. "Rochelle Hudson invested her money in real estate and is wealthy," one scribe noted.[159] But she had grown homesick for Hollywood, where she had kept an apartment all along. "I suppose I kept it as a sort of light in the window for myself," she admitted, "knowing that sooner or later I'd be back."[160] Offered a good price for her Arizona ranch, she decided she was ready for a new life—or a return to the familiar one.

Rochelle began to seek new opportunities in front of a camera. Of her periodic returns to acting in the early to mid–1960s, she said, "I'm not hungry, but I'm available."[161] The assignments weren't always glamorous; for instance, she headlined an episode of ABC's daytime series *Day in Court* in 1963.

There was also a new man in her life. Syndicated columnist Harrison Carroll (August 14, 1963) noted, "She is dating Palm Springs land architect Robert Mindell." A native of New York, a World War II veteran, Mindell was active in local politics, having won a race for vice-president of the Riverside County Democratic Council in 1961. Two years older than Rochelle, he had married once previously. Hudson and Mindell soon tied the knot, her fourth and final marriage. Celebrity interviewer Richard Lamparski wrote in 1970, "For the past eight years Rochelle has been the wife of a hotel executive."[162]

Eager to go on acting, Rochelle put out the word to old colleagues and friends like producer-director William Castle. As one journalist told it, "Last fall she walked into the office of William Castle, who had been her dialogue director in the old days. 'Got a part for me?' Rochelle asked him."[163] He did indeed, signing her to a featured role in *Strait-Jacket*, a campy melodrama about a middle-aged woman released from a long stay in a sanitarium after committing two axe murders.

Publicists were invited to a party celebrating the start of production on *Strait-Jacket*, where star Joan Crawford "confounded the calendar watchers with her svelte figure and radiant beauty." That was soon followed by Miss Crawford's introduction of her castmate Rochelle, "and when Rochelle stood up, the crowd gaped again. Ageless as Joan herself!"[164]

On the first day of shooting, "[t]he big door of Columbia's Sound Stage 22 swung open and a slight, familiar figure slipped quietly through and reported to director William Castle. 'Rochelle Hudson!' exclaimed cast and crew of Joan Crawford's starring horror movie, *Strait-Jacket*, and they swarmed around to greet one of the loveliest and most popular heroines of an earlier day."[165] Crawford reportedly welcomed Rochelle's presence on the set, telling her, "We're both old pros, so we won't have any trouble…. You still have the prettiest legs in Hollywood."[166] The film that resulted received mixed reviews, but made a healthy profit.

Though she still enjoyed acting, Rochelle said it wasn't integral to her existence. "Acting seems to be a narcotic to some people. It's not to me. I've never been that way. I can keep busy without ordering the tranquilizers." Still, she was reluctant to abandon it altogether, saying, "The most I've accomplished for the most people has been as an actress. So if I don't act it's not fair to that talent."[167] Her representatives, the Von-Young Agency of Hollywood, described her in the mid–1960s as 5'3", 115 pounds, blue-eyed, and suitable to play roles in the age range of 40 to 50. A brief biography of their client stated, "Rochelle swims, paints, plays piano, makes hook rugs and raises tropical fish in her spare time." She was booked as a "cameo guest star" on *Branded* (1965), the NBC-TV Western drama. A *Branded* publicity photo called her "a star of two decades ago," inaccurately describing her role in a Mae West film.

Studio publicity portrait of Rochelle as a featured player in *Strait-Jacket* (1964).

If her career was winding down, she still had her share of admirers, among them L.C. Melchior, who hosted a nostalgic radio show on KPEL-AM in Lafayette, Louisiana, and came to view Rochelle "like a second mother." Melchior visited the West Coast in the summer of 1963, and again the following year; he later recalled, "Rochelle Hudson took me to the homes of well-known people, and to movie studios. We found artifacts left from sets of the '20s and '30s. It was as if time stood still."[168] Hudson arranged for Melchior to be welcomed into the home of retired comedian Harold Lloyd, and gave him a glimpse into a Hollywood that was already passing into memory. Afterward, as Melchior's daughter recalled, "They communicated often via mail and talked on the phone a lot."[169]

In 1967, Miss Hudson made her final motion picture appearance, in a low-budget horror film variously known as *Gallery of Horror* and *Dr. Terror's Gallery of Horror*.

Final Act

Another vocational interest took root in Rochelle's life once her acting days were behind her. In 1968, a reporter wrote, "Rochelle Hudson sold her real estate in Arizona and has turned real estate broker in Brentwood."[170] She received a California real estate license that took effect on June 14, 1968. The following year, author Richard Lamparski stated that she had her own real estate brokerage firm in Palm Desert, California. By that time, she had few remaining ties to Hollywood, though she and old pal Alice Faye maintained contact.

She took up residence in the desert town where her mother had been residing for the past several years, as Madeleine Myers reported in the *Palm Desert Post*:

> A special welcome to two of our newest residents at 77–038 California Drive. They are Mr. and Mrs. Robert Lewis Mendell [sic] and the Mrs. is none other than the glamorous Rochelle Hudson of Movie fame. Rochelle is quite a successful Real Estate Gal these days and is now working with Walt Price of Golf Realtors.... Mae Hudson, mother of Rochelle and one of our first residents ... of course is so thrilled that lovely Rochelle and husband have decided to make [Palm Desert Country Club] their permanent home.[171]

Ads in *The Desert Sun* for properties represented by Golf Realty urged buyers to contact "your hostess, Rochelle Hudson." She became friendly with Price and his wife Lorena. According to the Prices' daughter Adriane Scheinost, "My mom actually got to know Rochelle better than my dad as both Mom and Rochelle were from Oklahoma. They both had been relocated to California at a young age. That gave them a connection." Adriane met the retired actress a few times at her parents' home, and she remembered, "Nothing regarding her past was ever discussed."[172]

In 1969, Rochelle and Mae entertained guests in Palm Desert: Mae's nephew Homer Deane Goddard, his wife Marie and their teenage daughter, named Rochelle in honor of her famous relative. While Mr. and Mrs. Goddard bunked at Mae's house, daughter Rochelle Ellen spent much of the day, and stayed overnight, at Rochelle's one-story house.

The young visitor, who'd seen several of Rochelle's movies, remembered that the actress, in her early fifties, "looked a little paunchy to me."[173] She recalled that Rochelle had allowed her hair to grow out, extending four or five inches below the neck, and tied it back with a ribbon. Young Rochelle was surprised to see the dark hair was now streaked with gray. Pouring glasses of soda for herself and her visitor, Miss Hudson then reached into a cabinet and pulled out a bottle, with which she topped off her drink. She also smoked throughout the visit.

During the teenager's stay, Rochelle took a phone call. A short time later, there was a knock at the door. The star opened the door to admit a neatly dressed middle-aged man with dark hair, who was carrying an empty box. It was Rochelle's husband. With barely a greeting to either Rochelle, Mindell took the box into the kitchen, and they could hear the sounds of him gathering and packing things. "Oh, he's taking the pots and pans," Rochelle announced calmly. A few minutes later, said Rochelle Goddard, "he walked out the front door, and that was it." Hudson explained to the teenager that he was her "soon-to-be ex-husband," Bob Mindell.

As a child, Rochelle Goddard had been presented with an 8×10 glossy of her famous relative looking glamorous in evening dress, which the actress had inscribed "From Big Rochelle to Little Rochelle." As the girl grew up, she had the opportunity to see a few Rochelle Hudson movies, including *Poppy* and *Curly Top*, usually after her mother had spotted a listing in *TV Guide*. When they met several years later, young Rochelle found her relative to be "a little bit of a quiet person," one who wasn't inclined to offer reminiscences about her Hollywood days. "She didn't talk a lot about her movie career," Goddard recalled. "You had to pull answers out of Rochelle." She did volunteer, however, that she had recently auditioned for a spot on *The Dean Martin Show*. Miss Hudson admitted that she had lost out to actress Kay Medford, who made multiple appearances on Martin's show in the early 1970s.

A James Dean fan, young Rochelle was a bit disappointed that Miss Hudson didn't have strong recollections of him from *Rebel Without a Cause*. Hudson explained that he wasn't on the set during the days when she shot her brief scenes. She recalled only that she saw him one day in the studio commissary, and had noticed him riding his bike around the lot. Of W.C. Fields, Hudson remembered, with perhaps a bit of understatement, "He did take sips of alcohol occasionally."

Rochelle filed paperwork to end her marriage to Robert L. Mindell, then employed as manager of the Elks Club in Cathedral City. Back in Kansas City, Rochelle's elderly father passed away in the fall of 1971. His obituary in the *Kansas City Star* (September 2, 1971) reported, "Ollie Lee Hudson, 99, of 10 E. 40th, died yesterday at the General Hospital. Mr. Hudson was born in Vandalia, Mo., and had lived here 30 years.... He leaves a daughter, Miss R. Elizabeth Hudson, Los Angeles."

Rochelle and her mother were still in frequent contact, living in close proximity. Mae grew concerned one day when her daughter was suddenly unreachable. She sought the help of Walter Price, who had a spare key to her home. Late on the afternoon of January 17, 1972, Price made a horrifying discovery: Rochelle was dead. According to newspaper accounts, "Walter Price, a real estate business associate, found the body Monday after being summoned by Miss Hudson's widowed mother, Mae Hudson, who got no response from her daughter by telephone or at the door."[174]

The cause of her death could not be immediately established. "The Riverside County sheriff's office said she may have suffered a heart attack and announced that an autopsy would be performed.... A friend, Evelyn Young, said Miss Hudson had been ill recently with a cold and laryngitis."[175] The autopsy attributed her death to pneumonia.[176] A recurring liver ailment was named as a contributing factor.

No funeral services were held. In lieu of flowers, contributions to the Motion Picture Relief Fund were suggested. Hudson's body was cremated and her ashes scattered. Her death came just as her fourth marriage was finally dissolved. "Miss Hudson's divorce from her fourth husband, Robert L. Mindell, became final 10 days ago," said the *Intelligencer-Journal*'s account. About four months later, Mindell married his third wife, Treva; they divorced the following year. He died in 1997. The late star's friend L.C. Melchior later recalled, "Rochelle Hudson died a few days before she was to come and visit me."[177] A few years after her death, Melchior paid tribute to the actress by naming his daughter Rochelle.

A society columnist for the *Palm Desert Post* (January 27, 1972) wrote, "Condolences to Mae Hudson on the death of her beloved daughter Rochelle Hudson. Rochelle's beauty and soft voice will be remembered.... Hats off to Mae Hudson for engineering such a successful place in life for her daughter."[178]

A few weeks later, Mae was contacted by the local sheriff's office to pass along a message from a lady named Fairy Kirkland, who had been trying to reach her. Mae remembered the young woman, who had worked for the family some 50 years earlier, and whom Rochelle had loved as a child. When they spoke, "Fairy felt Mae needed her and offered to come to California to take care of her. Mae declined the offer but said the happy tears of emotion welled in her heart to remember the loyal devotion."[179]

Even after her daughter's death, Mae did not allow Rochelle to be forgotten. A yearly scholarship, the Rochelle Hudson Memorial, was established, to be given by the Desert Symphony Auxiliary, the winner receiving a check for $250. Teenage piano student Jenny Cook of Rancho Mirage received the first Hudson scholarship, awarded at a ceremony in which the young woman performed a piano solo. Like Rochelle, the recipient had been something of a child prodigy; Jenny's mother, Mrs. Max Cook, started her daughter on the piano when she was four. "It's a lonely life when you're outstanding, and a lot of hard work," the proud mother stated.[180]

Rochelle's fans continued to remember her. North Carolina policeman Luther Hathcock corresponded with Walter Price and his wife for a few years after the star's death. The Prices responded to his interest by sharing some memorabilia, including a signed copy of her real estate license. Some time later, Mrs. Price made Hathcock a gift of "a painting of a green shady meadow with a stream running through it." He explained, "Rochelle had painted this art when she was a young schoolgirl."[181]

For a few years after her daughter's death, Mae continued to be socially active in the community. "A resident of Palm Desert Country Club since 1952, Mae Hudson ... was warmly welcomed at Woman's Club of the Desert November luncheon meeting and fashion show," noted one social page item in the fall of 1973.[182] In 1974, 92-year-old Mae attended a gala dinner party. A reporter wrote that she was still a participant in many desert cultural activities and called her "the vivacious, affable little dynamo...."[183] Another scribe wrote, "Mae has a figure that any teenager could envy, drives her own car, loves bridge and is [an] astute business woman."[184]

According to Adriane Scheinost, as Mae grew older, "both my parents would visit and keep an eye out on her." Mrs. Scheinost, who in the mid–1970s lived across the street from Mae, owned a St. Bernard at that time, and recalled, "Mae would come out and greet us when taking my girl for a walk. One of those times, she gave me some [photos] from a movie Rochelle worked on that also had a St. Bernard [*The Country Beyond*]."[185]

Visiting her great-aunt in the fall of 1973, Rochelle Goddard McNear, then 20, found that Mae observed a more formal lifestyle than her own upbringing had led her to expect. Comfortable in jeans and a sweatshirt one afternoon, the young woman was informed by Mae that dinner would be on the table soon. A few minutes later, she asked Rochelle, "Aren't you going to change? We dress for dinner here." During Rochelle's stay, Mae welcomed a visitor whom she introduced as her attorney. She added that she was working with him on preparing her will.

Within a few years, Mae's health began failing, and she died in Palm Desert on October 18, 1976. Her *Palm Desert Post* obituary (October 28, 1976) stated that she passed away "following a lengthy illness." She was survived by two nieces and three nephews. As Rochelle had no siblings and no offspring, Mae's death meant the end of that branch of the Hudson family tree. Her will left $10,000 to her nephew Homer Deane Goddard, but the bulk of her substantial estate (in excess of $1 million, according to Rochelle McNear) was bequeathed to the Motion Picture Relief Fund (now the Motion Picture and Television Fund).

Even today, Rochelle Hudson is remembered and appreciated by classic movie fans. Since her passing, the advent of home video and cable TV channels devoted to classic film have provided new audiences with opportunities to discover her work. In 1990, the National Film Registry's second annual list of important American motion pictures recognized *Rebel Without a Cause* as being of historic significance. *Imitation of Life* and *Wild Boys of the Road* were later added to the Registry.

The establishment of the Warner Archive in the late 2000s pioneered a welcome trend for releasing lesser-known oldies on DVD, such as Rochelle's *Harold Teen*. 20th Century–Fox likewise opened its vaults, unveiling *Show Them No Mercy!* and *Rascals*, among others. Even Rochelle's little-seen B movies have emerged. Barrie Roberts wrote when profiling her for *Classic Images* (February 1998), "Her very presence in 'B' films has long served to increase our pleasure in watching these little pictures." On any given day, there are typically several hundred items of Hudson memorabilia up for sale on eBay, indicating that interest in her continues to be strong.

If her motion picture career, ultimately, was not all it could have been, Rochelle nonetheless enjoyed a healthy run and gave some memorable performances (even when the films themselves did not live up to the same standard). It is our good fortune that so many of them can be seen and relished today.

Filmography

Major Film Roles

Fanny Foley Herself (1931)

Edna May Oliver (*Fanny Foley*), Hobart Bosworth (*Seely*), Florence Roberts (*Lucy*), Rochelle Hudson (*Carmen*), Helen Chandler (*Lenore*), John Darrow (*Teddy*), Robert Emmet [Emmett] O'Connor (*Burns*), Harry Stubbs (*Crosby*)
    Director: Melville W. Brown. *Supervisor*: John E. Burch. *Adaptation and Dialogue*: Carey Wilson. *Story*: Juliet Wilbur Tompkins. *Additional Dialogue*: Bernard Schubert. *Photographer*: Ray Rennahan. *Art Director–Costumes*: Max Rée. *Recordist*: George D. Ellis.
    RKO Radio Pictures; released October 10, 1931. 72 minutes.

    Vaudeville performer Fanny Foley earns $1000 a week on the stage. When her husband dies, Fanny's father-in-law Seely suggests that she turn her children over to him, suggesting she cannot properly look after them. Though Seely promises to leave the girls considerable fortunes in his will, Fanny instead enrolls them in boarding school. But when she plays an engagement nearby, her daughters, Lucy and Carmen, are embarrassed by her onstage antics.

    Insisting that Fanny must stop performing, the girls drop out of school and go to work so that they can support their mother. Not wanting them to sacrifice their futures, Fanny accepts her father-in-law's offer of a cottage on his property where they can live. She tells her daughters an old boyfriend of hers is their benefactor. The girls grow closer to their grandfather, to Fanny's sorrow.

    Carmen elopes with an impoverished young man, Teddy, and Fanny gives the young couple her support. Fanny realizes that she must mend the relationship with Seely to make things work out happily for all concerned.

    Presently categorized as a lost film, *Fanny Foley Herself* is an unusual example of an early sound film shot in Technicolor. With the Great Depression well underway, and vaudeville still a viable entertainment medium in 1931, some reviewers scorned the notion that Fanny's daughters would turn up their noses at their mother's stage success, or the substantial salary that came with it. "[Her] daughters are ashamed of her because she's an actress!" scoffed a reviewer for *Picture Play* (January 1932). "They're daughters you'd love to touch with a club."

Edna May Oliver (1883–1942) was on her way to becoming one of America's best-known character actresses. Publicity for *Fanny Foley Herself* reminded theatergoers of her recent film *Cimarron* (1931), a Best Picture Academy Award winner. Six months before *Fanny Foley*, Rochelle had played a minor role in Oliver's film *Laugh and Get Rich*. In *Fanny Foley*, she was entrusted by the studio with the featured role of Carmen, and increased screen time.

Reviews: "A fairly good comedy, with human interest…. The picture is not particularly exciting, but the heroine wins the sympathy of the audience by her love for her children…. Poor casting of the principal part has hurt it. No one will disagree that Edna May Oliver is an artist…. But she is miscast." *Harrison's Reports*, October 31, 1931

"Vaudeville is looked down upon by the scenario to make it appear the daughters and the father-in-law are wholly correct [that] the widowed mother is not fit to bring them up properly…. There are few laughs above a mild snicker, and plenty of the running time is sluggish. Miss Oliver is excellent throughout despite the material handicap…. The girls are Helen Chandler and Rochelle Hudson, latter a comparatively recent high school find of Radio's…. Color is soft and pleasing." *Variety*, October 27, 1931

Are These Our Children (1931)

Eric Linden (*Eddie Brand*), Beryl Mercer (*Eddie's Grandma*), Billy Butts (*Bobby Brand*), Rochelle Hudson (*Mary*), William Orlamond (*Heinrich "Heinie" Krantz*), Arline Judge (*Flo Carnes*), Roberta Gale (*Maybelle*), Mary Kornman (*Agnes*), Ben Alexander (*Nick Crosby*), Bobby Quirk (*Bennie Gray*), James Wang (*Sam Kong*), Robert McKenzie (*Oscar Cook*), Ralf Harolde (*Prosecutor*), Harry Shutan (*Defense Attorney*), Reginald Barlow (*Judge*), Earl Pingree (*Charlie*), Russ Powell (*Sam—Policeman*)

Director-Story: Wesley Ruggles. *Producer*: William LeBaron. *Adaptation and Dialogue*: Howard Estabrook. *Associate Producer*: Louis Sarecky. *Scenery-Costumes*: Max Rée. *Photographer*: Leo Tover. *Recordist*: Clem Portman. *Editor*: William Hamilton. *Music*: Max Steiner. *Photographic Effects*: Lloyd Knechtel.

RKO; released November 14, 1931. 84 minutes.

High schooler Eddie Brand is a young man of modest income but big dreams, with a sweetly loyal girlfriend, Mary. His buoyant outlook on the future takes a hit when he loses an oratorical contest. Embarrassed by the setback, he declares he's dropping out of school and going to work full-time. His devoted grandmother makes him promise to stay in school.

Dejected, he's easy prey for a "fast" girl, Flo, and he agrees to accompany her and her friends on a visit to a nightclub. The six young people dance to jazzy music, and the liquor flows freely. That first evening, Flo and her friends give Eddie a crash course in dangerous influences, from gambling to sources of easy money. Before long, he's neglecting Mary, impulsively quitting three jobs in a month's time, and coming home drunk in the wee hours. Grandma's gentleman friend "Heinie" Krantz, owner of a deli, promises to give Eddie a fatherly talk, but she isn't convinced he'll listen.

Out partying one evening, Eddie and his new friends run low on booze. Realizing they're near Heinie's delicatessen in the Jamaica neighborhood, Eddie bangs on the front door until he and his cohorts Bennie and Nick are admitted. Heinie stands up to the drunken Eddie, who impulsively shoots and kills him. Eddie is initially shaken, but when police are unsuccessful after a three-week hunt for the killer, he begins to relax, and even grow cocky. Soon, loose lips sink ships, and the entire sextet is thrown into prison. A newspaper headline reads, "Sheiks, Flappers Jailed in Killing."

A competently made motion picture, *Are These Our Children* seems to have as its principal goal to scare the hell out of parents of teenagers. As the film opens, a legend tells us, "Youth—love—and happiness—these make the world go round.... To all, each day, comes choice—every hour we must decide.... One way leads to shadows—the other into peace and light...." RKO promoted the film as "a penetrating drama of today."

Stage actor Eric Linden (1909–1994) makes an impressive film debut as Eddie. A fan magazine article proclaimed that director Wesley Ruggles "was having one of the hardest times in history trying to find a lead" to play the role, having unsuccessfully tested more than 100 young actors. Told about Linden's success on the stage in the East Coast, Ruggles arranged a test: "Eric passed with flying colors, hopped an airplane, and landed in Hollywood in less than forty-eight hours."[1] The part of Eddie required him to make a zero-to-60 transition from nice clean-cut boy to braggadocious reprobate, but Linden pulls it off. He's helped by some early script references to the young man's overweening ambition, as when he brags, "You better get used to seeing me in the papers, Heinie. I'm gonna be there plenty! ... I'm gonna be somebody!"

Fifteen-year-old Rochelle plays his goody-two-shoes girlfriend. Her character can only watch helplessly as Eddie loses interest in the kind of life she represents, but remains in his corner nonetheless, even at the eleventh hour. In early scenes, she seems to be pitching her speaking voice above its natural register, as if to sound completely young and naïve, but does this less as the film progresses. Her role doesn't require heavy emoting, but she does fine with a moment in which she is reduced to tears at what her former boyfriend has become. The *San Francisco Examiner*'s Ada Hanifin (November 12, 1931) took notice of Rochelle's contribution, limited though it was, commenting that she "probably would do unusually well if her part demanded it of her."

Studio publicity called Hudson "the extra girl who has been picked out of mob scenes for 'bits' several times. Not long ago she was given a small part. Now that she has been honored with a feminine lead and one that many RKO stars would relish, it is predicted that Miss Hudson is headed for stardom." Gossip column items reported that Rochelle and her leading man carried their on-screen relationship into at least a few dates.

Contrasted with Mary is Arline Judge (1912–1974), as the brassy, trashy Flo, who cheerfully leads Eddie down the road to Hell. With the Motion Picture Production Code not yet being fully enforced, Judge is free to make Flo a trampy threat to decency. The polar opposite of demure Mary, she gazes admiringly down Eddie's shirt front on their first night out, remarking on his lack of an undershirt, and is soon kissing him fervently. She later comments, "Gee, you're gorgeous!" At Eddie's trial, she's amusing in the midst of tragedy when she testifies that she knows the defendant "very, very well indeed."

Judge clearly made a strong impression on director Ruggles (1889–1972); they announced their engagement in September 1931 and wed the following month. After their 1937 divorce, Judge made six more trips to the altar, while continuing to amass film credits, often as women of uncertain virtue. Professionally, Ruggles had been widely acclaimed for his previous film, *Cimarron*, quite different from this film. *Are These Our Children* originated with a story idea of Ruggles', which he successfully pitched to RKO's William LeBaron.

Character actress Beryl Mercer (1876–1939) gives warmth and solidity to the role of Eddie's loving grandmother, who has raised him since the death of his mother. Her strongest moment comes with her heartfelt testimony on the witness stand at Eddie's trial.

Though this story undoubtedly seemed fresher 90 years ago, today's viewer may find it a bit too predictable. It begins to lag a bit in the middle, but the trial scenes and climax are still effective. Although the film's title would seem to be, as the late Alex Trebek often said, "in the form of a question," sources vary as to whether or not it actually concludes with a question mark. On-screen, it does not.

Reviews: "Likely to be hailed both as a masteral [sic] preachment against the 'wild youth' of the day and, on the other hand, as a pessimistic picture of modern youngsters. But it will be talked about, and that makes business…. Ruggles has done a sincere and competent job." *Motion Picture Herald*, October 17, 1931

"Despite its air of propaganda, and a title that lacks every element of popular appeal, *Are These Our Children* holds one until the closing scenes. Whether or not it may be classified as entertainment is apt to be a moot question, but the fact remains that the film is a product of quality and one to be taken seriously…. Eric Linden … is sensational in the [lead] and readily establishes himself as a juvenile actor of outstanding ability." Whitney Williams, *Los Angeles Times*, October 25, 1931

Beyond the Rockies (1932)

Tom Keene (*Blackjack*), Rochelle Hudson (*Betty Allen*), Marie Wells (*Ruby Sherman*), Julian Rivero (*Lavender Joe*), Ernie Adams (*Blinky*), Hank Bell (*Whiskey Bill*), William Welsh (*Frank Allen*), Tom London (*Kirk Tracy*), Ted Adams (*Emory*)
Director: Fred Allen. *Producer*: David O. Selznick. *Screenplay*: Oliver Drake. *Story*: John P. McCarthy. *Dialogue*: Bennett Cohen. *Photographer:* Ted McCord. *Editor*: William Clemens. *Art Director*: Carroll Clark. *Recordist*: Richard Tyler. *Assistant Director*: Dave Lewis.
RKO Pathé; released July 8, 1932. 54 minutes.

In the Old West, Blackjack and his scruffy-looking compadres, Lavender Joe, Blinky and Whiskey Bill, see that a stagecoach is being robbed and ride to the rescue. The driver wonders if Blackjack and his men are yet another gang, after they ask how much gold he's carrying. Following the coach into a nearby town, the four men receive a cold welcome from the townspeople, who are told that Blackjack has "a reputation of being a wizard with a gun." The sheriff is anticipating a confrontation, which he's ill-equipped to handle. Almost all the able-bodied men in town have gone to work for rancher Ruby Sherman. Taking advantage of her hired muscle, Ruby is gradually buying up all the smaller ranches, putting the livelihood of rancher Frank Allen and his daughter Betty at risk.

Betty wants to hire Blackjack and his men to insure that her father is able to safely transport his cattle for sale without interference by rustlers. Blackjack's three pals are surprised that he accepts the offer to work on the Bar A Ranch. With old habits dying hard, Blackjack's sidekicks are tempted to filch the cash the ranchers have on hand, but he doesn't allow this, saying, "We're on the level now."

When he learns that his gang members appropriated some cattle from the Sherman ranch, Blackjack insists they be returned. But in doing so, they are confronted by Ruby's men, and her foreman Kirk Tracy shoots and kills Whiskey Bill. At the local saloon, Blackjack finds Tracy and administers his own justice with his fists. He unwittingly drops a badge he was carrying, which Ruby finds and keeps.

Ruby fires Tracy and offers Blackjack the chance to become her new foreman. In the meantime, her men rustle some of the Allens' cattle. Tracking the missing cattle, Blackjack encounters Ruby and accepts her offer to serve as foreman. She offers to employ Lavender Joe and Blinky as well, but he tells them to stay put and help the Allens.

When Blackjack arrives at the Sherman ranch, Ruby has her men overpower Blackjack, making him realize his cover as a deputy marshal was blown when he dropped his badge. Blackjack escapes and hurries back to the Allen ranch, warning them that the Sherman gang plans to rustle their cattle across the border. Mr. Allen is skeptical of Blackjack's motives, thinking him disloyal, but Betty defends him. Reunited, Blackjack and his cohorts ride into danger on behalf of the Allens, with the opposition led by none other than Kirk Tracy.

Leading man Tom Keene (1896–1963) began his career in the silent era and became a staple of B Westerns. Originally acting under his real name George Duryea, he became Keene in 1930, and later in life took on yet another name, Richard Powers. He was evidently a childhood favorite of cult film director Edward D. Wood, Jr. (1924–1978), who had him make a cameo appearance as Col. Tom Edwards in *Plan 9 from Outer Space* (1958).

Rochelle, 16 years old, has a sizable though undemanding role as Betty Allen. B Westerns could be a good training ground for inexperienced young actresses, and she does fairly well with what little she is given to do. It's difficult to say whether to blame her or director Fred Allen (1896–1955) for her "I've got an idea" close-up, in which she first brainstorms hiring Blackjack. With everything short of a light bulb appearing over her head, it's done broadly enough that it would have gotten the message across easily even in a silent film—or for an audience of rowdy boys at a Saturday matinee.

She later said of this role, "When I found myself playing second fiddle to a horse, I was certain that when Hollywood saw the picture, I'd never get another part."[2] Her character gazes admiringly at the handsome Blackjack from their first meeting, and it's implied that they'll go off into the sunset together at the fadeout.

Marie Wells (1894–1949) has a somewhat more forceful role as villainous Ruby Sherman, who is described before we meet her as "the Cattle King, minus the pants." Julian Rivero (1890–1976) doesn't go overboard with the comic character of Lavender Joe, who boasts of his past crimes, but when called on it, says sheepishly that he is "the biggest liar in all of Mexico."

Screenwriter Oliver Drake (1903–1991) spent the bulk of his lengthy career turning out tales of the Old West. The Fred Allen who directed is not the acclaimed comedian; he's a longtime film editor, with many more credits in that capacity than in the director's chair.

Beyond the Rockies followed by only a few years another Western of the same title, released in 1926. That version, which starred Bob Custer, had a similar plot involving cattle rustlers (hardly a novel theme in the genre) but different character names and somewhat different incidents. No story credit is given to the original writers in the second film.

Reviews: "Here is a western crammed with blazing action, two-fisted fighting and all sorts of gun-play to please the most rabid fan. Tom Keene is a very personable lad, and knows how to handle himself in all the varied situations." *Film Daily*, September 16, 1932

"Basically this is the same old law officer parading as a bad man to catch the cattle rustlers. But the seedy old plot has been jazzed up.... As it stands it's a better than average western.... Keene makes a likable lead.... Rochelle Hudson is the heroine, but that means nothing in a western.... Script well developed and directed for the fullest effect." *Variety*, September 20, 1932

Hell's Highway (1932)

Richard Dix (*Duke Ellis*), Tom Brown (*Johnny Ellis*), Rochelle Hudson (*Mary Ellen*), C. Henry Gordon (*Skinner*), Oscar Apfel (*William Billings*), Stanley Fields (*F.E. Whiteside*), John Arledge (*Carter*), Warner Richmond (*"Pop-Eye" Jackson*), Charles Middleton (*Matthew*), Louise Carter (*Mrs. Ellis*), Sandy Roth (*Maxie*), Clarence Muse (*Rascal*), Fuzzy Knight (*Red*), Louise Beavers (*Rascal's Visitor*), Eddie Hart (*"Turkey Neck" Burgess*), Allan Cavan (*Hunt Club Manager*), Jed Kiley (*"Romeo" Schultz*), John Lester Johnson (*"Blubber Mouth"*), Robert Homans (*Sheriff*), Broderick O'Farrell (*Doctor*), Harry Smith (*"Buzzard"*)

Director: Rowland Brown. *Executive Producer*: David O. Selznick. *Screenplay*: Samuel Ornitz, Robert Tasker, Rowland Brown. *Photographer*: Edward Cronjager. *Art Director*: Carroll Clark. *Music Director*: Max Steiner. *Recordist*: John Tribby. *Editor*: William Hamilton.

RKO; released September 23, 1932. 62 minutes.

The job of building a new highway, the Liberty Road, has been awarded to contractor William Billings, who is given access to chain gang inmates to do the work.

The prisoners are driven mercilessly to meet Billings' deadline, including the use of a brutal "sweat-box" where malingerers and troublemakers are punished. When one young man, Carter, dies in the sweat-box, prison officials call it suicide.

When the cons are forced to go hungry because of a single missing spoon, Duke Ellis, a repeat offender who specialized in robbing banks, leads a revolt. Just as work resumes, a new batch of prisoners is processed into the camp, among them Duke's 18-year-old brother Johnny. Johnny hero-worshiped Duke and attempted to assault the man he blames for Duke's imprisonment.

Prisoner Matthew, who professes his gifts as a seer, is recruited to aid Duke's escape plan, which involves guard "Pop-Eye" Jackson. Matthew persuades Jackson to open the prison gate temporarily, so that he can consult the stars. Duke passes up the chance to escape that night when he sees Johnny, but Jackson exploits the opened gate to kill his wife. Two of the escaped prisoners are accused of the crime.

Johnny gets into a fight with another chain gang member and is thrown into the sweat-box. Duke exploits his hold over Jackson to get his kid brother reassigned to an easy office job, but in return he is expected to help keep the other prisoners working. When the Ellis brothers' mother visits them, she brings along Johnny's girlfriend Mary Ellen, who isn't impressed by Duke's bluster, and makes him realize he bears responsibility for leading Johnny astray.

Whiteside, a guard sent to the camp to investigate conditions there, is favorably impressed by Johnny and recommends that he be paroled. But in the meantime, Johnny, opening the office mail, learns that Duke is being extradited to Michigan, where as a repeat offender he will be imprisoned for life. Johnny sneaks a rifle to Duke, who tells him to put it back. Before Johnny can do so, another prisoner snatches it, and in minutes a deadly prison break, as well as a fire stoked by kerosene, are underway.

Hell's Highway made it to theaters only weeks ahead of Warner Brothers' *I Am a Fugitive from a Chain Gang*. The film opens by panning across authentic newspaper headlines from publications like the *Seattle Post-Intelligencer*, decrying the abuses taking place in chain gangs. An on-screen legend reads, "Dedicated to an early end of the conditions portrayed herein—which, though a throw-back to the Middle Ages, actually exist today." Almost relentlessly grim (as befits the subject matter), the film does make its points strongly, and is rarely dull. While never trying to represent the chain gang members as wronged innocents, it does make it clear that their treatment is deplorable, and that there is a profit motive at work that deserves exposure.

Richard Dix (1893–1949) is believable in the leading role of Duke Ellis, projecting strength and intensity and even evoking compassion despite his character's failings. As his fresh-faced brother, Tom Brown (1913–1990) embodies the teenager who his brother realizes may not yet be beyond redemption.

We get our first glimpse of 16-year-old Rochelle near the film's halfway point, when we see the photo of Mary Ellen that Johnny carries. In her single in-person scene, we see that Mary Ellen is a sweet, caring young lady, but no fool. Baited by

Young Rochelle is pictured with Tom Brown on this *Hell's Highway* (1932) lobby card.

Duke about women causing men to steal, Mary Ellen calmly replies, "Johnny don't have to steal for me." She brings about an epiphany for Duke when she adds, "The only thing that's wrong with Johnny is that he thinks you're something wonderful."

Among the strong supporting performances is that of Charles Middleton (1874–1949). Still a few years away from his career-defining role as Ming the Merciless, Middleton gives a certain tense edge to the eccentric Matthew, who explains that life under lock and key is easier than facing his three wives. Louise Beavers (1902–1962) is unbilled in her small role as Rascal's lady, while Eddie Hart (1898–1972) is cast as what one reviewer termed "a nance camp laborer."

According to *Variety* (September 27, 1932), the film's original downbeat ending was revised after previews to allow for a glimmer of optimism.

Reviews: "Because of the subject with which it deals there is nothing dainty about *Hell's Highway*. It's bitter drama of bitter men, but despite its harshness it should prove to be a sensational picture…. Given the backing of a truth-telling campaign, with the name of Dix, who is really great in the picture … you can count strongly on *Hell's Highway*." *Motion Picture Herald*, August 20, 1932

"Coming in the van [*sic*] of a threatening chain gang cycle, this tense drama should draw attention. The action deals with the tortuous conditions in a convict labor camp, where mean treatment causes prisoners to break for liberty…. There is enough human interest to give the picture a little appeal for women, though it is too strong stuff for kids." *Film Daily*, September 27, 1932

The Savage Girl (1932)

Rochelle Hudson (*The Girl*), Walter Byron (*Jim Franklin*), Harry C. Myers (*Amos P. Stitch*), Adolph Milar (*Erich Vernuth*), Theodore [Ted] Adams (*Chauffeur*), Floyd Shackelford (*Oscar*), Charles Gemora (*Gorilla*), Herbert Evans, John Ince (*Club Members*)

Director: Harry L. Fraser. *Supervisor*: Burton King. *Story, Continuity and Dialogue*: Brewster Morse. *Photographer*: Edward Kull. *Assistant Director*: Harry Knight. *Editor*: Fred Bain. *Sound Technician*: Homer Ackerman. *Music Supervisor*: Lee Zahler.

Monarch Film Corp./Commonwealth Pictures; released December 5, 1932. 66 minutes.

Author and explorer Jim Franklin, an expert on Africa and its wild animals, speaks to a New York City men's club about his experiences. Wealthy (and somewhat inebriated) Amos P. Stitch, of the Westchester County set, tells him that he wants a zoo at his estate. Jim agrees to take Stitch on an expedition to Africa, with the latter paying all expenses while they collect the animals. When their taxicab driver to the New York docks tells them he's always wanted to see Africa, he and his vehicle are simply added to the luggage. To find out if it's true that elephants are afraid of mice, Stitch buys several rodents at the last minute to take along.

Upon landing, Jim engages an assistant, Erich Vernuth, who warns him that the area he proposes to visit is dangerous, with "bad natives." Vernuth also mentions a white "jungle goddess" who lives companionably among the animals; "No white man has ever seen her." Among the several natives hired to carry their belongings is Oscar, a Harlem native wishing he could get back home.

When the travelers make camp, a chimpanzee alerts the jungle goddess to their arrival. She watches and is pleased when Jim helps an animal with an injured paw, but is upset to see that their wooden cage has trapped a lion. She follows the men back to their camp. In the morning, the hunters awaken to see that the cage is empty. Vernuth reminds his boss of the legend of the jungle goddess, but Jim is skeptical.

When the girl falls into a tiger pit, Jim comes to her rescue. Carrying her back to their camp, he places her in an empty hut. Vernuth, having knocked back a few drinks, tries to molest her. Jim punches and then fires Vernuth, who vows to come back with an unpleasant surprise. The girl, grateful to Jim, begins to warm up to him. Eventually she and Jim get better acquainted. Vernuth incites the natives, who kidnap Jim and prepare for a human sacrifice. The lecherous Vernuth once again plots to force his attentions on the terrified girl.

The Savage Girl offers an hour of undemanding action, centering on a female counterpart to Tarzan. (MGM's *Tarzan the Ape Man*, starring Johnny Weissmuller and Maureen O'Sullivan, had been released the previous spring.) From the outset, it takes a somewhat whimsical tone, as an on-screen legend tells us, "Come with us on the trail of the beautiful white Jungle Goddess. Laugh with us—cheer with us—thrill with us ... and, with complete mental abandon, accept it for its contribution to pure enjoyment."

Rochelle makes her entrance as the jungle goddess one-third of the way into the film, looking quite fetching in her brief leopard skin and a lengthy, somewhat messy, wig. Initially, her dialogue consists solely of unintelligible murmurs, directed mostly at her four-legged friends, and an occasional lusty scream once she encounters the hunting party. Later, she utters a few hesitant English words, repeating bits of Jim's speech. When she's first captured, he says, "She's just as ferocious as many a wild animal I've tried to capture. You should have seen her try to bite me." But he soon sees a more appealing side of her.

Rochelle's performance calls for her to use her eyes, her lithe movements, and her varied facial expressions as she reacts to new experiences. Though many of the animals seen in the jungle seem to come to us courtesy of stock footage, she does cuddle a few of the smaller ones in close-up shots. The film's pressbook had her saying, "The part was doubly difficult because there was so much I had to 'say' by actually saying nothing! But Mr. Fraser, the director, was kindness itself."[3]

Walter Byron (1899–1972), who played some of his early film roles under his birth name Walter Butler, was active as a film actor for nearly 20 years, though he often played minor roles. He's adequate as Jim, who's supposedly perfectly at ease in the wilderness, telling a New Yorker early in the film, "I'm more afraid of your taxicabs, congested traffic and subway rushes than I am of lions, crocodiles and elephants." As Amos Stitch, Harry C. Myers (1882–1938) plays a man who's slightly tipsy from start to finish, but does prove to be more reliable than expected when the chips are down. Charles Gemora (1903–1961), who enjoyed a lengthy career as one of Hollywood's most expert impersonators of gorillas, turns up to play a heroic one near the end of the film.

In the *Motion Picture Herald*'s "What the Picture Did for Me" column (February 11, 1933), a Milwaukee exhibitor reported, "Something new and different from the usual, with plenty of comedy relief which is just what the public wants. Photography and sound very good. We ballyhooed this one and did a very splendid business."

Reviews: "This is frankly a thrill meller for consumption in spots where they like their entertainment dished up with broad and telling strokes. There is nothing arty or subtle about it. It is a rehash of all the pop elements that have gone into scores of other jungle pictures.... Rochelle Hudson plays the [lead] part, clothed in a scanty leopard skin. That is about the only wild thing about her. She goes through her part in a matter of fact manner." *Film Daily*, January 6, 1933

"[T]here isn't much name strength, but word of mouth should help this one. Harry Myers is excellent as the comedian, and the animal background offers exploitation possibilities ... [An] audience pleaser." *New York State Exhibitor*, January 25, 1933

She Done Him Wrong (1933)

Mae West (*Lady Lou*), Cary Grant (*Captain Cummings*), Owen Moore (*Chick Clark*), Gilbert Roland (*Serge Stanieff*), Noah Beery, Sr. (*Gus Jordan*), David Landau (*Dan Flynn*), Rafaela Ottiano (*Russian Rita*), Dewey Robinson (*Spider Kane*), Rochelle Hudson (*Sally Glenn*), Tammany Young (*Chuck Connors*), Fuzzy Knight (*Rag Time Kelly*), Grace La Rue (*Frances*), Robert E. Homans (*Doheney*), Louise Beavers (*Pearl*)
    Director: Lowell Sherman. *Associate Producer*: William LeBaron. *Screenplay*: Mae West, Harvey Thew, John Wright. *Music and Lyrics*: Ralph Rainger. *Photographer*: Charles Lang. *Editor*: Alexander Hall. *Art Director*: Robert Usher. *Costumes*: Edith Head. *Assistant Director*: James Dugan. *Sound*: Harry Lindgren.
    Paramount; released January 27, 1933. 65 minutes.

In the Gay '90s, glamorous, seductive Lady Lou is the star attraction at Gus Jordan's nightclub. Though she and Jordan are romantically involved, there are other men in her life: jailbird Chick Clark, who stole diamonds for her, and a handsome newcomer, personable Captain Cummings, a preacher who runs the mission next door.

A young woman, Sally, is stopped just in time from committing suicide at Gus' place. Faint, she's taken upstairs to Lou's quarters, where the latter correctly surmises that her trouble involves a man. Lou arranges for her to have fresh clothes and turns her over to Russian Rita, who says there is a job Sally can do.

When Rita's partner Serge Stanieff pledges his love for Lou, and presents her with jewelry, a jealous Rita attacks Lou with a dagger, and he is killed in the ensuing fight. Further complications find Lou messily entangled with multiple rivals for her affection. An unexpected one reveals his true identity and plans to figure in her future.

She Done Him Wrong is one of the most enduring classics of Mae West (1893–1980), whose bravura performance leaves little room for anyone else in the cast to shine. Cary Grant (1904–1986), still in the early stages of his film career, is seen to good effect, however, as the charming Captain Cummings.

Present in the film for only a few minutes, Rochelle plays a character who gets from Lou some hard-earned wisdom about dealing with men. Afraid her reputation has been sullied by involvement with a married man, Sally is reassured by Mae's famous line, "When women go wrong, men go right after them." In an interview, Rochelle praised West: "She makes you feel that you have an important part in a play, even though she herself is the star."[4] She also recalled of this film, "Of course no one recollects anyone in that but Mae West."[5]

She Done Him Wrong was a somewhat controversial film at the time of its release, testing and expanding the boundaries of how explicit movie dialogue could—or should—be. Some exhibitors were hesitant to play it, fearful of community backlash, though few denied that it was funny. West's films quickly became a box office bonanza for Paramount, but her wings were clipped somewhat by the adoption of the Production Code, making her later films tamer and less fun.

Reviews: "Mae West's first starring film is steeped in sin and sex—but boys and girls, the laughs are there ... a strange mixture of melodrama, muck and belly laughs, with the laughs predominating.... The entire cast ... was excellent." *Hollywood Reporter*, January 10, 1933

"For a picture of its type it is entertaining; but it certainly is not for the family circle or for squeamish adults.... Mae West is in a class by herself, since she can do and say vulgar things, sing ribald songs, and still not be particularly offensive because of her likeable personality." *Harrison's Reports*, February 4, 1933

Love Is Dangerous (1933)

John Warburton (*Steve*), Rochelle Hudson (*Gwendolyn*), Bradley Page (*Dean Scarsdale*), Judith Vosselli (*Emily Scarsdale*), Dorothy Revier (*Pat Ormsby*), Albert Conti (*R.J. Ormsby*), Herta Lynd (*Paula*), May Beatty (*Gloria*), Lorin Raker (*Tom*)
   Director: Richard Thorpe. *Producer*: George R. Batcheller. *Screenplay and Dialogue*: Stuart Anthony. *Story*: Beulah Poynter. *Photographer*: M.A. Andersen. *Editor*: Roland Reed.
   Chesterfield; released March 15, 1933. 67 minutes.

Teenage Gwendolyn is infatuated with an older man, Steve, from the time she sees his photograph, but he proves resistant to her charms. After his initial rebuff, Gwendolyn connives to meet up with him at his mother's estate, accompanied by her sister, who is frustrated by her husband's jealousy. Romantic complications take a back seat to crime when a man is shot and Gwendolyn becomes the prime suspect. Steve hopes that posing as Gwendolyn's husband will help divert police attention from her.

Love Is Dangerous was originally announced and went into early release as *Love Is Like That*, also the title of Beulah Poynter's romance novel from which it was adapted. *Hollywood Filmograph* (December 3, 1932) reported that producer George Batcheller had taken an option on Poynter's book, published in 1930 by Chelsea House. The studio's synopsis said the film

> concerns the seriocomic consequences of a romantic youngster's campaign to win a handsome, woman-hating bachelor. Tossing aside all the traditional rules, this determined little damsel rushes right in and begins pummeling the heart of her adored, if somewhat chilly, Adonis. ...[S]he causes several misunderstandings along the way and becomes involved in an attempted murder mystery.

A small *Film Daily* advertisement (July 9, 1933) noted that the film's title had been belatedly amended, possibly in response to the bruising reviews it received from the trade publications that gazed upon it. Trying for a do-over, a different publicity approach was adopted: "Like a lesson in love along with your movie fare, girls? ... [T]his dramatic mystery romance presents a practically fool-proof program for getting involved in a couple of major domestic mixups, not to mention a murder attempt."

Leading man John Warburton (1903–1981), British by birth, had a modestly successful film career that lasted for several decades. Probably the luckiest survivor of this cinematic debacle was director Richard Thorpe (1896–1991), who directed everything from Tarzan films and Elvis Presley vehicles to *Ivanhoe* (1952) in a career that lasted into the 1960s. Chesterfield Pictures, which had been in existence since 1925, was a Poverty Row studio that struggled to gain a toehold in the movie marketplace. Thorpe directed much of its early 1930s output.

Three years after its release, Rochelle was dismayed when she saw a re-release of *Love Is Dangerous*. "I hardly recognized myself on the screen," she told columnist Sidney Skolsky (April 9, 1936). "My eyebrows were shaped differently, my hair didn't appear the same, my face was round and chubby."

Reviews (both under the original title): "Cumbersome … plot and insipid dialog. Cast can't do much with it, and picture ranks as an extremely poor indie effort. The performers evidently had complete free wheeling in manner and diction…. Little Rochele [*sic*] Hudson goes after her man despite rebuffs that would wilt a bill collector…. Unimaginative story unfolds forced situations to make the artificalty [*sic*] practically 100%." *Variety*, May 9, 1933

"Mediocre program fare. The story is thin, and the actions of the characters do not arouse sympathy for them. The heroine is a scatter-brained young girl [who] should have been spanked and sent back to school." *Harrison's Reports*, May 6, 1933

Notorious but Nice (1933)

> Marian Marsh (*Jenny Jones Charney*), Betty Compson (*Millie Sprague*), Donald Dillaway (*Richard Hamilton*), Rochelle Hudson (*Constance Martin*), John St. Polis (*John Martin*), J. Carrol Naish (*Joe Charney*), Dewey Robinson (*Tuffy Kraft*), Henry Kolker (*Defense Attorney Clark*), Robert Ellis (*Prosecutor*), Robert Frazer (*Park Man*), Wilfred Lucas (*Judge*), Michael Mark (*Bill Decker*), Jane Keckley (*Mrs. Kelly*), Frank Glendon (*Clark's Associate*), Clarence Geldert (*Old Man*), Edward Piel [Peil] (*Doctor at Sanitarium*), Nancy Cornelius (*Nurse*), Bess Flowers (*Miss Price*), Frank LaRue (*Haskell*), Henry Hall (*Visiting Doctor*), Hal Price (*New Tenant*), Rolfe Sedan (*Café Waiter*), Lee Phelps (*Millie's Pal*)
> *Director*: Richard Thorpe. *Producer*: George R. Batcheller. *Story*: Adeline Leitzbach. *Screenplay and Dialogue*: Carol Webster. *Photographer*: M.A. Andersen. *Editor*: Roland Reed. *Sound Technician*: Pete Clark. *Art Director*: Edward C. Jewell. *Assistant Director*: Melville Shyer.
> Chesterfield; released August 5, 1933. 70 minutes.

Young Jenny Jones and Richard Hamilton are in love, but she is hesitant to accept his marriage proposal. She reminds him that her boss, John Martin, is still the executor of his late father's estate, and doesn't want Dick to endanger his inheritance by doing anything of which the older man would disapprove. Not only does Martin plan to thwart the marriage, his beautiful daughter Constance wants Dick for herself. Martin sends him on a business trip to Montana to delay things, but before he leaves, Dick shows Jenny a cottage where he hopes they can live after they're married.

Summoning Jenny to his law office, Martin accuses her of lying about her past, noting that she told him she came from his hometown, which isn't true. Jenny admits she did so because she was in need of a job, but refuses to explain anything else about herself. After they argue, with Jenny branding him an "unspeakable cad," she is out of work. Jenny's neighbor, Millie Sprague, a brassy type who knows her way around, offers to get her a job at the nightclub where she works, but Jenny is reluctant.

Thanks to Millie, who's being paid by John Martin to intercept Dick's letters, Jenny hears nothing from him while she vainly seeks another job. Evicted from her apartment, Jenny is faint with hunger when a stranger offers her a meal. They end up at a slightly disreputable café, where the man presses liquor on her. Told he will find his fiancée there, Dick turns up just in time to punch the guy out. He's tossed into a cab and spirited away before Jenny can explain.

Refused the chance to speak with Martin at his office, Jenny collapses on the stairs of her old apartment building. Millie summons a doctor, who says she must be hospitalized. Disgusted by Martin's treatment of Jenny, Millie abruptly switches teams, telling him he will be paying for her care, if he knows what's good for him. While Jenny recuperates, she receives cards and flowers in Dick's name, but they are actually sent by Millie. When she calls Dick's residence and learns that he's away on an ocean voyage, Jenny is heartbroken.

Desperate to support herself, Jenny gives in to Millie's offer to get her a "hostess" job. Joe Charney, the club owner, takes a liking to her. Jenny holds out for the security of marriage, and soon becomes Joe's wife. Though Joe plies her with jewelry in lieu of soft words ("I'm not so good at saying those pretty things"), he suspects she hasn't gotten over Dick, while she implores him in vain to stick to honest living.

When Dick, now Constance's fiancé, escorts her to Joe's joint one evening, he crosses paths with Jenny, but she's prevented from clearing up any of the misunderstandings that separated them. She's summoned to Joe's office; moments later, shots ring out. His men burst in to find him dead. With a secret she won't disclose even to her defense attorney, Jenny goes on trial looking to be a shoo-in for the electric chair.

Notorious but Nice is an entertaining B movie that gains momentum and interest as it goes along. Another product of the small-time Chesterfield Pictures, it drew a substantially more favorable response than Rochelle's maiden outing for the studio. Its sets, costumes and performances are largely on par with lesser films from bigger companies, and it keeps the viewer interested throughout. Rochelle's featured role as Constance finds her playing one of her nastier screen characters, as John Martin's spoiled socialite daughter. Though pretty and well turned-out, she's distinctly charmless, answering Jenny's polite "How do you do?" with, "Is it any of your business?" Constance flatly refuses to believe Jenny and Dick are engaged; when Jenny declines Martin's attempt to bribe her, saying she has "nothing to sell," Rochelle's character looks her over and snaps, "I'll say you haven't!" She later resurfaces as a spectator at Jenny's murder trial, where she's in for at least one surprise.

Cast as the film's heroine, Marian Marsh (1913–2006) was, like Rochelle, a WAMPAS Baby Star in 1931. Though her career seemed to be progressing nicely in the early 1930s, with triumphs such as her lead role in *Svengali* (1931), she was dropped by Warners' after demanding better pay. She's well cast as the good-hearted heroine who has been knocked about pretty thoroughly by life. Making no pretense of a privileged upbringing, Jenny is thrilled when she glances into the backyard of the modest cottage Dick wants to buy her, exclaiming, "Washtubs! Hooray!" (She tells him he'd understand if he'd washed out socks in sinks as often as she has.) Rochelle and Marsh were reunited a few years later in *Missing Daughters* (1939).

Given the liveliest role, Betty Compson (1897–1974) nearly walks away with the film playing the jaded but feisty Millie Sprague, who goes from being one of Martin's stooges to becoming Jenny's stalwart pal. Miss Compson, a major star at Paramount in the 1920s, was past the peak of her stardom by the time she accepted this role, though one reviewer rather grudgingly conceded that she "probably still has some followers." Millie isn't cowed by any man, including Dick's butler: When he moves to hustle her out of the apartment, she snaps, "You lay a hand on me and I'll sock you so hard your shirt'll run up your spine like a window shade!" She continued acting in films through the late 1940s, though mostly in lesser roles.

Donald Dillaway (1903–1982) is pretty bland as Dick, leaving moviegoers to wonder if he's really worth all the trouble two women expend over him. J. Carrol Naish (1896–1973) gives a restrained performance as the gangster Joe Charney, who convinces us he's genuinely taken with Jenny. Louise Beavers appears briefly as the Charneys' maid.

Reviews: "Chiefly by reason of a sequence or two embodying a certain amount of suspense activity, this independently-produced picture reaches the average program classification of screen drama. With hard-working performers doing reasonably well, the story moves at a fair pace, but contains rather little that is not more or less usual story material of its type. …With a promise of fair entertainment and a good courtroom scene the exhibitor should get his best results." *Motion Picture Herald*, November 11, 1933

"Director Richard Thorpe has turned out a neat production with lavish settings, intelligent readings, and suspenseful situations. A bit slow to get its stride, it gradually works into plenty of action terminating with a well-written courtroom scene…. The cast is fine and the settings are colorful." *Film Daily*, August 23, 1933

Doctor Bull (1933)

Will Rogers (*Dr. George Bull*), Rochelle Hudson (*Virginia Banning Muller*), Louise Dresser (*Mrs. Herbert Banning*), Vera Allen (*Janet Cardmaker*), Ralph Morgan (*Dr. Verney*), Marian Nixon (*May Tupping*), Howard Lally (*Joe Tupping*), Andy Devine (*Larry Ward*), Berton Churchill (*Herbert Banning*), Tempe Pigott (*Grandma Banning*), Elizabeth Patterson (*Aunt Patricia Banning*), Nora Cecil (*Aunt Emily Banning*), Patsy O'Byrne (*Susan*), Veda Buckland (*Mary*), Effie Ellsler (*Aunt Myra Bull*), Helen Freeman (*Helen Upjohn*), Louise Carter (*Mrs. Ely*), Si Jenks (*Gaylord*), Marcia Mae Jones (*Ruth*), Charles Middleton (*Mr. Upjohn*), Francis Ford (*Mr. Herring*), Sarah Padden (*Mary*), Ethel Griffies (*Miss Ace*)

Director: John Ford. *Based on* "The Last Adam" *by* James Gould Cozzens. *Adaptation*: Paul Green. *Screenplay*: Jane Storm. *Photographer*: George Schneiderman. *Sound*: Eugene Grossman. *Art Director*: William Darling. *Wardrobe*: Rita Kaufman. *Music Director*: Samuel Kaylin.

Fox; released September 22, 1933. 79 minutes.

George Bull has been practicing medicine in the small town of New Winton for a good many years, with a caseload that often leaves him overstretched and weary.

As an on-screen legend that opens the film proclaims, "Doctor Bull brings his neighbors into the world and postpones their departure as long as possible. He prescribes common sense and accepts his small rewards gratefully. His patients call him Doc."

Though his neighbors rely on him to be available around the clock, they don't always approve of his somewhat old-fashioned ways. He shows little patience with hypochondriacs like soda jerk Larry Ward, and takes it philosophically when he realizes there's nothing to be done for a patient. Dr. Bull is particularly devoted to the care of Joe Tupping, a young man confined to bed with a mysterious case of paralysis. Although his friend Dr. Verney tells him Joe's outlook is bleak, Doc Bull keeps trying.

Doc's relationship with attractive widow Janet Cardmaker, according to postmistress Helen Upjohn, has "been the main topic of conversation in this town for the last five years." Local gossips are scandalized that the two keep company, showing no signs of getting married. Also much talked-about is Virginia, college-age daughter of the wealthy Banning family. When she returns from a house party at the university, she is upset but won't tell her mother why. She confides to Dr. Bull that she has fallen in love with a fellow student, John Muller, though her mother has arranged for her to marry the son of a Senator.

As a bout of illness breaks out in town, Dr. Bull takes a specimen to Dr. Verney's lab. The results show that a typhoid outbreak is imminent, having apparently originated in a construction company that's contaminating the water supply. Doc rolls up his sleeves and gets busy inoculating the local children, but there are objections. At a town meeting, over Janet's anguished protest, the citizens vote to remove Doc as their health officer. Though a serum he tested causes a turning point in Joe Tupping's case, Doc says he's through practicing medicine.

Leisurely paced and somewhat episodic, *Doctor Bull* is entertaining without setting off any noteworthy sparks. As film historian Scott Eyman noted, "In terms of conventional plotting, practically nothing happens, but [director John] Ford assembles such a series of charming tableaus that he creates a beautiful evocation of another time and place in a country long gone."[6] The unrelenting gossip and hypocrisy of a small town, not a new theme even in 1933, is presented plainly but not without some understanding. Humorist Will Rogers (1879–1935) effectively plays a character well-suited to his established persona. He also drops the occasional wry remark. Seeing several of his fellow churchgoers gazing into an adjoining cemetery, he comments, "What's the matter? Somebody get out?" At times, Dr. Bull's actions seem less than admirable, as when he is in no apparent hurry to visit the seriously ill Mamie Talbot, arriving just about in time to pull the sheet over her head. He barely hesitates before injecting his paralyzed patient with an experimental serum, reasoning that it worked fine on a cow.

Doctor Bull was the first of four films in which Rochelle and Rogers co-star. Only a few months after its release, they were reunited in *Mr. Skitch* (1933). Their on-screen pairing might have continued longer, had Rogers not died tragically in a plane crash in 1935. Rochelle makes her entrance as Virginia more than a half-hour into the film. Before we see her, we hear about her; one townsperson says, "All that girl does is run around." Shocking the neighbors when she hangs out at the local beer joint, smoking cigarettes and guzzling booze, she finds a sympathetic ear with Dr. Bull, whom she tells, "You're the best friend I ever had, Doc." From that point forward, Rochelle largely disappears from the film.

Vera Allen (1897–1987) gives gravitas and dignity to the role of Janet, who lovingly tolerates Doc's foibles while giving him some much-needed companionship. This film provides a boatload of work for older character actresses, though few of them have any standout moments. Marian Nixon (1904–1983) and Howard Lally (1900–1967) make the Tuppings a sympathetic and engaging pair. Froggy-voiced Andy Devine (1905–1977) was paid to play an irritating character, and was more than up to the task.

Reviews: "*Doctor Bull* is definitely down-to-earth entertainment for the masses, and perhaps for the classes. The locale, the settings, are of the home variety, being the typical small town in Connecticut, extremely familiar, pleasant and appealing.... Rogers lends his own peculiarly appealing brand of half-whimsical, half-philosophical humor.... Not startling, not in any way brilliant, the film is good entertainment, especially for the Rogers followers." *Motion Picture Herald*, October 14, 1933

"Once in a while Will Rogers finds a vehicle that fits him superbly.... From the standpoint of general entertainment and story value, *Doctor Bull* does not come up to the standard of *State Fair* or previous Rogers' starring vehicles. But the role ... gives him great opportunity to reveal his keen savvy of human nature. The Sage of Beverly Hills cannot be topped for the characterization of a country doctor.... It is a spotty picture, combining a gentle, delicate romance with some slapstick comedy, as well as some flights into the musical comedy field." *Illustrated Daily News* (Los Angeles), September 29, 1933

Wild Boys of the Road (1933)

Frankie Darro (*Eddie Smith*), Edwin Phillips (*Tommy Gordon*), Rochelle Hudson (*Grace*), Dorothy Coonan (*Sally*), Sterling Holloway (*Ollie*), Arthur Hohl (*Dr. Heckel*), Ann Hovey (*Lola*), Minna Gombell (*Aunt Carrie*), Grant Mitchell (*James Smith*), Claire McDowell (*Mrs. Smith*), Robert Barrat (*Judge R.H. White*), Willard Robertson (*Detective Captain*), Ward Bond (*Red*), Marlo Dwyer (*Harriet Webster*), Charley Grapewin (*Mr. Cadman*), Eddy Chandler (*Brakeman*), Alan Hale, Jr. (*Boy*), Lee Shumway (*Mike*), Jack McHugh (*Mack*), Milton Kibbee (*Movie Usher*)

Director: William A. Wellman. *Producer*: Robert Presnell, Sr. *Screenplay*: Earl Baldwin. *Story*: Daniel Ahearn. *Editor*: Thomas Pratt. *Art Director*: Esdras Hartley. *Photographer*: Arthur L. Todd. *Orchestra Conductor*: Leo F. Forbstein. *Music*: Bernhard Kaun. *Production Manager*: William Koenig. *Assistant Director*: Dolph Zimmer.

First National Pictures; released October 7, 1933. 68 minutes.

Teenaged Eddie Smith and his best pal Tommy Gordon are doing their best to have a good time at the height of the Depression, but money is tight. After taking their girlfriends home from a school dance, Tommy confesses that his widowed mother is unemployed and can no longer afford to support him. Eddie arrives at home to find his parents going over bills, and his father tells him he has been laid off from his job. Eddie sells his beloved jalopy to raise cash for his family.

Feeling they are a burden on their parents, Eddie and Tommy jump aboard a moving train that night, hoping to find work in Chicago. Awakening the next morning and unable to find some of their provisions, the boys spot another stowaway in the same car. The stranger, who gives Eddie a bloody nose when he starts a fight, is a tough, tomboyish girl named Sally. After finding their sandwiches, Eddie shares one with Sally, and they become friendly.

In Chicago, as multiple kids get off the train, they're stopped by police, who intend to take them directly to Juvenile Hall. Since Sally has a letter from her aunt, who lives in Chicago, and she tells the policeman Eddie and Tommy are her cousins, the trio is allowed to stay. Sally's brassy Aunt Carrie, happy to see them, gives them a welcome meal. But moments later, her apartment, which is functioning as a bordello, is raided. The youngsters make a hasty escape through the window.

The trio joins forces with other kids riding the rails, until there is a band of 20 or more of them. Outside Columbus, Ohio, they are confronted by railroad detectives, and the situation escalates into a brawl. One girl who stays behind in a railroad car is sexually assaulted. Overpowering the detectives, the young people jump aboard again and take vengeance on the rapist.

Just short of the Columbus station, the gang members leap off the train. Amidst the mayhem, Tommy is knocked off his feet and is unable to crawl free of the tracks in time. Eddie finds a doctor and pleads with him for help, but Tommy's leg has to be amputated. The gang sets up an impromptu camp outside a factory. The police try to get them to leave peaceably, but bring out fire hoses when the boys and girls refuse.

Rousted out of Ohio, the gang finally ends up camping at the municipal dump in New York City. Finally getting a job, Eddie needs decent clothes. Attempting to panhandle for the money, Eddie falls prey to criminals who take advantage of his need. Before long, he, Tommy and Sally are facing a judge in Juvenile Court, awaiting their fate.

Wild Boys of the Road makes compelling entertainment out of a dramatic situation taken from daily American life of the period. Director William A. Wellman took a strong personal interest in the story and crafted a fast-moving film that is at times quite moving.

Frankie Darro (1917–1976) gives a fine performance in the lead role of Eddie, believably tough when the scene calls for it, but also likable and sympathetic. He was still a teenager when he starred in *Wild Boys of the Road*, but his diminutive height (5'3") allowed him to continue playing youthful characters for some years afterward. He's ably supported by second lead Edwin Phillips (1911–1981), who had a very brief film career, bowing out after a featured part in *Soak the Rich* (1936).

Dorothy Coonan (1913–2009) was cast as the boyish Sally at the insistence of director Wellman, who rejected more glamorous types such as Jean Parker for the role. Primarily a dancer, she became romantically involved with the director. According to their son William Wellman, Jr., "It was rumored around the studio that Dottie and Bill were secretly married and living together before *Wild Boys* went into production. However, no documentation or official record ever surfaced until after Wild Bill had passed, and Dottie admitted to the hush-hush nuptials."[7] They remained married until his death.

Despite her prominent billing, Rochelle is present only in the first few minutes of the film, cast as Eddie's high school girlfriend Grace. The role requires nothing more of her than being pretty and graceful.

Wellman fiercely resented the studio's interference with the film, which included rejecting the downbeat ending originally intended. Years later, he told an interviewer, "Jack Warner is one of the most despicable men I've ever met.... I hate him.... It was supposed to be a sad ending, really.... He changed that."[8]

In 2013, *Wild Boys of the Road* was named to the National Film Registry.

Reviews: "Granted that boys on the road is a vital public question and that this picture gives it absorbing treatment, the outstanding fact is that it makes a depressing evening in the theatre, one that the general public would gladly avoid.... It should never have been done at all for general commercial release.... The acting is so gripping and the incidents so graphic that they conspire to make the hour's running of the subject one of considerable discomfort to the spectator. The picture presents a distressing condition only too absorbingly." *Variety*, September 26, 1933

"Although [the movie] undertakes to picture a sociological and economic situation which to an extent has passed from the public mind, it is still sufficiently timely to offer excellent selling opportunities to the exhibitor.... In many cases the picture may strike directly home to the community, a thought not to be overlooked by the showman.... There is thrill, excitement and suspense in the film which ... makes a strongly sentimental, definitely human story ... [A]n excellent cast." *Motion Picture Herald*, September 30, 1933

Walls of Gold (1933)

Sally Eilers (*Jeanie Satterlee Ritchie*), Norman Foster (*Barnes Ritchie*), Ralph Morgan (*J. Gordon Ritchie*), Rosita Moreno (*Carla Monterez*), Rochelle Hudson (*Joan Street*), Frederick Santley (*Tony Val Raalte*), Marjorie Gateson (*Cassie Street*), Mary Mason (*"Honey" Satterlee*), Margaret Seddon (*Mrs. Satterlee*), Gloria Roy (*Maid*), Charles Coleman (*Weeks*), Rolfe Sedan (*Barber*), Adrian Rosley (*Louie*)

Director: Kenneth MacKenna. *Producer*: Sol M. Wurtzel. *Based on a Novel by* Kathleen Norris. *Adaptation*: Wallace Sullivan, Edmond Seward. *Screenplay*: Lester Cole. *Photographer*: George Schneiderman. *Sound*: S.C. Chapman. *Music Director*: Samuel Kaylin. *Gowns*: Royer.

Fox; released October 21, 1933. 74 minutes.

Jeanie Satterlee, who operates an employment agency, discovers a mutual attraction with handsome Barnes Ritchie when they meet, but he is not interested in marriage. Barnes' wealthy uncle, Gordon, warns him away from Jeanie, claiming she's an opportunist, but then begins to court her himself. Jeanie can't help being impressed by the lavish gifts pressed on her by the older man, and accepts his argument that a good friendship makes a solid basis for matrimonial happiness.

Jeanie soon fears that she made a mistake in accepting Gordon's proposal, while Barnes consoles himself by romancing her younger sister Honey. As Jeanie has second thoughts about her own marriage, Honey announces her pregnancy. She dies in childbirth. Jeanie, whose husband didn't want a baby, is allowed by Barnes to care for her infant niece. After an ugly incident involving one of Gordon's paramours at a party, Jeanie tells him she wants a divorce. But Gordon, sure she means to be reunited with Barnes, refuses.

Walls of Gold was adapted from Kathleen Norris' bestselling novel of the same name, published earlier in 1933; Norris' name appeared at the head of the title in the opening credits. The June 13, 1933, *Variety* noted Fox's acquisition of the screen rights; the film was hastily assembled, going into production by August. In Norris' book, the lead character was known to her friends as "Jimmy."

Rochelle is seen in a featured role as Joan, a young maid in the employ of Gordon Ritchie—and also one of his mistresses. She has a prominent role to play in the climactic scene that finds her older lover getting his belated comeuppance. In Norris' book, Joan is not a servant but rather a houseguest: "youth incarnate; gold curls neat on a neat little head ... trim little body that she dressed with the utmost cleverness, and with charming bright neat little manners to match."[9] Leading man Norman Foster was reunited with Rochelle three years hence, when he plays her love interest in *Everybody's Old Man*. This is her only film for director Kenneth MacKenna (1899–1962), who racked up more credits as an actor. At the time *Walls of Gold* was shot, he was married to actress Kay Francis, but they divorced after a three-year union.

Reviews: "Essentially entertainment for the better class audiences, for the drama has a grown-up and somewhat sophisticated plot, but it is delicately handled. Miss Eilers has one of her best roles, and one of the most difficult she was ever asked to handle, and does splendidly.... An unusual love drama." *Film Daily*, October 21, 1933

"It's the old, old story of the girl who sells herself for money and rues the bargain. Haltingly told without ever reaching proper suspense, with a weak and misguided romantic interest, poor direction, only fair photography and good sets.... Badly directed acting.... About everyone muffed on this." *Variety*, October 24, 1933

Mr. Skitch (1933)

Will Rogers (*Ira Skitch*), Rochelle Hudson (*Emily Skitch*), ZaSu Pitts (*Maddie Skitch*), Florence Desmond (*Herself*), Harry Green (*Sam Cohen*), Charles Starrett (*Harvey Denby*), Eugene Pallette (*Cliff Merriweather*), Cleora Robb (*Winnie Skitch*), Glorea Robb (*Minnie Skitch*), Wally Albright (*Ira Skitch, Jr.*), George Irving (*Harvey's Uncle*), John Elliott (*Crenshaw*), Frank Melton (*Perry*), Charles Dow Clark (*Store Manager*), Robert Homans (*Norville*), Spencer Charters (*Mr. "Umpchay"*),

Howard Lally (*Indian Guide*), Charles Middleton (*Frank*), Si Jenks (*Furniture Mover*), Charles Lane (*Hotel Clerk*), Morgan Wallace (*Jones*)

Director: James Cruze. *Screenplay*: Ralph Spence, Sonia Levien, based on the story "Green Dice" by Anne Cameron. *Photographer*: John Seitz. *Sound*: W.D. Flick. *Settings*: William Darling. *Costumes*: Rita Kaufman. *Music Director*: Louis De Francesco.

Fox; released December 22, 1933. 68 minutes.

Hard times have hit the Skitch family of Flat River, Missouri, whose house is being repossessed. While father Ira tries to accept it philosophically, his teenage daughter Emily is humiliated when her boyfriend Perry abruptly drops her. With few prospects for work locally, Mr. Skitch decides to pack up his wife Maddie and four children, relocating to California.

On the road, they meet Florence Desmond, a young British woman also on her way to the coast, in search of success as a performer. The Skitch family stops at Yellowstone Park, where Ira tells his nervous wife it's time for him to get tough in order to support his family. Meanwhile, Emily takes a swim and nearly drowns in the rushing eddies. Observing her through a telescope, handsome West Point cadet Harvey Denby comes to her rescue. He's immediately attracted to Emily, but she keeps him at arm's length, wary of men after her experience with Perry.

Making money any way he can, Ira gets acquainted with chatty Sam Cohen, who says he's traveling to regain his health. Bears invade their campsite, terrifying Maddie and the younger kids, but they are quickly rescued. Moving on to the Grand Canyon, Ira tries getting work as a tour guide, and meets Harvey, who wants to be reunited with Emily. Harvey doesn't know it's Ira's daughter he's seeking, but soon finds out. Emily runs away in embarrassment when her family reveals how poor they really are, but Harvey doesn't care.

In Calverna, California, Ira gets a temporary job as waiter in a casino. There he sees Florence Desmond cozying up to a well-to-do chump to earn her keep. Ira befriends loud, crude Cliff Merriweather, "the greatest gambler west of the Mississippi," and proves to have surprising luck at the roulette table. With money in hand, Ira announces they're returning to Missouri and getting their old house back. But before they can hit the road, there are complications that threatens their plans and the growing romance between Harvey and Emily.

Mr. Skitch is a lightly entertaining "road trip" film that passes an hour (and change) pleasantly. It begins on a downbeat note, surely familiar to many Great Depression moviegoers, as Ira Skitch and his family are forced to give up their home and furniture, and figure out a way to survive. As the synopsis suggests, the story is somewhat episodic, but it introduces us to some interesting characters, and remains watchable throughout.

The role of a small-town handyman, with wife and kids, fits Will Rogers neatly, and he has some amusing moments along the way, with clever asides from time to time. He and ZaSu Pitts (1894–1963) make an interesting marital match, her typical jittery, flustered demeanor balanced by his (usually) calm, gentle approach. Pitts' comedic skills are put to good use without being excessively milked; her interaction with bears at the dinner table is fun.

Rochelle is believable and charming as their young daughter. Inclined to be a bit dramatic, as someone her age might, she tells her would-be beau Harvey, "I'm through with love.... I've had all the experience I want with men. The world will never know what I've been through." Her somewhat revealing swimming outfit makes it clear that Rochelle was growing up quickly, and had what it took to play leading-lady roles. Charles Starrett (1903–1986), who went on to fame as a B-Western hero, is personable as her would-be suitor.

Harry Green (1892–1958) garners a few smiles, if not belly laughs, as Sam Cohen, a quirky character who is demonstrably Jewish while managing to largely skirt the worst anti–Semitic humor of the period. Florence Desmond (1905–1993), supposedly playing "herself," is permitted to exhibit her talents for vocal mimicry, most notably a Garbo impersonation. Eugene Pallette (1889–1954) makes a brief late-in-the-game appearance as a boisterous, slightly inebriated gambler.

Twins Cleora (1922–2013) and Glorea (1922–2020) Robb are unbilled for their relatively sizable featured roles as Skitch daughters Winnie and Minnie. The two girls are walking encyclopedias, spouting off knowledge at every opportunity, which

Charles Starrett and Rochelle Hudson are starry-eyed young lovers in *Mr. Skitch* (1933).

leads Ira (Rogers) to observe to his wife, with more ruefulness than rancor, "Ma, there's such a thing as educating children up too high."

Reviews: "Not a big picture, but a good comedy of program grade. It has much human interest, good comedy moments, and in addition to all this some excellent out-door shots of the Grand Canyon and of points west.... There is nothing outstanding, and it is not as amusing as some other Rogers pictures, but it keeps the audience entertained." *Harrison's Reports*, December 30, 1933

"*Mr. Skitch* is not a good picture but it should be a moderate grosser on Will Rogers' name plus that of ZaSu Pitts.... Despite the basic absurdities and threadbare plot mechanics of the film, its laughs carry along with a certain commendable zip.... Whole thing is frankly a Midwestern small town Cinderella fairy tale based on the mortgage-haunted depression.... Critics can make mincemeat of *Mr. Skitch*, for by standards of excellence, it is a grave sinner. Yet this is probably wiped away for the general public by the laughs. Performances are generally good." *Variety*, December 26, 1933

Harold Teen (1934)

>Hal Le Roy (*Harold "Teenzy" Teen*), Rochelle Hudson (*Lillian "Lillums" Lovewell*), Patricia Ellis (*Mimi Snatcher*), Guy Kibbee (*Joe "Pa" Lovewell*), Hugh Herbert (*Ed Rathburn*), Hobart Cavanaugh (*Pop*), Chic [Chick] Chandler (*Lilacs*), Douglas [Douglass] Dumbrille (*H.H. Snatcher*), Eddie Tamblyn (*Shadow*), Clara Blandick (*"Ma" Lovewell*), Mayo Methot (*Sally LaSalle*), Richard Carle (*Parmalee*), Charles Wilson (*"Mac" McKinsey*), Spec O'Donnell (*Jones*), Cliff Saum (*Man Repossessing Car*), Billy Dooley (*Photographer*), Willis Marks (*Doorman*), Henry Otho (*Stagehand*), Eddie Shubert (*Morris*), Ethel Wales (*Miss Gilly*), Richard Powell (*Rathburn's Assistant*), Harriett Forbstein (*Sadie Rawlins*), Harry Seymour (*Yost*), Jane Wyman (*Graduate*), Victoria Vinton (*Blonde in Sugar Bowl*)
>
>*Director*: Murray Roth. *Producer*: Robert Lord. *Screenplay*: Paul Gerard Smith, Al Cohn. *From the Comic Strip by* Carl Ed. *Music and Lyrics*: Irving Kahal, Sammy Fain. *Editor*: Terry Morse. *Art Director*: John Hughes. *Photographer*: Arthur L. Todd. *Gowns*: Orry-Kelly. *Vitaphone Orchestra Conductor*: Leo F. Forbstein.
>
>Warner Bros.; released April 7, 1934. 66 minutes.

Harold Teen, one year out of high school, works as a cub reporter for his hometown newspaper, the *Covina Crier*. Wanting to congratulate his girlfriend Lillums on graduating high school, he buys her a bottle of perfume he can't really afford. Planning to give her a ride after the graduation rehearsal, he's stymied when his car is repossessed, leaving his rival Lilacs to transport her instead. Not a very competent journalist, Harold completely misses a big story right in front of his face, and tells his frustrated editor that he "didn't pay much attention" to the overturned bus that left 18 people injured.

At the graduation ball, Harold and Lillums quarrel when her dog snaps at his heels, and she accuses her date of kicking the pup. Wanting to get back in her good graces, Harold sends away for the Ed Rathburn home study course in dancing. Meanwhile, Lillums' parents fret because they can't afford to send her to the college she'd like to attend.

A newcomer to Covina, H.H. Snatcher is taking over management of the bank, and decides Harold is worth cultivating as a source of favorable publicity. Flattered by Snatcher's attentions, Harold babbles about him until Lillums is tired of hearing the name. Taking Lillums for a canoe ride, Harold manages to tip them over into the lake, much to her disgust. Snatcher fishes her out of the water, sees her home and sends her flowers.

Jealous of his rival, Harold accuses Lillums of encouraging the older man's attentions because of his wealth, calling her a "mercenary gold-digger." With the teen couple on the outs, Harold is easy prey for Snatcher's daughter Mimi, who decides he will be "just dandy to play with." When Lillums sees Mimi and Harold kissing at the soda shop, it seems that young Mr. Teen has lost his best girl forever.

Mimi organizes a talent show for the young people of Covina and imports well-known Broadway director Ed Rathburn (whose mail order dance lessons Harold is still taking) to direct the production. Rathburn initially casts Mimi in the starring role, thinking this is what her financier father would want, but is quickly captivated by Lillums. Opening night of the big show finds romantic alliances being rearranged, and Harold offered an unexpected opportunity to show what he does best.

Largely forgotten today, "Harold Teen" was a highly popular comic strip of its day, introduced in 1919 and enjoying a 40-year run. This is the second film adaptation, following by six years a silent version starring Arthur "Dagwood" Lake as the title character. The 1934 film, which opens with frames comparing the live-action actors with their funny-page counterparts, was described in its trailer as "a peppy collegiate musical comedy."

The music and dance routines in this version of *Harold Teen* are, on the whole, more effective than the comedy, which tends toward the actively cornball or worse. The scenes involving a high school boy made the butt of jokes because he stutters are offensive now, and may well have been in 1934. At least most of the weak gags go by quickly, as when various girl-boy couples are given one each to deliver in the graduation ball sequence.

BOY: Honey, who's gonna take you home tonight?
GIRL: The undertaker, if you don't stop squeezing me!

Rochelle is second-billed as Harold's love interest Lillian "Lillums" Lovewell, a character almost exactly her own age. She's pert and likable, a good-hearted though not highly intelligent young lady. Her grasp of the language is occasionally shaky, as when she comments on feeling older with her diploma, saying, "Graduating makes me feel very maternal." Later, when Harold refers to H.H. Snatcher as a tycoon, she argues, "A tycoon is a storm on the ocean."

The goofy, well-intended but clumsy character of Harold Teen could easily be an ancestor of Archie Andrews, or perhaps Henry Aldrich's older brother. Here he's played by Broadway dancer Hal Le Roy (1913–1985), who had previously appeared in several Warner Brothers shorts. Le Roy has a gawky face and skinny build that suit the character nicely, but it's not until near the end of the film that he has an opportunity to show off his energetic dancing that won him acclaim on stage.

A bushy-haired Chick Chandler (1905–1988), nearly 30 when the film was shot, is featured as Harold's high school rival, who tools around town in a jalopy painted with wisecracks along the lines of "Here's your rattle, baby!" At 58, and in dowdy costumes, Clara Blandick (1876–1962) seems a bit mature to play the mother of a teenage girl. In 1949, she and Rochelle both appeared in the industrial film *Roots in the Soil*.

Reviews: "Seldom happens that a story from a cartoon derivation makes good. But *Harold Teen* is anemic even for a cartoon adaptation.... It's too childish even for the boys and girls for whom the appeal apparently is directed.... Nothing to hold the interest and no suspense. Played mostly for comedy gags, visual and verbal, with the former having the best of it.... Rochelle Hudson makes a personable Lillums." *Variety*, June 5, 1934

"This is fairly good entertainment for the younger element, but it will bore adults. It has been produced well and has some comedy, but the story ... is rather thin and presents just juveniles, in their petty affairs and social activity.... Some human interest is felt for the hero and the heroine, but not enough to hold the interest throughout." *Harrison's Reports*, March 17, 1934

Such Women Are Dangerous (1934)

Warner Baxter (*Michael Shawn*), Rosemary Ames (*Helen Hallock*), Rochelle Hudson (*Vernie Little*), Mona Barrie (*Wanda Paris*), Herbert Mundin (*Horatio Hollingsworth Wilson*), Henrietta Crosman (*Aunt Sophie Travers*), Lily D. Stuart (*Ellison*), Irving Pichel (*Stanley*), Jane Barnes (*Nancy Ryan*), Matt Moore (*George Ryan*), Richard Carle (*Thomas H. Delahanty*), Murray Kinnell (*Jan Paris*), Frank Conroy (*Bronson*), Fred Santley (*Hinton*), John Sheehan (*Granigan*), William Augustin (*Coroner*), Edward LeSaint (*Judge*), Rita Owin (*Nurse*), Sam Flint (*Doane*), Monte Vandergrift (*Detective*), Stanley Blystone (*Turnkey*), George Offerman, Jr. (*Messenger Boy*)

Director: James Flood. *Producer*: Al Rockett. *Screenplay*: Jane Storm, Oscar M. Sheridan. *From the story "Odd Thursday" by* Vera Caspary. *Additional Dialogue*: Lenore Coffee. *Photographer*: L.W. O'Connell. *Costumes*: Rita Kaufman. *Settings*: Gordon Wiles. *Sound*: George Leverett. *Music Director*: Louis De Francesco. *Editor*: Dorothy Spencer.

Fox; released June 8, 1934. 81 minutes.

Michael Shawn has earned fame and fortune writing sappy romantic novels. His devoted secretary Helen Hallock wishes he would turn his talents to something more significant, but he reminds her that he has nine million female fans and therefore a very comfortable existence.

The other women in Michael's life include singer Wanda Paris, who lives across the way. At first, he is annoyed when her musical efforts disturb his work, but when he storms over to confront her, they find a mutual attraction. Also trying to make a claim on his time is Vernie Little, a naïve young woman from Indiana who arrives in New York determined to make his acquaintance. A devoted fan of Michael's work, she presses him to advise her on the novel in verse she's writing. Helen, on Michael's behalf, tries to let Vernie down gently, but she reacts angrily, saying that the older woman just wants him for herself.

Giving Michael a lift into the countryside one day, Vernie stops outside a furnished cottage for rent, which she immediately envisions as a cozy home for the two of them. A sudden downpour leaves Michael with a bad cold upon his return to town, and Vernie is dismayed to see how Helen and Wanda dance attendance on him. Growing impatient, Michael tries to pay Vernie's fare back to Indiana, telling her, "You're a child, and rather a silly child."

Though Vernie believes Wanda is her chief competition for Michael's affection, he's upset to learn that the glamorous singer in fact has a husband and a little boy. Meanwhile, having delivered an ultimatum to Michael, Vernie sets a plan into motion that will ultimately have him arrested and charged with murder.

Such Women are Dangerous, also known as *Too Many Women* and, in its early stages, as *Nine Million Women*, is a well-made film that offers Rochelle one of the best dramatic outings of her early career. Her character, Vernie Little, makes far too much of her initial meeting with Michael at a women's club affair, and travels cross-country to be with him. "You're the first man who's ever touched my soul," she declares breathlessly, as she proceeds to barge relentlessly into his life. Vernie refuses to listen to the well-meant advice of Michael's sensible secretary, who tells her, not unkindly, "You're a little girl who's playing at being the heroine of a storybook."

Mustachioed Warner Baxter (1889–1951), seen four years earlier in *Such Men Are Dangerous*, is well-cast as the slightly older, jaded man who's still quite attractive to women. Baxter won an Academy Award as Best Actor for his role as the Cisco Kid in 1928's *In Old Arizona*. As he aged, he slipped into B-movie roles, having a steady gig for much of the 1940s as Dr. Robert Ordway in Columbia's Crime Doctor series.

Rosemary Ames (1906–1988) plays Michael's loyal assistant Helen, who has few illusions about his conduct but loves him nonetheless. Patiently taking dictation of his latest literary effort, she tells him frankly, "I think your women behave rather strangely. First they throw their clothes off, and then their figures are full of tremors. And then they have a rather sickening weakness for kissing." Disliking the "junk" he grinds out, she tells him that devoting his talent to it is "like harnessing a racehorse to a plow." Ames, a Fox contract player for about three years, was dropped by the studio in 1935 and left films permanently. Mona Barrie (1909–1964) gives a creditable performance as Wanda, the glamorous singer with little regard for honesty, and a firm focus on her own wishes.

The script provides well-rounded characters for a good cast to play. Though Rochelle does engage our sympathy as the foolish Vernie, she's not just an injured innocent; we see clearly that she makes a nuisance of herself, and is capable of being selfish (as when she boldly pushes aside other women waiting their turn at Michael's book signing). Michael, solidly played by Baxter, is not a one-note cad who uses women, but a basically decent guy who goes through life with a distracted air, and fails to appreciate the best qualities of his faithful secretary. In the first couple of reels, we seem to be watching what could be a romantic comedy, but things take a dramatic turn as it progresses.

Quite a bit of sharp dialogue enlivens the film. One of Michael's enraptured fans at a book signing complains, "After reading one of his books, it's all I can do to *look* at my husband!" His plain-spoken Aunt Sophie, played by character actress Henrietta Crosman, is cheerfully termed by Michael "my little bundle of sex appeal." Answering one of Michael's comments about his readership, Helen says dryly, "You have women neatly catalogued, don't you?"

A gossip columnist quoted Rochelle as saying, with the film in the can, "The stand-ins for Warner and me are so sore they won't even speak to us, because we refused to let them work for us in the big love scenes. You see, the fellow who has been standing in for Warner for five years ... has quite a crush on the girl who does that job for me. We had lots of fun and had to take the scene over about twenty times."[10]

Reviews: "*Such Women Are Dangerous* has the advantage of a cleverly devised plot, worked out convincingly on an entirely credible basis.... The first half of the picture is a little slow.... The latter half of the picture swings into a nice speed and tempo and ends with fine excitement.... Baxter, as the kind, gentle, romantic novelist, will disappoint not a single fan. Miss Hudson offers an appealing and finely etched characterization of the girl.... James Flood directed intelligently." *Hollywood Reporter*, April 12, 1934

"This modern story builds and maintains continual interest. [With] such proved theatre values as romance, drama, light comedy, suspense, semi-mystery and thrill, the novel story-telling technique gives the picture an intriguing charm.... Baxter and Miss Hudson turn in fine and convincing performances.... Title, cast and entertainment values suggest potent showmanship exploitation possibilities to attract popular attention." *Motion Picture Daily*, April 12, 1934

Bachelor Bait (1934)

Stuart Erwin (*William Watts*), Rochelle Hudson (*Cynthia Douglas*), Pert Kelton (*Allie Summers*), "Skeets" Gallagher (*Bramwell Van Dusen*), Burton [Berton] Churchill ("*Big Barney" Nolan*), Grady Sutton (*Don Beldon/Diker*), Clarence H. Wilson (*D.A. Clement Graftsman*), Dick Winslow (*Lionel Pierpont Wells, Jr.*), Anne Shirley (*Miriam Ann Johnson*), William Augustin (*Judge with Cigar*), Landers Stevens (*Wells, Sr.*), Phil Dunham (*Wilson*), Otto Hoffman (*Postal Clerk*), Frank O'Connor (*William's Boss*), Hazel Forbes (*Margery*), Lynton Brent (*Photographer*), Carol Tevis (*Miss Winters*), Zeffie Tilbury (*Miss Turner*), Will Stanton (*Drunk*), Amelia Batchelor (*Van's Secretary*), Bill Wolfe (*Mr. Wolfe*), Rolfe Sedan, William H. O'Brien (*Waiters at the Ritz*), Nora Cecil (*Mrs. Trutmanner*), Tom London (*Detective*), Paul Kruger (*Newspaper Reporter*), Ethan Laidlaw, Bruce Mitchell (*Policemen*)

Director: George Stevens. *Executive Producer*: Pandro S. Berman. *Associate Producer*: Lou Brock. *Screenplay*: Glenn Tryon. *Story*: Edward Halperin, Victor Halperin. *Photographer*: David Abel. *Art Directors*: Van Nest Polglase, Carroll Clark.

Music Director: Max Steiner. *Costumes*: Walter Plunkett. *Recordist*: Clem Portman. *Editor*: James B. Morley.

RKO; released July 27, 1934. 74 minutes.

William Watts, a good-natured but ineffectual clerk at the county's marriage license bureau, is fired abruptly. Encouraged by his friendly neighbor Cynthia Douglas, an unemployed stenographer, he decides to open a matrimonial bureau, his newspaper ad promising that for a $5 fee, "young men of good habits" can apply to be paired with a prospective mate who "will love you, cherish you, and you will always be together." Responses pour in immediately, impressing not only William but the taxi driver who helps him lug home the mail—and reveals himself to be lawyer Bramwell Van Dusen. Fast-talking Van Dusen, known as "Van," encourages William to forge ahead with the business he says should be called "Romance, Incorporated." His eye for a profitable venture nicely balances William's sincerity about the importance of bringing people together.

The business expands rapidly, Cynthia joining the staff as a secretary. William refuses a buy-out offer from pushy Barney Nolan of the Civil Betterment Bureau. Meanwhile, Van's brassy ex-wife Allie shows up seeking money. Claiming he doesn't have it, he offers instead to find her a well-heeled mate among the agency's clients.

Hearing of a new client, naïve but wealthy rube Don Beldon, Van suggests a match with Allie, but William believes that what Don needs is a "sweet, unsullied girl." Unable to find the perfect candidate, William suddenly decides that Cynthia fits the bill perfectly, oblivious to the fact that she's attracted to *him*. Cynthia agrees to go on dates with Beldon, provided that William chaperone them. The trio goes for tea at the Ritz, but Van and Allie crash the party. Refusing to take no for an answer, Allie horns in on the weekend cruise William had arranged for Don and Cynthia. She isn't happy to be stuck with the nebbishy William as a companion.

Van insists to his partner that Cynthia is in love with him, but he's unconvinced ("She wouldn't look at me"). But William is coaxed into declaring his feelings. Unfortunately, after the mishap that found William and Allie spending the weekend at sea, Cynthia thinks he has betrayed her, and accepts Don's marriage proposal. Allie insists that she's already staked out a claim on the Oklahoma millionaire. Both ladies are surprised when he unveils his true identity.

Film Daily (May 7, 1934) announced that the film's original title, *The Great American Harem*, had been jettisoned. At that point, William A. Seiter was expected to direct.

Stuart Erwin (1903–1967), who built a career on his portrayals of well-intended but somewhat bumbling men, is perfectly suited to the *Bachelor Bait* lead. William Watts lacks confidence, but he has worthy qualities that he puts to good use despite his shy demeanor, and a moral compass that helps him hold his ground. Erwin later moved from films to television, becoming the star of a popular sitcom variously known as *The Trouble with Father* and *The Stu Erwin Show*.

He's surrounded by a cast brimming with fine character actors, including "Skeets" Gallagher (1891–1955), whose fast-talking, wisecracking Van Dusen provides a winning comic contrast to Erwin. Gallagher also sparks in his scenes with Pert Kelton (1906–1968), cast as his smart-mouthed wife from a marriage that lasted three weeks. Kelton attracts notice from her first line, when she breezes into the agency and has a confrontation with her ex-husband's secretary:

> SECRETARY: Is Mr. Van Dusen expecting you?
> ALLIE: No, I come as a complete surprise.

When Van introduces her to William, hoping to land her a wealthy husband, Van cracks, "For once, try not to be yourself." That seems to be a lost cause, which only makes the movie a great deal more fun, as when she tells Grady Sutton's character, "I feel a little naked without an escort," or dismisses William as "the finest example of embalming I've ever seen." (She adds, "I'll bet he wears his bathing suit in the bathtub.") Sutton (1906–1995) is well-cast as the shy, gawky client who turns out to be something other than what he appears to be.

Just as Erwin and Gallagher's characters were opposites, Rochelle, who had recently turned 18, plays a loyal young woman who's nothing like Kelton's hard-boiled Allie, one who could provide exactly the type of gentle, innocent love interest that Erwin needs. Though Van describes Cynthia as a "little white mouse," Rochelle's fresh-faced beauty cannot be so easily dismissed. Like Erwin's character, hers can stand up for herself when the occasion demands. Rochelle had just embarked on a short vacation in Oklahoma when she was summoned back to California to play *Bachelor Bait's* female lead.

Relatively little mention is made of the Great Depression in this light-hearted, escapist comedy, though at one point Cynthia remarks of the job market, "You'd be surprised at the number of people out of employment. People who've never been out of work before." This film came early in what would become a distinguished directorial career for George Stevens (1904–1975), whose later films included *I Remember Mama*, *A Place in the Sun* and *The Greatest Story Ever Told*.

Reviews: "A nice, pleasant little comedy that takes time out every once in a while to bowl you over completely with several hilarious wisecracks, thrown in amongst the mild humor which is its general tone.... Rochelle Hudson is charmingly lovely as the sweet little gal.... The direction is okay in a tough job of putting action into a picture that occasionally talks itself right off the screen." *Hollywood Reporter*, June 5, 1934

"A knockout comedy with plenty of hearty laughs plus nice love interest ... one of the best all-around good jobs in screen comedies to come along in some time ... the picture is headed to bring heaps of joy to the movie fans of the land.... In addition to Erwin's fine performance, there is comedy work by Pert Kelton ... and the sweet performance of Rochelle Hudson...." *Film Daily*, July 20, 1934

Judge Priest (1934)

Will Rogers (*Judge William Pitman Priest*), Tom Brown (*Jerome Priest*), Anita Louise (*Ellie May Gillespie*), Henry B. Walthall (*Rev. Ashby Brand*), Stepin Fetchit (*Jeff*

Poindexter), David Landau (*Bob Gillis*), Rochelle Hudson (*Virginia Maydew*), Roger Imhof (*Billy Gaynor*), Frank Melton (*Flem Talley*), Charley Grapewin (*Sgt. Jimmy Bagby*), Berton Churchill (*Sen. Horace Maydew*), Brenda Fowler (*Caroline Priest*), Francis Ford (*Juror #12*), Hattie McDaniels [McDaniel] (*Aunt Dilsey*), Grace Goodall (*Mrs. Maydew*), Winter Hall (*Judge Floyd Fairleigh*), Si Jenks (*Juror #10*), Louis Mason (*Sheriff Birdsong*), Paul McAllister (*Doc Lake*), Matt McHugh (*Gabby*), Paul McVey (*Trimble*), Duke R. Lee (*Deputy*), Margaret Mann (*Governess*), Ernest Shields (*Milan*)

Director: John Ford. *Producer*: Sol M. Wurtzel. *Screenplay*: Dudley Nichols, Lamar Trotti, based on Irvin S. Cobb's Judge Priest character. *Photographer*: George Schneiderman. *Sound*: Albert Protzman. *Editor*: Paul Weatherwax. *Settings*: William Darling. *Gowns*: Royer. *Music*: Cyril J. Mockridge. *Lyrics*: Dudley Nichols, Lamar Trotti. *Music Director*: Samuel Kaylin.

Fox; released September 28, 1934. 80 minutes.

In Kentucky, circa 1890, Judge William Pitman Post is an easygoing soul who presides informally over his courtroom. He hears a case involving an African-American man, Jeff Poindexter, accused of being a chicken thief. Rather than sending him to prison, the judge gives him a job, though his duties mostly seem to consist of acting as the jurist's companion on fishing trips and the like.

Judge Priest, known to his friends as Billy, is delighted to find that his nephew Rome is home from law school with a degree, ready to undertake his career. Rome also hopes to romance their next-door neighbor, pretty schoolteacher Ellie May Gillespie, who is also pursued by local barber Flem Talley. While Billy favors the match, his snobbish sister-in-law Carrie doesn't think Miss Gillespie's family background is acceptable. Her mother died in childbirth, and the identity of her father is unknown.

Carrie wants her son to romance socially prominent Virginia Maydew, daughter of the pompous former Senator Horace Maydew, who has announced that he will be opposing Judge Priest in the upcoming election. Visiting the grave of his late wife Margaret one evening, Billy notices Bob Gillis, a taciturn man who works for the local blacksmith, bringing flowers to the tomb of Ellie May's mother. Billy later tries chatting up Bob about his background, but learns nothing.

At the Episcopal Church's ice cream social benefiting veterans, Ellie May is serving customers while Rome is buttonholed by lovely, flirtatious Virginia. Billy contrives to interrupt her pursuit of his nephew, and allow Rome the opportunity to spend some time with Ellie May. Later, at Flem's shop, Billy hears the boisterous barber boasting crudely about his plans to enjoy Ellie May's favors. Customer Bob Gillis, without saying a word, punches Flem.

Having a quiet drink at the local saloon, Gillis is jumped by Flem and two of his pals. Gillis, who pulled a knife to defend himself in the fight, is arrested. Rome excitedly announces that Gillis will be his first client as an attorney, though his mother strenuously objects. When Flem's attorney, Senator Maydew, protests that Judge Priest cannot be impartial, Billy reluctantly steps down.

With Maydew seemingly winning the jury over to his side, Rome urges Gillis to tell the truth about hitting Flem to defend Ellie May's honor. Gillis refuses to bring her name into it, or to explain on the witness stand the reason for his animosity toward Flem. Seeing Gillis headed toward a prison term, Judge Priest takes action. At the eleventh hour, he draws on the recollections of the local minister and has himself appointed his nephew's associate counsel.

Will Rogers has one of his best roles in this film directed by the great John Ford (1894–1973), who previously helmed *Doctor Bull*. The star's folksy mannerisms and homespun wisdom are well-suited to the role of the small-town judge who has his own sense of fair play, though he readily admits that he took up his career because he had "a hankering for the spirit of the law, not the letter." He's amusing as the magistrate who glances through the funny papers as the prosecutor blathers on at Jeff's trial.

Rochelle takes the small featured role of Virginia Maydew, a lovely and flirtatious Southern belle who has her eye on Rome. Encountering him at an ice cream social shortly after his return to town, she coos, "I think you've forgotten where I live." Polite if slightly noncommittal, Rome doesn't take her attentions too seriously, saying, "Haven't you got every boy in town on your string?" Tom Brown and Anita Louise make a charming romantic couple.

Contemporary audiences may well be of two minds about the featured roles given to two of the most noteworthy African-American performers of the day, Stepin Fetchit (1902–1985) and Hattie McDaniel (1893–1952). Both play stereotyped characters—he's the bone-lazy, slow-witted man who's accused of stealing chickens, while she is cast as Judge Priest's housekeeper, who sings cheerfully as she takes down his laundry from the line. Their characters exist in a world where Confederate war veterans, including their benevolent employer, are the town's heroes. But Rogers and Fetchit work very well together, and it's noteworthy that the judge, lacking many of the prejudices of the era depicted, simply takes pleasure in Jeff's companionship. McDaniel, playing her umpteenth domestic servant, is given ample opportunity to showcase her singing voice, even if one of the numbers in question is "My Old Kentucky Home," with its original lyrics about "darkies." When Rogers joins in on one of her songs, it makes a charming scene, whatever baggage a 21st-century viewer may attach to it.

Berton Churchill (1876–1940) provides effective contrast to Rogers' character, playing the stuffy blowhard Senator Maydew. Character actor Francis Ford, the director's brother, earns a few laughs as the seedy-looking juror who deflates some of Maydew's bluster with his neatly timed use of a nearby spittoon, which causes a bell-like sound as each piece of discarded tobacco lands. A subtler performance is given by Henry B. Walthall (1878–1936) as the kindly Reverend Brand, who plays an unexpected role on the witness stand near the end of the film, delivering a stirring speech that is a dramatic highlight.

Judge Priest was adapted by screenwriters Dudley Nichols and Lamar Trotti from the writings of humorist Irvin S. Cobb, whose name appears above the film title.

An opening legend, attributed to Cobb, notes, "The figures in this story are familiar ghosts of my own boyhood.... There was one man Down Yonder I came especially to admire for he seemed typical of the tolerance of that day and the wisdom of that almost vanished generation. I called him Judge Priest." In a few years, the paths of Cobb and Will Rogers intertwined again, when the latter's early death resulted in Cobb getting one of his most noteworthy film roles in *Everybody's Old Man*.

John Ford remade *Judge Priest* as *The Sun Shines Bright* in 1952.

Reviews: "An excellent comedy; it will be enjoyed by the whole family. It is simple, dealing with plain people. Will Rogers is at his best, appearing as the Southern country judge who not only arranges love affairs but runs the town court, disposing of cases as he sees best.... In its series of situations, showing Rogers in his daily contacts with people of the small town, there is much that is human and warm, and understandable to all types of audiences." *Harrison's Reports*, August 25, 1934

"Irvin Cobb's story dealing with an eccentric and interesting Kentucky judge is the basis of this story, which ought to please any audience and which is as clean as a hound's tooth. It possesses an infectious brand of comedy to supplement Rogers' own unfailing supply.... The casting job is good and the dialogue natural and clever." *Film Daily*, August 18, 1934

Imitation of Life (1934)

Claudette Colbert (*Beatrice Pullman*), Warren William (*Stephen Archer*), Rochelle Hudson (*Jessie Pullman*), Ned Sparks (*Elmer Smith*), Louise Beavers (*Delilah Johnson*), Fredi Washington (*Peola Johnson*), Baby Jane [Juanita Quigley] (*Baby Jessie*), Alan Hale (*The Furniture Man*), Henry Armetta (*The Painter*), Wyndham Standing (*Jarvis—Butler*), Sebie Hendricks (*Peola, Age 4*), Dorothy Black (*Peola, Age 10*), Marilyn Knowlden (*Jessie, Age 8*), Clarence Wilson (*Mrs. Bristol*), Noel Francis (*Mrs. Eden*), Paullyn Garner (*Mrs. Ramsey*), Lenita Lane (*Mrs. Dale*), Alma Tell (*Mrs. Craven*), Daisy Bufford (*Waitress*), Norma Drew (*Teacher*), Henry Kolker (*Dr. Preston*), Franklin Pangborn (*Mr. Carven*), Teru Shimada (*Pancake Shop Customer*), Claire McDowell (*Teacher Outside Classroom*), Joyce Compton (*Young Woman at Party*), Alyce Ardell (*French Maid*), Edgar Norton (*Butler at Party*), Curry Lee (*Chauffeur*), William B. Davidson (*Man Buying Cigar*), Paul Porcasi (*Manager of Jackson's Restaurant*), Marcia Mae Jones, Jane Withers (*Peola's Classmates*)

Director: John M. Stahl. *Producer*: Carl Laemmle, Jr. *Screenplay*: William Hurlbut. *From the Novel by* Fannie Hurst. *Photographer*: Merritt Gerstad. *Art Director*: Charles D. Hall. *Music Director*: Heinz Roemheld. *Special Effects*: John P. Fulton. *Editors*: Philip Cahn, Maurice Wright.

Universal; released November 26, 1934. 111 minutes.

Bea Pullman is a young widow struggling to support herself and her toddler daughter Jessie. She is surprised when Delilah Johnson, a black woman, arrives in response to a classified ad for a cook and housekeeper, having come to the wrong address. Delilah explains that she's looking for a home for herself and her daughter Peola, and would be willing to work for room and board. Delilah quickly makes herself indispensable to Bea, who's worn out from her job selling maple syrup, and wishes she could spend more time at home with her child.

After raving over Delilah's homemade pancakes, Bea makes a deal to rent a storefront near the boardwalk, so that the two of them can go into business together with "Aunt Delilah's Homemade Pancakes." She sweet-talks a painter and a furniture man into helping her fix up the shabby store for the smallest amount possible. Within a few years, the business is flourishing.

Peola, who is very light-skinned, rebels at being identified as black, and is humiliated when Delilah visits her classroom. Her mother tries to persuade Peola to accept her identity, but the girl persists in allowing people to assume she's white.

An enthusiastic customer, Elmer Smith, suggests to Bea that she should market the pancake mix. Delilah agrees to the incorporation plan, but doesn't want to be separated from Bea and Jessie. Aunt Delilah Pancake Flour is a roaring success. The ensuing wealth takes Bea and the others into a grander social world, but Peola, now a young woman, is unhappy, not knowing where she fits in. "I want to be white, like I look," she tells her distraught mother.

Hosting an elegant party at her home, Bea meets suave Stephen Archer, an ichthyologist. At first, he doesn't realize that she's "the pancake queen" herself. He's charmed by her, but Elmer tells him she has no time in her life for romance. Nonetheless, Stephen and Bea soon become an item. He proposes marriage and she happily accepts, but asks that they not announce their engagement until Jessie has a chance to get acquainted with him. When Jessie comes home from college, Bea makes plans to show her a good time, with Stephen's help. But when Delilah learns that Peola has dropped out of school down South, with her current whereabouts unknown, Bea accompanies her on a trip to investigate.

Delilah finds Peola working as a restaurant cashier and passing for white. Her mother is heartbroken when Peola denies knowing her. When Peola turns up at Bea's house, she tells her mother they must go their separate ways, so that she can live the life she wants.

In Bea's absence, her fiancé and her daughter have grown closer. After seeing the town with Stephen, Jessie tells her mother she doesn't want to return to school. Stephen is dismayed when Jessie tells him she's fallen in love with him. Meanwhile, with her daughter seemingly lost to her forever, Delilah's health gives way.

Imitation of Life was adapted from Fannie Hurst's (1885–1968) same-name novel, which was serialized in *Pictorial Review* magazine starting in late 1932 (under the title "Sugar House") and published by Harper & Brothers a few months later. The resulting film was nominated for three Academy Awards, including Best Picture. Miss Hurst was pleased with the results, writing to director John M. Stahl that his movie demonstrated "insight, sympathetic understanding and a quality too subtle to analyze."[11] Other Hurst novels adapted by Hollywood include *Back Street*, *Humoresque* and *Four Daughters*.

The film's success rests heavily on the performances of leading ladies Claudette Colbert (1903–1996) and, especially, Louise Beavers (1902–1962), the latter playing a far more challenging and rewarding role than most of those she was given in a

Jessie (Rochelle Hudson, standing) senses the growing attraction between Stephen (Warren William) and her mother Bea (Claudette Colbert) in *Imitation of Life* (1934).

long film career. Several columnists and industry insiders decried the racial prejudice that left Beavers out of contention when nominations for that year's Best Actress Academy Award were chosen. The importance of her performance also failed to be reflected in her paycheck, reportedly $300 per week (with Colbert, by comparison, picking up in excess of $10,000 a week).

Fredi Washington (1903–1994), who plays the adult Peola, was only a year younger than Beavers. The finale gives employment to a few other reliable African-American actors of the day, with Hattie McDaniel and Fred "Snowflake" Toones among those appearing in bit roles. Jane Withers and Marcia Mae Jones, both to enjoy considerable success as child actresses, can be glimpsed as students in Peola's classroom.

Rochelle makes her entrance just over an hour into the film, taking over the role of Jessie as a college student who, in Stephen's words, is "half-child, half-woman." Still believable as either a teenager or a young woman, she's well-suited to playing Jessie, herself stuck between adolescence and maturity. Jessie is like a greatly toned-down version of Veda from *Mildred Pierce* (1945), slightly spoiled by the money her mother's business brings in, and prone to eye Mom's man hungrily. She handles the dramatic sequences well, and shares the screen with Colbert at the fade-out. According to *Universal Weekly* (October 13, 1934), "Vera West, Universal's costume creator ... originated five different costumes for Rochelle Hudson ... all very costly as were the furs, shoes, and underthings that completed the ensembles. All these with hats, handbags and accessories were specially made for the film."

Child actress Marilyn Knowlden (born 1926), who played Rochelle's character as a young girl, later recalled star Colbert "looking in the mirror at Rochelle Hudson.... Juanita Quigley ... and myself, laughing as she compared her own nose and profile with that of the three of us. Her verdict: we were perfectly cast as her daughter, Jessie."[12]

Director Stahl (1886–1950) won acclaim not only for this film but for his others, which included *Magnificent Obsession* (1935) and *The Keys of the Kingdom* (1944). He had a gift for handling emotional scenes without letting them descend too far into melodrama or overwrought performances. In September 1934, *Universal Weekly* reported that shooting for the film was complete after 12 weeks, the last few days being spent shooting the classroom scenes.

In 2005, the picture was named to the National Film Registry by the Library of Congress. It was remade in 1959, under the direction of Douglas Sirk, with Lana Turner and Juanita Moore playing the female leads and Sandra Dee stepping into Rochelle's character, renamed Susie.

Reviews: "Put this down as one of [the] best pictures of the year. As usual, director John Stahl has injected the human note.... Rochelle Hudson is good as the daughter of Miss Colbert... [An] outstanding human interest story expertly directed and admirably acted." *Film Daily*, November 23, 1934

"A screen victory that may well fling glory to its personnel, especially those who have contrived behind the screen to bring it to the screen.... There was sufficient testimony of tears last night to prove that *Imitation of Life* will be the joy of its women audiences.... Miss Colbert has never done anything finer or more heart-touching ... to which may be added the excellent efforts of Rochelle Hudson and Dorothy Black." Edwin Schallert, *Los Angeles Times*, November 28, 1934

The Mighty Barnum (1934)

Wallace Beery (*Phineas T. Barnum*), Adolphe Menjou (*Bailey Walsh*), Virginia Bruce (*Jenny Lind*), Rochelle Hudson (*Ellen Saunders*), Janet Beecher (*Nancy Barnum*), Tammany Young (*Todd*), Herman Bing (*Farmer Schultz*), Lucille La Verne (*Joice Heth*), George Brasno (*Tom Thumb*), Olive Brasno (*Lavinia Thumb*), Richard Brasno (*Gilbert*), May Boley (*Bearded Lady*), John Hyams (*J.P. Skiff*), R.E. "Tex" Madsen (*Cardiff Giant*), Ian Wolfe (*Swedish Consul*), Davison Clark (*Horace Greeley*), George MacQuarrie (*Daniel Webster*), Charles Judels (*Maitre D'*), Cornelius Ballard (*Barnum's Driver*), Emilie Cabanne (*Mrs. Astor*), Wilbur Higby (*Mr. Astor*), Robert Dunbar (*Mr. Vanderbilt*), Greta Meyer (*Mme. Lind's Maid*), Claude Payton (*Spieler*), Paul Panzer (*Barber*), E.H. Calvert (*House Detective*), Bert Lindley (*Mayor of New York*), Frederick Vroom (*Henry Wadsworth Longfellow*)

Director: Walter Lang. *Producer*: Darryl F. Zanuck. *Story and Screenplay*: Gene Fowler, Bess Meredyth. *Associate Producers*: William Goetz, Raymond Griffith. *Photographer*: Peverell Marley. *Editors*: Allen McNeil, Barbara McLean. *Art Director*: Richard Day. *Musical Score*: Alfred Newman. *Sound*: Frank Maher, Roger

Heman. *Assistant Director*: Freddie Fox. *Costumes*: Omar Kiam. *Men's Wardrobe*: William Bridgehouse. *Women's Wardrobe*: Peg O'Neil. *Still Cameraman*: Kenneth Alexander. *Set Dresser*: Julie Heron.

20th Century Pictures; released December 23, 1934. 86 minutes.

In 1835, Phineas T. Barnum is a New York shopkeeper with a fondness for the bizarre, much to the dismay of his practical wife Nancy. Not only is her husband bankrupting the business by trading stock for such novelties as a three-headed frog, he insists on taking in the perennially inebriated Bailey Walsh, whom he believes to be a great idea man. As their financial situation grows precarious, Nancy obtains $250 from her father and insists they return to Connecticut, where she grew up. She entrusts the cash to Phineas, who uses it to rent a former livery stable and go into partnership with Walsh on a museum of curiosities. Barnum's niece Ellie, who has taken a shine to Bailey, accepts the challenge of sobering him up.

Promoter J.P. Skiff brings them their first star attraction: Joice Heth, a woman said to be 160 years old, and the onetime nurse to George Washington. Soon, Barnum & Bailey's establishment becomes "the mecca of New York's curiosity seekers." The wily Skiff tells Barnum and Bailey that Heth is a phony, an escaped slave from Georgia. Barnum refuses to pay the blackmail, so Skiff takes the story to the newspapers. Newspaperman Horace Greeley prints his accusation that Barnum's new star, Madame Zorro the bearded lady, is a phony as well. When the bearded lady is proved to be a man, there's a riot in the museum. Bailey falls off the wagon.

Down but not out, Barnum is overjoyed to meet a midget known as Tom Thumb, who has an equally small lady friend. Soon Barnum and Bailey's novelties are attracting crowds throughout Europe, and he is even presented to Queen Victoria. With their fortunes on the upswing, Barnum eagerly awaits the arrival of Jumbo the elephant, which Bailey went to Europe to acquire. Instead, Bailey returns with a renowned singer, Jenny Lind, known as "The Swedish Nightingale," who has signed an exclusive contract to make her American debut under Barnum's management.

Barnum is immediately infatuated with the beautiful singer and tries to transition from his rough-hewn self to a musical impresario. When Jenny's U.S. debut is a success, Barnum begins concentrating all his attentions on her, neglecting his other attractions. Nancy realizes that she and Barnum have drifted apart. No luckier in love is Ellie, who tells Bailey she's about to turn 21 but realizes he has forgotten the promise he made to her some years earlier.

When Barnum forgets his wedding anniversary, Nancy leaves him. But his troubles are only beginning, as he inadvertently insults Mme. Lind. Bailey and the singer sail for England, while Barnum faces bankruptcy and an uncertain future.

The Mighty Barnum, as the opening crawl tells us, depicts "a Connecticut Yankee with amazing dreams and the heart of a child, a self-styled 'Prince of Humbugs,' whose carnival drums are still heard round the world." After a few moments of stock footage showing the Barnum & Bailey Circuses of the 1930s, the story flashes back 100 years to depict the rise from humble beginnings of Phineas T.

Barnum (1810–1891). What follows is a mishmash of comedy, drama, spectacle and a few moments that are nearly as odd as Barnum's beloved curiosities. The film was adapted by Gene Fowler and Bess Meredyth from their stage play.

Wallace Beery (1885–1949) was born to play flamboyant characters like Barnum; his expansive performance brings out the showman's eccentric personality and likability even when he's up to something shady, as he often is. This was not Beery's first time playing Mr. Barnum; he had done so four years earlier in *A Lady's Morals* (1930), a story focused primarily on the life of Jenny Lind. Screenwriter Fowler, who visited the set as production got underway, reported,

> On Stage 4 Mr. Wallace Beery … is learning his lines. He wears sideburns and a merchant's apron. He perspires, partly because of the hot weather and partly because he is having a tussle with his verses. Once Beery has absorbed his lines, however, the hefty veteran can be relied upon to endow his work with something more valuable than a parrot's memory, something more interpretive than thought-up grimaces of a Hollywood automaton.[13]

Janet Beecher (1884–1955) plays the sorely tried Mrs. Barnum, a dignified sort who with good reason cracks her sharp tongue at what she's expected to tolerate. About the nicest thing she calls Beery's Barnum is "my slippery nitwit." Thoroughly appalled by his fondness for what he calls "my collection of freaks," she reacts with horror when he mistakenly thinks she's expecting a blessed event, telling him, "I'd be afraid. Probably have five legs!" Beecher was still a newcomer to films, after a successful career as a stage actress.

Rochelle has perhaps the unlikeliest romantic interest of her screen career in Adolphe Menjou (1890–1963), not only more than 25 years her senior, but distinctly unappealing in his early scenes as a grubby, unshaven mess that Nancy aptly terms "a gutter souse." Inexplicably, Ellie tells Bailey she "could cry for joy" when he professes to return her affections and promises to wait for her to come of age. Insult is added to injury when her romantic attachment goes awry. Though she receives a fair amount of screen time, this is largely an unrewarding role for Rochelle, who's given some lovely period costumes but very little to chew on, dramatically.

Virginia Bruce (1909–1982) appears well after the film's halfway point to play the lovely Jenny Lind, with a singing voice furnished by Francia White. George Brasno (1911–1982) and his sister Olive (1917–1998) appear as Mr. and Mrs. Tom Thumb.

In the film's pressbook, producer Darryl F. Zanuck, co-founder of 20th Century Pictures, denigrated the practice by many studios of casting every film from its list of contract talent, saying that too often, "players are shoved into parts which do not necessarily fit them, merely to absorb their salaries." For the 42 speaking roles in *The Mighty Barnum* (aside from star Beery), Zanuck said, "We made individual casting arrangements with forty-two players, each fitted for the particular role he is playing."

Among the promotional angles suggested to exhibitors by studio publicists: "There are plenty of tattooed men, and some tattooed women, in your community. If you can find a way to uncover these strangely marked people, and display them in conjunction with your campaign, you'll help yourself in a way characteristically Barnum."

Reviews: "P.T. Barnum's life ... proves engrossing if not sensational screen entertainment as here produced. It possesses all the elements, except an occasional lack of speed, to insure returns of average to good.... Beery's performance is the heart of the picture.... Adolphe Menjou, playing the reformed drunk who is to become Bailey, is capital in his assignment, with Rochelle Hudson for charming love interest.... Picture runs 87 minutes, leaving plenty of room for further cutting." *Variety*, December 25, 1934

"Fairly good entertainment for the masses; but the younger element may be disappointed at the lack of romantic interest in the story. The first half is a little slow and it takes too much time to establish Beery's character.... It is not, as the title implies, the story of a 'mighty' man but rather of one who made his fortune more by luck than by brains. But the production is excellent and this covers up the story's defects.... Many of the situations are exciting." *Harrison's Reports*, December 29, 1934

I've Been Around (1935)

Chester Morris (*Eric Foster*), Rochelle Hudson (*Drue Waring*), G.P. Huntley, Jr. (*Franklin "Nick" De Haven*), Phyllis Brooks (*Gay Blackstone*), Gene Lockhart (*Sammy Ames*), Isabel Jewell (*Sally Van Loan*), Ralph Morgan (*John Waring*), William Stack (*Doctor*), Henry Armetta (*Italian*), Dorothy Christy, Verna Hillie (*Girls*)
Director: Philip Cahn. *Producer*: B.F. Zeidman. *Original Story and Screenplay*: John Meehan. *Photographer:* John Mescall. *Art Director*: Harrison Wiley. *Editor*: Ray Curtiss. *Process Photographer:* John P. Fulton.
Universal; released March 5, 1935. 63 minutes.

Aviator-businessman Eric Foster and debutante Drue Waring are engaged, but while he's away on a lengthy business trip, she becomes infatuated with *bon vivant* polo player Franklin "Nick" De Haven. Drue, from a well-to-do Long Island family, is unaware that De Haven is an opportunist who's interested in her money. When Mr. Waring tells De Haven not to expect to live off the family fortune, De Haven's interest in Drue wanes. On the rebound, Drue impulsively marries Eric shortly after he returns home. Then, on their wedding night, she admits she doesn't really love him. An angry Eric arranges a party at which he announces he is leaving his wife, and then proceeds to drown his sorrows in liquor and night life overseas.

Back in town on New Year's Eve, Eric meets his pal Sammy Ames, who's surprised to see that he's sober. Sammy tells Eric where Drue is now living, but he arrives to find her entertaining De Haven and his friends. De Haven is on the verge of marrying another woman, but Eric misunderstands his presence. Drue despairs at the prospect of losing her estranged husband, whom she has now realizes is the right man for her.

One *I've Been Around* set visitor was a fan magazine reporter who found cast members shooting one of the climactic scenes, on a set designed as "a very elaborate bedroom." He admired the set design, which provided the illusion of the world outside Drue's window, complete with snow and a distant church steeple, "built in miniature on a scale that makes it look exactly the [proper] height." He added, "They are all ready to shoot the scene when suddenly the camera man yells, 'The steeple is out of the picture!' So everything is held up for ten minutes while some sweating laborers move the church steeple six inches to one side. Then the scene proceeds."[14]

According to studio publicity, "Miss Hudson does such a splendid job that you hate her for most of the picture." She and her leading man, Chester Morris, were reunited several years later when they teamed in one of his Boston Blackie vehicles. Seen here in key supporting roles are Gene Lockhart (1891–1957) as Sammy, Isabel Jewell (1907–1972) as Sammy's girlfriend Sally, and Ralph Morgan (1883–1956) as Drue's father.

Reviews: "There is little rhyme or reason for the rambling romantic monkeyshines that make up *I've Been Around*. As if the title were not sufficiently unattractive, the story itself impressed this department as being on an even lower scale of allurement. It will do badly, very badly, everywhere and there is no reason why any theatre should go out of its way to look for bad business.... You may now go back to your knitting, Mr. Exhibitor, and look the other way when they try to induce you to play this one." *Film Bulletin*, February 5, 1935

"One of those run-of-the-mill stories that has snatches of everything that was excellent in some previous film, but that somehow remains as unconvincing as a cardboard lover.... [Huntley, Morgan and Lockhart] all perform with a sincerity that contributes much to redeeming an otherwise commonplace picture." *Boston Globe*, February 9, 1935

Life Begins at 40 (1935)

Will Rogers (*Kenesaw H. Clark*), Richard Cromwell (*Lee Austin*), George Barbier (*Col. Joseph Abercrombie*), Rochelle Hudson (*Adele Anderson*), Jane Darwell (*Ida Harris*), Slim Summerville (*T. Watterson Meriwhether*), Sterling Holloway (*Chris*), Thomas Beck (*Joe Abercrombie, Jr.*), Roger Imhof (*Pappy Smithers*), Charles Sellon (*Tom Cotton*), John Bradford (*Wally Stevens*), Ruth Gillette (*Mrs. Cotton*), T. Roy Barnes (*Simonds*), Claire Du Brey (*Mrs. Meriwhether*), Robert P. Kerr (*Bank Teller*), Paul McVey (*Judge*), Creighton Hale (*Drug Clerk*), Jed Prouty (*Charles Beagle*), Guy Usher (*Sheriff*), Edward McWade (*Doctor*), Barbara Barondess (*Abercrombie Maid*), Lillian Lawrence (*Effie*), Kathrin Clare Ward (*Housewife*), Billy Engle (*Well-Wisher*)

Director: George Marshall. *Producer*: Sol M. Wurtzel. *Screenplay*: Lamar Trotti. *Contributing Dialogue*: Robert Quillen. *Suggested by the Book by* Walter B. Pitkin. *Photographer*: Harry Jackson. *Sound*: Bernard Freericks. *Art Directors*: Duncan Cramer, Albert Hogsett. *Gowns*: Lillian. *Music Director*: Samuel Kaylin.

Fox; released March 22, 1935. 85 minutes.

Kenesaw Clark, a low-key, easygoing type, edits a small town newspaper, the *Plain View Citizen*. He enjoys his quiet life, including next door neighbor Ida Harris, with whom he is friendly despite their occasional quibble, and her boarder, young schoolteacher Adele ("Dell") Anderson. Dell is being courted by Joe Abercrombie, son of stuffy banker Col. Abercrombie. She's in no rush to accept Joe's marriage proposal.

Leaving the newspaper office one evening, Ken sees a young man skulking around Abercrombie's bank after hours. It's Lee Austin, who recently served a three-year prison sentence after being found guilty of stealing money from the bank, where he used to work. Lee tells Ken he was framed and wants to clear his name. Ken, who knew Lee's parents and believes in his honesty, offers him a room in his house and a job as his assistant on the newspaper. He also makes sure that Lee and Dell get acquainted. The young man tells Dell frankly about his past.

Col. Abercrombie, who's running for re-election as head of the school board, is angered to see that Ken has hired the man he believes is a thief. Abercrombie threatens to call in the loans Ken took out for newspaper equipment unless Ken fires Lee. When Ken refuses, Abercrombie installs his son Joe to run the *Plain View Citizen*. Ken decides the town needs an opposition newspaper and digs out an old printing press to launch the *Wildcat*, with Lee as business manager and Ida as society editor.

Ken exposes the haughty Abercrombie to ridicule by announcing that lazy layabout T. Watterson Meriwhether will oppose him for his school board seat. Meriwhether grows to like the idea and, with the help of his friends and family, turns Abercrombie's campaign gala, a hog show, into a debacle.

Lee and Dell grow closer, and she gives a nonchalant answer to his question about whether she really intends to marry Joe. When Joe publishes an editorial accusing Dell of consorting with criminals, Lee punches his rival. Dell confesses to Ken that she is in love with Lee, but he doesn't feel it's fair for him to propose when he is hampered by a prison record. Ken promises the young people that there will soon be new developments.

Based on the 1932 novel by Walter B. Pitkin (1878–1953), a Columbia University faculty member, *Life Begins at 40* is a noteworthy slice of Americana, with a bit of social commentary that goes down easy amidst the film's homespun charm and gentle comedy. The script contains plenty of smiles, beginning with the slogans of the *Plain View Citizen*: "All the news $1 a year entitles you to," and its successor, the *Wildcat* ("Published every Thursday—we hope").

Will Rogers has another tailor-made role as Kenesaw Clark, sharing bits like, "What's fairness got to do with marriage?" Seeing one of his older acquaintances with a lady on his arm, he observes, "Man never gets too old for a blonde." Given what film fans know was in store for the star, however, it's poignant to hear his character say, "Well, you come to the wrong fellow to talk about dying. Take me now. I'm just beginning to live." Rochelle later recalled, "Uncle Bill stubbed his tongue on a scene twelve times and then, on the thirteenth try when he got it perfectly, I just stood there with my mouth open, staring at him and unable to say a word. 'Well,' he drawled with a sly grin, 'I guess I sort of gave you a precedent to go by, didn't I?'"[15]

This was Rochelle's fourth and final film with Rogers, who died several months after its release. It provides her with a far more substantial role than she had in *Judge*

Priest. Her beauty and appeal are on display throughout; she and co-star Richard Cromwell (1910–1960) make a very endearing young couple. Despite the dated sentiment, she's delightful as the small-town girl who says of her beau, "I lie awake nights, thinking about darning his socks." Cromwell's character is listed as "Lee Austin" in the closing credits, but a newspaper headline seen during the film spells his name "Austen."

Jane Darwell (1879–1967) gives a lively performance as Ida Harris, her warm smile surfacing periodically despite her sometimes prickly relationship with Rogers' Ken Clark. George Barbier (1865–1945) embraces the role of the unscrupulous colonel, getting a few laughs when a duel with Ken proves an assault on his dignity, but also effective in more dramatic moments.

Reviews: "This is more of the good old hokum, but thoroughly palatable and sure to go over with the whole family trade. Will Rogers is in good form as a philosophical country editor.... Right up with the best of the Will Rogers pictures, meaning swell entertainment for all." *Film Daily*, April 5, 1935

"Again Will Rogers delivers rib-rocking, heart-socking entertainment, loaded with laughter touched off by the comedian's inimitable brand of Americanese.... Chuckles, giggles, belly laughs and roars tumble over one another ... in a production that exudes a salt-of-the-earth flavor and emerging as gorgeous entertainment.... *Motion Picture Daily*, February 2, 1935

Les Misérables (1935)

Fredric March (*Jean Valjean*), Charles Laughton (*Inspector Emile Javert*), Sir Cedric Hardwicke (*Bishop Bienvenue*), Rochelle Hudson (*Cosette*), John Beal (*Marius*), Frances Drake (*Eponine*), Florence Eldridge (*Fantine*), Jessie Ralph (*Mme. Magloire*), Mary Forbes (*Mlle. Baptiseme*), Florence Roberts (*Toussaint*), Jane Kerry (*Mme. Thenardier*), Ferdinand Gottschalk (*Thenardier*), Charles Haefeli (*Brevet*), Marilynne [Marilyn] Knowlden (*Little Cosette*), John Bleifer (*Chenildieu*), Leonid Kinskey (*Genflou*), Harry Semels (*Cochepaille*), Eily Malyon (*Mother Superior*), Ian MacLaren (*Head Gardener*), Vernon Downing (*Brissac*), Lyons Wickland (*Lamarque*), John Carradine (*Enjolras*), Margaret Bloodgood (*Factory Forewoman*), Sidney Bracey (*Mayor's Clerk*), Everett Brown (*Convict*), Francis Powers (*Lawyer*), Arthur Evers (*Court Clerk*), Robert Greig (*Prison Governor*), Perry Ivins (*M. Devereux*), Paul Irving (*Innkeeper*), Pietro Sosso (*Jean's Valet*), Nick Shaid (*Old Beggar*), Lorin Raker (*Valsin*), G. Raymond Nye (*Jacques*), Mary MacLaren (*Nurse*), Olaf Hytten (*Pierre*), Reginald Barlow (*Henri*).

Director: Richard Boleslawski. *Producer*: Darryl F. Zanuck. *Associate Producers*: William Goetz, Raymond Griffith. *Screenplay*: W.P. Lipscomb. *From the Novel by* Victor Hugo. *Photographer*: Gregg Toland. *Art Director*: Richard Day. *Editor*: Barbara McLean. *Music Director*: Alfred Newman. *Sound*: Frank Maher, Roger Heman. *Costumes*: Omar Kiam. *Assistant Director*: Eric Stacey.

20th Century Pictures; released April 20, 1935. 109 minutes.

In 1800 France, Jean Valjean is on trial for theft. Despite his explanation that he stole bread only to feed his sister and her children, he is sentenced to a ten-year prison sentence on the galleys. Meanwhile, police officer Emile Javert applies for a promotion but is considered a questionable candidate. Emotionally, he talks about wanting to rise above the life his parents led, and his devotion to enforcing the law. He pleads his case successfully and his promotion is approved.

Jean undergoes brutal treatment working the galleys, with Javert as supervisor. When another prisoner is trapped under a heavy beam, Jean rushes to his rescue. Javert is unimpressed. When Jean's sentence is finally concluded, he is released into society, but his fellow man coldly rejects an ex-convict. Bedraggled, hungry and tired on a rainy night, Jean is taken in by a priest, Bishop Bienvenue, despite the misgivings of the bishop's staff. Tormented by nightmares of his prison life, Jean leaves during the night, stealing some silver plates. He's soon caught by the police, who bring him back to Bienvenue, who falsely says that the plates were a gift. With the bishop's blessing, Jean embarks on a second chance at life.

Rechristening himself Monsieur Madeleine, Jean becomes the owner of a glass factory with a large staff. A pillar of his community after five years, he is asked to accept the job of mayor and magistrate. After some hesitation, he accepts. Shortly afterwards, he learns that Javert has been appointed police inspector for the district. Javert doesn't appear to recognize Jean.

Fantine, a young woman dismissed from her job at the glass factory because she was believed to have given birth to an illegitimate child, begs Javert for help

One of Rochelle's best films, *Les Misérables* (1935), found her playing opposite Fredric March.

reclaiming her child from the owners of an inn where she works. Javert, knowing Fantine is impoverished, is coldly unsympathetic. Desperate, Fantine bursts into Jean's home to confront him. Over Javert's protests, Jean is determined to help her, arousing the inspector's suspicions about Jean's past. Javert's interest is further piqued when he sees Jean helping to lift a cart that has turned over atop a man, stirring memories of the similar incident that took place during Valjean's prison term. Jean rescues eight-year-old Cosette from the inn, and a life of unrelenting hard work, much to her mother's joy.

Jean is surprised one evening by a visit from Javert, who believes himself to have committed a crime by reporting to his superior that "M. Madeleine" was in fact Jean Valjean. Now that Valjean has reportedly been arrested elsewhere, charged with violating parole, Javert assumes that he made a mistake and must be punished. Jean refuses to press charges.

Unable to let the other man be wrongly jailed, Jean goes to the trial and reveals his true identity. Planning to escape England, Jean tries to provide for Cosette and her mother, but Javert is immediately on the scene, confiscating the cash Jean tried to leave with Fantine. Already seriously ill, Fantine dies. Jean overpowers Javert long enough to flee his house, with Cosette in tow.

In Paris, Jean arranges for Cosette to be educated in a convent, where she grows into a lovely teenager. The pair observes a protest against unduly harsh prison sentences, with young law student Marius giving a passionate speech. Cosette visits Marius at his organization's headquarters, and they are attracted to one another. Soon they are in love, and he wants to ask her father for her hand. But the indefatigable Javert is on the scene. With riots breaking out between police and revolutionaries, Marius and Cosette are separated. Once again, Jean is faced with the prospect of running for his life, but Cosette protests that she cannot leave Marius, making inevitable the final confrontation between Jean and Javert.

Les Misérables is an excellent, lavish rendition of Victor Hugo's classic novel, anchored by the fine performances of Fredric March (1897–1975) and Charles Laughton (1899–1962), and enhanced by the cinematography of the gifted Gregg Toland. The film could, perhaps, have laid the key story points in viewers' laps with a bit more subtlety, but it makes engaging drama throughout. March, in addition to his star turn as Jean Valjean, also appears briefly as the prisoner Champmathieu, who is mistaken for him. Laughton's performance as Javert is commendably subtle, though the character's hateful villainy comes across nonetheless. March's real-life wife, actress Florence Eldridge (1901–1988), is effective in her supporting role as Fantine.

Once again, as in *Imitation of Life*, child actress Marilyn Knowlden and Rochelle share a role, with young Miss Knowlden quite impressive as the younger Cosette. Rochelle arrives on the scene more than an hour into the film, as Valjean's life enters its "third phase." Despite her late arrival, she proceeds to have one of her best dramatic showcases. She easily conveys the rapport that exists between Cosette and her adoptive father, and the conflict she feels when Valjean asks her to escape with him—and without the man she loves. Rochelle's blossoming talent allows her to keep pace with March in their scenes together, while her delicate beauty is at its peak in the costumes she wears. She and John Beal (1909–1997) achieve a touching rapport as star-crossed lovers, but it is with March that she has her best scenes.

Director Richard Boleslawski (1889–1937) guides his cast members skillfully, eliciting strong work throughout, and capturing the dramatic sweep of the story without excess. Both Laughton and the picture itself were Oscar-nominated.

Reviews: "A great picture from a great and human document.... It has been done with the utmost good taste with a cast that is flawless.... Rochelle Hudson and John Beal are just right as the young lovers.... Boleslawski's direction brings a fine feeling of the period and the spirit of the story ...[Gregg Toland] has captured each moment as though it were a painting in movement." *Hollywood Reporter*, March 30, 1935

"This is a feature in which quality abounds. It has strength and power, and also considerable sweep.... It is somber and heavy, but admirably worthwhile, and will undoubtedly be relished by the great screen public.... Miss Hudson and Miss [Frances] Drake are capable and convincing." Edwin Schallert, *Los Angeles Times*, May 11, 1935

Curly Top (1935)

Shirley Temple (*Elizabeth Blair*), John Boles (*Edward Morgan*), Rochelle Hudson (*Mary Blair*), Jane Darwell (*Mrs. Denham*), Rafaela Ottiano (*Mrs. Higgins*), Esther Dale (*Aunt Genevieve Graham*), Etienne Girardot (*Mr. Wyckoff*), Arthur Treacher (*Reynolds*), Maurice Murphy (*Jimmie Rogers*), Billy Gilbert (*Morgan's Cook*), Leonard Carey (*Morgan's Secretary*), Herbert Evans (*Morgan's Chauffeur*), Lynn Bari (*Girl at Beach*), Stanley Andrews, Edward LeSaint (*Trustees*)

Director: Irving Cummings. *Producer*: Winfield Sheehan. *Screenplay*: Patterson McNutt, Arthur Beckhard. *Music*: Ray Henderson. *Lyrics*: Ted Koehler, Edward Heyman, Irving Caesar. *Photographer*: John Seitz. *Dances*: Jack Donohue. *Sound*: Eugene Grossman. *Editor*: Jack Murray. *Art Director*: Jack Otterson. *Gowns*: Rene Hubert. *Music Director*: Oscar Bradley. *Wardrobe*: Sam Benson. *Assistant Director*: Booth McCracken.

Fox; released July 26, 1935. 75 minutes.

Little Elizabeth Blair lives at the Lakeside Orphanage, where her older sister Mary earns their keep by working in the kitchen. High-spirited Elizabeth finds herself in trouble with the strict superintendent Mrs. Higgins on a regular basis, for committing infractions like "singing and dancing without permission." The child of show biz parents killed in an auto wreck, Elizabeth is known to her family as "Curly Top."

One rainy night, when Elizabeth sneaks her pony Spunky into the dormitory, she incurs the wrath of Mrs. Higgins, who declares that the horse and Elizabeth's pet duck will be sold. Kindhearted Mrs. Denham thinks her boss is too hard on the little girl, but can't intercede.

The orphanage is visited by a group of trustees, among them grouchy old Mr. Wyckoff and handsome young lawyer Edward Morgan, described in a newspaper

Rochelle (left) was cast as elder sister to Shirley Temple in *Curly Top* (1935).

headline as "Bachelor Heir to Millions." Wyckoff thinks Elizabeth is incorrigible when he catches her impersonating him, and suggests she be sent to a public institution. Edward is charmed by Elizabeth, and also takes a shine to Mary, who passionately defends her sister.

Edward impulsively decides to adopt Elizabeth, and honors the deathbed promise Mary made to her parents that the two girls would never be separated. Edward tells them that a well-do-client, Hiram Jones, is their benefactor, not wanting Elizabeth to feel that she is indebted to him. Edward and his loving aunt welcome the two into their home, where Elizabeth is lavished with gifts. Grateful for her good fortune, she arranges a gala charity bazaar to benefit the other orphanage girls.

Aunt Genevieve sees plainly that Edward is in love with Mary. Asked for her hand in marriage by a presentable suitor, Jimmie Rogers, Mary declines, as she is not in love with him. But when she overhears Edward say he isn't interested in her, Mary changes her mind. Elizabeth, who has already decided that her sister should marry Edward, wants to see them find their happy ending.

At the height of the Great Depression, Shirley Temple (1928–2014) became America's #1 box office star, adding a fortune to Fox coffers. This typical vehicle shows why, as she demonstrates her amazing skill at singing, dancing and generally providing a dream image of an adorable child. *Curly Top* has barely enough plot to cover its

75-minute running time, and exudes a heavy dose of saccharine, but it's doubtful any of young Miss Temple's fans were bothered. In her memoir, the actress herself was as harsh a critic as any, writing, "*Curly Top* ... was uncomfortably banal."[16]

Third-billed Rochelle is teamed with John Boles (1895–1969) as the picture's romantic leads. Both characters have an opportunity to sing, with Rochelle's Mary being showcased in a solo number called "The Simple Things in Life." The song is a bit ironic, since it follows on the heels of the Blair girls being showered with everything of a material nature they could possibly want, and finds Rochelle decked out in quite a fancy getup, but she sells it nicely. Boles makes tolerable a character who spouts lines like, "There's no human problem that can't be solved by love," though it's Edward's checkbook that seems to fix most of them.

Character actor Etienne Girardot (1856–1939) is, surprisingly, not struck by a bolt of lightning when his nasty Mr. Wyckoff has the temerity to call America's Sweetheart "a bad and wicked child." Of the two women who run the orphanage, Jane Darwell is on the side of the angels as the compassionate matron Mrs. Denham, while Rafaela Ottiano (1888–1942) plays her cold-hearted supervisor. Arthur Treacher (1894–1975), as the stuffy butler who is won over by Elizabeth, says "My word!" almost as many times as Temple says, "Oh, my goodness!" Up-and-coming Lynn Bari has a tiny role here.

Reviews: "A great showmen's and audience picture, ...*Curly Top* is sure to be a box-office cleanup wherever and whenever played. The heart-warming story ... presents the amazing starlet in a manner certain to thrill exhibitors and delight the public.... Shirley's singing and dancing are gems of showmanship which are bulwarked by the singing of Boles and Miss Hudson.... Every effort is devoted to making Shirley the focal point [yet] Irving Cummings' direction ... makes Boles and Miss Hudson outstanding as well." *Motion Picture Daily*, July 16, 1935

"*Curly Top* is cinch [box office] for almost any house. Should be a matinee cleanup ... and almost just as good at night. Holds plenty for almost any type of audience.... Boles and Miss Hudson are okay for the adult romance appeal.... Miss Hudson does her chore with due restraint and feminine appeal.... The Ray Henderson tunes are sturdy and almost any one of them may assert itself for general popularity." *Variety*, August 7, 1935

Way Down East (1935)

Rochelle Hudson (*Anna Moore*), Henry Fonda (*David Bartlett*), Slim Summerville (*Seth Holcomb*), Edward Trevor (*Lennox Sanderson*), Margaret Hamilton (*Martha Perkins*), Andy Devine (*Hi Holler*), Russell Simpson (*Squire Amasa Bartlett*), Spring Byington (*Louisa Bartlett*), Al Lydell (*Hank Woolwine*), Astrid Allwyn (*Kate*), Sara Haden (*Cornelia Peabody*), Billy Benedict (*Amos*), Harry C. Bradley (*Mr. Peabody*), Phil La Toska (*Abner*), Clem Bevans (*Doc Wiggin*), Vera Lewis (*Mrs. Poole*), Ann Doran (*Rosie*), Kay Hammond (*Emma Stackpole*), William Borzage (*Musician*), Brenda Fowler, Lucille Ward, Claire Whitney (*Guests at Quilting Party*)

Director: Henry King. *Producer*: Winfield Sheehan. *Screenplay*: Howard Estabrook,

William Hurlbut. *From the Play by* Lottie Blair Parker. *Photographer*: Ernest Parker. *Sound*: Joseph Aiken. *Editor*: Robert Bischoff. *Art Director*: William Darling. *Gowns*: William Lambert. *Music Director*: Oscar Bradley.

Fox; released October 25, 1935. 80 minutes.

Hard-working David Bartlett dutifully helps his parents on their Maine farm, but longs to escape for a life in the city. His father, Squire Bartlett, a stern, deeply religious man, wants his son to carry on with the farm.

While working in the fields, David meets a new arrival, a lovely young woman who introduces herself as Anna Moore. She tells David's mother Louisa that she's the daughter of Louisa's late school friend Prudence Moore. With the squire's grudging approval, Anna is taken on as a hired girl, making a favorable impression with her good manners and work ethic.

David's second cousin, lovely Kate, comes home from Boston and is welcomed by the Bartletts. The squire hopes his son will settle down on the farm with Kate. However, a slick-talking neighbor, Lennox Sanderson, wants Kate for himself. He and Anna are startled when they cross paths. Although they know each other, he advises that they not say so, urging her, "Pretend we've never seen each other." Though she's dismayed to find that Lennox lives nearby, Anna says the Bartletts have given her a needed refuge, and she won't give up her job. She and David are also beginning to acknowledge their mutual attraction.

The whole town turns out for an ice-skating party to celebrate David's birthday, but he wants to spend time with Anna. Lennox catches her alone and suggests they work together to achieve their desired aim—Kate for him, David for her. But she feels Kate, who has been kind to her, should be warned about Lennox, and bursts into tears when David proposes, telling him she can't marry him.

While shopping in the village, Anna is recognized by gossipy spinster Martha Perkins, who tells her crony Cornelia that Anna is "a notorious woman." On the evening of the birthday party, Martha arrives at the farm, eager to tell Mr. and Mrs. Bartlett that their hired girl has been deceiving them. Martha insists that she encountered this young woman in the town of Beldon, where she was going by the name Mrs. Lennox and had a baby.

Despite an impending ice storm, Squire Bartlett makes the journey to Beldon, where the kindly Mr. Peabody confirms that a young boarder in his home had a husband none of the locals ever saw, and a baby that didn't survive. Back on the farm, a grim Bartlett promptly fires Anna, over David's protests. David still wants to marry her. Humiliated by the confrontation, Anna identifies Lennox Sanderson as the cad he is, and then flees into the stormy night.

Way Down East had already enjoyed several incarnations before Fox brought it back to movie screens in 1935. Lottie Blair Parker's play was a modest success on Broadway in 1898 and became the basis for films in 1908 and 1914. In 1920, D.W. Griffith directed Lillian Gish and Richard Barthelmess in a third version, one of the hallmarks of silent cinema.

Henry Fonda was Rochelle's leading man in *Way Down East* (1935).

This remake falls short of Griffith's masterpiece, but it's a highly competent and engaging retelling of the story, even if movie audiences found it a bit shopworn by the fourth time around. The action-packed climax, putting the heroine at risk from breaking ice floes atop a roaring river, is well-staged if inevitably melodramatic. For the most part, director Henry King (1886–1982), always at home with stories of Americana, keeps the histrionics in check.

Fresh-faced Henry Fonda (1905–1982) and Rochelle make an appealing pair of young lovers. She stepped into the role, getting a welcome career break, after Janet Gaynor fell ill. Leonard Maltin, while regretting that Gaynor had to be replaced, called Rochelle "quite capable" as Anna, noting particularly the scene in which she and Fonda talk about drinking water from tin cans vs. gourds: "Not many actors could bring the genuineness to such dialogue that these two do."[17] King saw it differently, saying some years later, "We got Rochelle Hudson to replace Janet because she fit in her clothes perfectly. Rochelle didn't have the personality for the role. Rochelle was a good little actress, but not good for that part."[18]

Rochelle handles the dramatic scenes more than capably, and her beauty cannot be disguised even by drab costumes. Though she has her biggest scenes in the last few minutes of the film, she's also effective in smaller moments, even those without dialogue, as when she shows a highly emotional reaction to holding another woman's baby. Fonda acquits himself well in his second major film outing.

A set visitor observed the staging of the ice floes sequence, and wrote, "Imagine, if you can, an 1,800 horse-power generator launching a stream of water at the rate of 96,000 gallons a minute while tons of huge ice cakes crash and break in the madly churning flood. And just to complicate matters, eight enormous wind machines blow the gypsum snow into a violent gale.... No blizzard of nature could be more furious, nor more perilous."[19] He reported that the stars refused to let their stunt doubles perform in their place.

Way Down East benefits from a strong ensemble of character players, notably Margaret Hamilton (1902–1985), who ably juxtaposes drama and comedy as Martha. Though she hankers for the romantic attentions of local storekeeper Seth, she's always on the lookout for any juicy scandal, especially concerning anyone else's love life. She bridles at elderly Hank Woolwine's claim that she gossips, but he says, "As long as you're able to be about, they won't need no newspapers in this town." Sara Haden (1898–1981) plays a smaller role as another scandalmonger.

Spring Byington (1886–1971) gives the character of David's mother warmth and charm. Russell Simpson (1880–1959) plays her stolid, humorless husband with an iron-clad moral code. Broader performances come from Andy Devine as the Bartletts' simple-minded, clumsy farmhand, and Al Lydell (d. 1937) as a local geezer always looking to treat his rheumatism with spirits. Astrid Allwyn (1905–1978) is cheated of billing in the opening titles, though she plays a fairly significant role as Cousin Kate.

As Rochelle told it to a reporter, "The cast had a lot of fun making *Way Down East*, despite the discomfort of snow scenes in midsummer. Slim Summerville kept them in an uproar most of the picture."[20]

Reviews: "An entertainment feature certain to thrill the nation's theatregoers.... The great, old story lives anew, with modern screen advantages embellishing its gripping drama, inspiring love interest and natural humor.... The action is convincingly handled by Miss Hudson, Fonda, Simpson, his wife, Spring Byington, Miss Hamilton, and Trevor, who all make sincere simplicity powerful... [S]plendid direction." *Motion Picture Daily*, August 15, 1935

"Miss Hudson achieves a dramatic performance which has been more or less heretofore unsuspected.... She comes through in her dramatic opportunities in a manner that's pleasantly surprising and highly creditable.... Oscar Bradley's musical score is swell. His musical tempos, to translate the temperaments and moods of characters or situations, make for a fine orchestral cloak. Ernest Palmer's photography is almost portraiture in some of its snow-topped scenic backgrounds." *Variety*, November 6, 1935

Show Them No Mercy! (1935)

Rochelle Hudson (*Loretta Martin*), Cesar Romero (*Tobey*), Bruce Cabot (*Pitch*), Edward Norris (*Joe Martin*), Edward Brophy (*Buzz*), Warren Hymer (*Gimp*), Herbert Rawlinson (*Kurt Hansen*), Robert Gleckler (*Gus Hansen*), Charles C. Wilson

(*Clifford*), William B. Davidson (*Chief Haggerty*), Frank Conroy (*Reed*), Edythe Elliott (*Mrs. Hansen*), Orrin Burke (*Judge Fry*), Jimmy Butler (*Boy at Service Station*), Boothe Howard (*Lester Mills*), Edward LeSaint (*Gas Station Owner*), Phil Tead (*Ticket Clerk*), Edward Keane (*Doctor*), Lester Dorr (*Milkman*)

Director: George Marshall. *Producer*: Darryl F. Zanuck. *Story*: Kubec Glasmon. *Adaptation*: Henry Lehrman. *Associate Producer*: Raymond Griffith. *Photographer*: Bert Glennon. *Art Director*: Jack Otterson. *Editor*: Jack Murray. *Costumes*: Arthur M. Levy. *Sound*: W.D. Flick, Roger Heman. *Music Director*: David Buttolph.

20th Century–Fox; released December 6, 1935. 76 minutes.

Crowds gather outside the home of the wealthy Hansen family, whose son Tom has been kidnapped. The Hansens can raise the $200,000 ransom demanded, but they refuse to allow investigators from the Bureau of Investigation to pay it in marked bills.

Lost on a back road during a torrential thunderstorm, their car stuck in the mud, young marrieds Joe and Loretta Martin (accompanied by their baby and their dog) are forced to seek shelter. The nearest house is unoccupied, and seems abandoned, but there are fresh stores of food and other supplies.

After the Martins go to sleep, they are startled by the unexpected arrival of four armed men who tell them they can stay the night, provided they leave in the morning. A radio broadcast announces that Tom Hansen has been safely returned after the ransom was paid, and the Martins realize they are sharing the house with the kidnappers. In the morning, gang leader Tobey tells the Martins they cannot leave, though their infant daughter is sick. Instead, Joe will accompany Tobey on a shopping trip into a nearby town, where the young husband will try spending some of the ransom money, to find out whether it is marked. They manage to pass some bills without difficulty, but a radio bulletin subsequently alerts Tobey and his cohorts that the money is indeed marked. The Martins' dog Sport playfully grabs a pile of dough and runs off with it, causing Pitch, another gang member, to shoot at him. Joe is digging an escape route from the bedroom in which they're confined.

Arguing amongst themselves as the threat of an FBI dragnet closes in, the kidnappers finally decide to go their separate ways, with Tobey remaining at the hideout. On the run, the men find themselves pursued, and may finally get their just deserts, with some help from a wounded but resourceful terrier.

The crime of kidnapping was a hot topic in the 1930s, thanks largely to the Lindbergh baby case which horrified the nation. *Show Them No Mercy!* depicts the role of the FBI in handling crimes that cross state lines, with bureau chief J. Edgar Hoover name-dropped in one scene. Since the kidnapping is already a *fait accompli* as the film opens, we don't learn much that might encourage budding criminals in the audience, and the victim Tom Hansen never appears on-screen. As studio publicity put it, "The nation is lashing out at the racketeers and mobsters preying on its citizenry, and turns the weapons of terror back on the men who first used them." The publicists described the film as "an account of the nation's war on crime, interspersed with moments of comedy and romance."

In the planning stages, the film immediately drew the attention of censors who had tightened up restrictions on kidnapping stories in the wake of the Lindbergh tragedy. Geoffrey Shurlock provided Fox's Darryl F. Zanuck with a document outlining pertinent rules, including one that forbade stories about kidnapped children, as well as standards stating that "no profit accrues to the abductors or kidnapers" and that "the kidnapers are punished." In a letter back to Shurlock, Zanuck wrote that the studio intended to make the first picture "that will conclusively and definitely prove to even an imbecile that kidnapping, even if successfully engineered, is utterly futile."[21]

Show Them No Mercy! racks up the tension by putting the Martins, their baby and their dog in jeopardy, at close quarters with the hardened criminals. Rochelle and Edward Norris make an endearing, sympathetic young couple, establishing a good rapport that makes them credible as husband and wife. While Rochelle's Loretta quickly gains our sympathy as a demure young wife and mother, there's sterner stuff at her core, as we find out when Rochelle delivers a stirring speech to her captors:

> If I ever get out of here, I'll not only talk, I'll shout. I'll yell from the housetops. I'll tell everyone who you are and what you are! I'll remember your faces as long as I live. I hope I'll have the satisfaction of seeing you hanged…. Go ahead, kill me. But don't torture my baby!

The good guys vs. the bad guys: Captive couple Loretta and Joe (Rochelle Hudson, Edward Norris, left) are at the mercy of Tobey (Cesar Romero) and Pitch (Bruce Cabot, right) in *Show Them No Mercy!* **(1935).**

The character of Loretta also plays a key—and slightly surprising—role in the film's violent climax.

Norris (1911–2002) had been active as a film actor for only two years, *Show Them No Mercy!* providing an opportunity to move beyond the minor roles he'd previously played. He was borrowed from MGM for this assignment. He remained busy as an actor into the early 1960s, mostly working on television after 1950. He later said, "My leading lady, Rochelle Hudson, was wonderful to work with, very sincere."[22]

Cesar Romero (1907–1994) and Bruce Cabot (1904–1972) are cast as the most ruthless of the quartet of kidnappers, director George Marshall making good use of occasional close-ups to capture their faces in moments of particular tension. Romero told columnist Eleanor Barnes that he welcomed the chance to play something other than "just a nice boy opposite some girl"; the reporter added, "He regarded the role as an opportunity and he used it to good advantage."[23] Though Romero gives a credible performance as a tough guy (slightly undermined by his habit of periodically warbling happy ditties to himself), Cabot's Pitch is perhaps the more intimidating of the two, especially when he gets drunk and starts eyeing the lovely Loretta thoughtfully. It may have been a mistake to give his character that particular name, since "Pitch" can easily be misheard, causing it to seem as if his cohorts are saying things like, "Take it easy, bitch!"

Scenarist Kubec Glasmon (1897–1938) found himself in demand after the James Cagney screen adaptation of his unpublished novel *The Public Enemy* became a massive hit in 1931. His career was cut short by his death of a heart attack at the age of 40. George Marshall (1891–1975) had been directing films since the mid-1910s, and had many credits in comedy in the sound era. One of his last directorial assignments was a brief stint on the television series *Here's Lucy*.

In early announcements, the film was known by the title *Snatched*, sometimes with an exclamation point affixed to the end. A *Motion Picture Herald* item (July 13, 1935) listed it as one of the first features to be issued under the banner of 20th Century–Fox, following the merger of Twentieth Century Pictures and Fox Films. It was retitled *Tainted Money* for British release.

Reviews: "Fans who like tense drama will get a good stretch of it in this kidnaping yarn. It carries suspense from start to finish.... The cast does good work, with [Bruce] Cabot making a particularly hateful killer, and a terrier dog plays an interesting part in the story. Some comedy is also sprinkled along the route." *Film Daily*, December 7, 1935

"A new method of preserving the showmanship and entertainment vitality of the gangster–G-Man conflict, yet introducing a powerful dramatic contrast, is uncovered here.... As typical menacing melodrama is vividly portrayed by gangsters Cesar Romero, Bruce Cabot, Edward Brophy and Warren Hymer, heart-touching drama is played by Rochelle Hudson, Edward Norris and their baby." *Motion Picture Daily*, October 26, 1935

The Music Goes 'Round (1936)

Harry Richman (*Harry Wallace*), Rochelle Hudson (*Susannah Courtney*), Walter Connolly (*Hector Courtney*), Douglass Dumbrille (*Bishop*), Lionel Stander (*O'Casey*), Henry Mollison (*Stephen Gray*), Etienne Girardot (*Brewster*), Walter Kingsford (*Cobham*), Wyrley Birch (*Josh*), Victor Kilian (*Marshall*), Dora Early (*Eleanora*), Gene Morgan (*Nelson*), Eddie Anderson (*Lucifer*), Al Herman (*Stage Manager*), Jack Mack (*Manager*), Art Berry, Sr. (*Butler*), Granville Bates (*Political Candidate*), Ann Bupp (*Girl in Audience*), Betty Farrington (*Girl's Mother*), Edward Earle (*Station Manager*), Alma Fern (*Maid*), Russell Hicks (*Mr. Cohn*), Carrie Daumery (*Dowager in Audience*), Ned Norton (*Telegraph Operator*), Victor Potel, Fred "Snowflake" Toones (*Garage Attendants*), Edward Farley, Michael Riley and Their Band, Michael Bartlett, Herman Bing, The Four Blackbirds (*Themselves*)

Director: Victor Schertzinger. *Story*: Sidney Buchman. *Screenplay*: Jo Swerling. *Music and Lyrics*: Lew Brown, Harry Akst, Victor Schertzinger. *Additional Lyrics*: Red Hodgson, Edward Farley, Michael Riley. *Associate Producer*: Max Winslow. *Photographer*: Joseph Walker. *Editor*: Gene Milford. *Music Director*: Howard Jackson. *Dance Director*: Larry Ceballos. *Art Director*: Stephen Goosson. *Special Camera Effects*: E. Roy Davidson. *Costumes*: Samuel Lange.

Columbia; released February 27, 1936. 86 minutes.

Broadway star Harry Wallace is ten days away from opening his new revue, and quarreling with his producer, Mr. Bishop, about a comedy number he wants to add. Sensing that his headliner is nearing burnout, Bishop suggests he take a little time off. Harry promptly borrows his gardener's car and leaves town for parts unknown, while newspapers play up his disappearance.

Down South, car trouble forces Harry to stop in the small town of Adamsville, Mississippi. Wandering down to the riverside, he is intrigued by a job notice for an actor. On a docked showboat, beautiful Susannah Courtney is trying out applicants to play three minor roles in the Courtney Players' latest shipboard production. Harry, calling himself Harry Linden, impresses her with his reading of "I love you," and is hired for a dollar a night plus room and board.

The Courtney Players, operated by Susannah and her father, specialize in corny, old-fashioned melodramas, including their latest, "Love Conquers Pride; or, The Belle of Charleston." Attracted to his new boss, Harry asks her if she would consider letting him step into the leading man role, opposite her, should her co-star Stephen Gray drop out. She rebukes him when he ad-libs a kiss in one scene.

Susannah and her father are staying one step ahead of the bills, and the boat crew goes on strike when they are unable to pay wages. She warns Harry that he may need to find another job. He wires New York and urges his valet, O'Casey, and Bishop to come down as soon as possible.

Harry arranges a musical parade and succeeds in getting a full house of locals to attend the Courtney show. When Stephen Gray is diagnosed with measles, Harry steps into the lead opposite Susannah. Harry had promised his New York pals "the comedy sensation of all time." Bishop indeed finds the show hilarious, and he and Harry persuade the entire company to come north, where their drama will be incorporated into his upcoming show.

In New York, the Courtney Players are installed at Harry's Long Island estate, where they rehearse separately from the other revue cast members, unaware of how their overheated drama will be used in the show. On opening night, with Susannah's father drunk, *Bishop's Follies of 1936* opens. Prominently featured is the novelty number "The Music Goes 'Round and Around." Guilt-stricken, Harry tries to tell Susannah what's in store for her and her co-stars; she's humiliated when their dramatic sequence inspires laughter and catcalls from the audience. Furious, she tells them they are "nothing but a bunch of dressed-up hoodlums." She and the other Courtney Players promptly abandon the show and go home to Mississippi, while Harry tries to make things right with the woman he loves.

Top-billed Harry Richman (1895–1972) was a popular entertainer, graduating from vaudeville to Broadway, and eventually to films, where he made a hit of the title song in *Puttin' on the Ritz* (1930). Though it's occasionally possible to see glimpses of what endeared him to audiences at the time, *The Music Goes 'Round* is a film that hasn't aged well. His nasal speaking voice is off-putting, as are his musical numbers, singing about "darkies."

Rochelle is cast as young, naïve Susannah Courtney, who her father says was "born on this showboat." She has charm and appeal, though her romance with Richman (who seems to be wearing more makeup than she is) doesn't convince. She is amusing in the sequences in which Susannah performs in the show-within-a-show, giving a performance that's just exaggerated enough to be endearing, yet not over the top. Her teary speech when she tells off the snobbish Broadway audience, as Susannah watches her dreams crumble, is touching.

A few gossip column items tried to publicize a romance between Rochelle and her leading man. She debunked the rumors, telling columnist Sidney Skolsky (April 5, 1936), "I had to be told by a director when to kiss him." According to the actress and her mother, Rochelle had had a couple of dinners with Richman, and they worked on songs together. "I think Harry is very nice," Hudson said. "He's not wild at all, like they say, and I feel safer with him than I would with some of these young Hollywood hangers-on."[24]

Actor-singer Michael Bartlett (1903–1979) and character actor Herman Bing (1889–1947) make cameo appearances as themselves, each recruited from the audience to sing a chorus of "The Music Goes 'Round and Around" during the revue sequence. Lionel Stander (1908–1994) has a couple of amusing moments as Harry's rough-hewn valet, who pitches woo to stuffy actress Eleonora, whom he calls "Ellie." Eddie "Rochester" Anderson (1905–1977), a year or so shy of his career-defining breakthrough with Jack Benny, plays the clichéd character of Lucifer.

Director Victor Schertzinger (1888–1941) was a noted symphonic conductor whose directorial credits in the sound era ran largely to musicals. His final, posthumous credit as director came with *The Fleet's In* (1942).

Studio publicity leaned heavily on the appeal of the novelty song from which the film took its title, announcing breathlessly in trade ads, "Columbia Pictures scores an electrifying beat by acquiring full and exclusive rights to the world-rocking song sensation." *Radio Mirror* (April 1936) devoted an entire feature to what was described as "that elfin tune which sneaks up and twists your tongue and brain about insanely," claiming that "a bewildered, delirious country was singing, dancing, playing the mad tune—and still is."

Reviews: "Just a fair musical comedy. If spectators can overlook the triteness of the plot, they may find a few features to amuse them.... The fault with the picture lies in the fact that the story dwells too much on the actions of the showboat people.... The story, too, is implausible, for the producers seem to expect the audience to believe that Rochelle Hudson takes what she is doing seriously." *Harrison's Reports*, February 29, 1936

"Some tall hurdling will have to be done to bring this one into the money.... Inclusion of 'The Music Goes 'Round' [the song] has resulted in balling up what most likely had been a pleasant little romance of modest dimensions... [T]he most is made of the few laugh moments that the script offers.... Miss Hudson does an ingratiating job." *Variety*, February 26, 1936

Everybody's Old Man (1936)

Irvin S. Cobb (*William Franklin*), Rochelle Hudson (*Cynthia Sampson*), Johnny Downs (*Tommy Sampson*), Norman Foster (*Ronald Franklin*), Alan Dinehart (*Frederick Gillespie*), Sara Haden (*Susan Franklin*), Donald Meek (*Finney*), Warren Hymer (*Mike Murphy*), Charles Coleman (*Mansfield*), John Miltern (*Larson*), Walter Walker (*Haslett*), Maurice Cass (*Dr. Phillips*), Frederick Burton (*Aylesworth*), Delma Byron (*Miss Martin*), Hilda Vaughn (*Helen*), Hal K. Dawson (*Jameson*), Lynn Bari (*Miss Burke*), Gennaro Curci (*Gondolier*), Ann Moultrie (*Stenographer*), Patricia Farr (*Telephone Girl*), Leonid Snegoff (*Russian*), Eric Wilton (*Butler*), Stanley Mack, Anne Nagel, Fred Wallace (*Clerks*), Sam Ash, John Guston, Cyril Ring, Emmett Vogan (*Salesmen*)

Director: James Flood. *Executive Producer*: Darryl F. Zanuck. *Screenplay*: Patterson McNutt, A.E. Thomas. *Suggested by the Story by* Edgar Franklin. *Photographer*: Barney McGill. *Art Director*: Mark-Lee Kirk. *Settings*: Thomas Little. *Assistant Director*: William Forsythe. *Editor*: Lloyd Nosler. *Costumes*: Gwen Wakeling. *Sound*: E. Clayton Ward, Roger Heman. *Music Director*: David Buttolph.

20th Century–Fox; released March 20, 1936. 82 minutes.

Sixtyish William Franklin has devoted 40 years of his life to his company, Franklin's Foods, making it a resounding success. His chief motivation has always been his longtime rivalry with Tom Sampson, owner of Sampson's Soups. Former business partners, they also competed for the hand of Mary Travers, who became Mrs. Sampson. Learning that Tom has died suddenly of a heart attack, Franklin finds himself at loose ends, and decides to turn over the operation of his company to his nephew Ronnie.

Franklin spends a few months traveling in the company of his sister Susan. In Paris, a friendly cab driver offers to give Franklin (minus his sister) a taste of the city's night life. At a somewhat disreputable club, Le Rat Mort (The Dead Rat), Franklin encounters the late Mr. Sampson's son and daughter, Tommy and Cynthia, who seem to be hell-bent on spending their inheritance in record time. Lending a hand when a drunken Tommy gets into a brawl, Franklin becomes friendly with both Sampsons. He tells them his name is George Spelvin.

Learning that Sampson's Soups is hovering on the edge of bankruptcy, Franklin urges Ronnie to acquire the company, but he refuses. Going through a lawyer, Franklin offers $750,000 for the firm, later raising it to $2 million because he likes Cynthia, who strongly resembles her mother. His attorney tells him that, despite the poor financial standing of Sampson's Soups, general manager Gillespie declined his offer. Thinking he sees potential in the young Sampsons, despite their spendthrift ways, Franklin asks the judge overseeing their estate to put him in charge of it.

Tommy and his sister are initially delighted, assuming "Spelvin" will merely act as a figurehead. Instead, he cuts off their liquor supply, discharges the servants they can no longer afford, and forces them to face their bleak economic outlook. After rousing their anger, he informs them that, thanks to their inattention, the Sampson company has lost more than $200,000 in the past year. He challenges them to step up to the plate and show some maturity, along with pride in their family name. Tommy agrees to take a more active role in running the factory, with Franklin's help. Meanwhile, Cynthia gets a job at the Franklin plant, using her mother's maiden name, so that she can spy on their operation.

The Sampson siblings (Rochelle Hudson, Johnny Downs) find their cozy lives disrupted in *Everybody's Old Man* (1936).

Franklin shows Tommy that Gillespie has been deliberately running the company into the ground, intending to then acquire it at a cheap price. Cynthia catches the eye of Ronnie. Sampson's Soups is soon so prosperous that Ronnie is on the verge of crying "uncle," unaware that, in fact, his uncle is precisely the cause of the crisis.

Everybody's Old Man, though competently made and performed, rarely rises above mild entertainment. The project began as a potential vehicle for Rochelle's frequent co-star Will Rogers. But his sudden death kiboshed those plans. Then the film was revived with humorist and author Irvin S. Cobb (1876–1944) stepping into the lead. Cobb is surely one of the homelier actors ever handed a starring movie part, as his character acknowledges, saying he has a face "sorta built to scare little children with." He lacks Rogers' amiable warmth, and the script featured few instances of the homespun humor moviegoers associated with Rogers.

Second-billed Rochelle plays the smarter and more sensible of the Sampson siblings. Her character rises to the occasion when Franklin sees that she has untapped potential, telling her, "You're not the girl that's been bullyin' me, and drinkin' too much, and telephonin' for more gin." She's a virtual lookalike for her mother, as shown in a portrait using Rochelle's image (seen periodically throughout the film). Hudson has a few dramatic opportunities, and realizes them well. She's credible as the foolish young woman who matures under the right influence, and as the young lady whose tears make it impossible for Ronnie to fire her. Handsome Johnny Downs (1913–1994) makes a believable brother for her, delivering a capable performance. Classic cinema's most aptly named character actor Donald Meek (1878–1946) appears as a typically milquetoast assistant in the Franklin executive offices.

Rochelle and Irvin S. Cobb were guests on the March 6, 1936, broadcast of radio's *Hollywood Hotel*, hosted by Dick Powell, and re-enacted scenes from *Everybody's Old Man*. A studio ad mat showed Cobb saying, "Fact is … don't like my face much myself!" to which was added the line, "But millions of movie-goers can't be wrong … and you've laughed him into stardom!"

A Nevada exhibitor reported sadly to the *Motion Picture Herald*'s "What the Picture Did for Me" column (November 7, 1936), "A good program picture. However, it did nothing at the box office."

Reviews: "This is a most ordinary film, destined to land on second spots of dual bill programs…. Its only chance resides in rural areas and subsequent runs where sophistication is frowned upon…. It bears a very obvious resemblance to [George] Arliss' *Working Man* of a few seasons back…. [Irvin S.] Cobb has little to offer as an actor and he will never come within a million miles of Rogers' warming appeal. The gentle, mildly humorous yarn moves along leisurely and with little action." *Film Bulletin*, March 25, 1936

"Irvin S. Cobb's first crack with top billing gets over big…. Excellent comedy with strong cast support…. With Cobb's benevolent motive based on love for the dead mother of the young profligates, the piece gets off enough tear-stimulation to balance the comedy. Rochelle Hudson and Johnny Downs do well as the sister and brother." *Film Daily*, March 27, 1936

The Country Beyond (1936)

Rochelle Hudson (*Jean Alison*), Paul Kelly (*Sgt. Cassidy*), Robert Kent (*Corp. Robert King*), Alan Hale (*Jim Alison*), Alan Dinehart (*Ray Jennings*), Andrew Tombes (*Senator Rawlings*), Claudia Coleman (*Mrs. Rawlings*), Matt McHugh (*Constable Weller*), Paul McVey (*Fred Donaldson*), Holmes Herbert (*Inspector Reed*), Chester Gan (*Cook*), Buck (*Buck*), Prince (*Wolf*), Chief Thunderbird (*Indian Chief*), Fred Walton (*Station Agent*), George Reed (*Porter*), Lew Harvey (*Pierre*)

Director: Eugene Forde. *Executive Producer*: Sol M. Wurtzel. *Screenplay*: Lamar Trotti, Adele Comandini. *Photographer*: Barney McGill. *Editor*: Fred Allen. *Art Director*: Duncan Cramer. *Costumes*: William Lambert. *Assistant Director*: Aaron Rosenberg. *Music Director*: Samuel Kaylin. *Sound*: Eugene Grossman, Harry M. Leonard.

20th Century–Fox; released April 24, 1936. 73 minutes.

Sergeant Cassidy of the Canadian Mounted Police is assigned to train a newcomer, Corp. Robert King. As the son of the CMP's commissioner, King is regarded with skepticism by his new supervisor. The two men are at odds from the outset. The fun-loving King encounters pretty Jean Alison, and tries to get better acquainted, but Buck, her Saint Bernard, intercedes.

Cassidy is assigned to investigate a robbery at a trading post, which included a fatal attack on the watchman by a dog. King manages to get himself attached to the investigation, against Cassidy's wishes. Thanks to Buck, stolen furs are found in the cellar of the lodge of Jean's father Jim Alison, who is arrested. Alison persuades his daughter to help him escape so that he can clear his name. Jean tricks King into letting her dad go free.

The film's poster art described it as "a breathless adventure amid the Northlands' trackless wilds!" This was the second screen adaptation of author-conservationist James Oliver Curwood's 1922 novel, following a 1926 silent version with Olive Borden and Ralph Graves. Curwood's name was emblazoned above the title in the remake. Director Eugene Forde (1898–1986) may be best-known for helming multiple entries in Fox's Charlie Chan series.

Robert Kent (1908–1955) was one of Rochelle's most frequent co-stars; they made five Fox pictures together in a two-year period. *The Country Beyond* represented his first lead role. According to studio publicity, he was cast after being spotted in a Los Angeles stage production of *Kind Lady* with May Robson.

Receiving almost as much media attention as the two-legged cast members was Buck, the Saint Bernard seen previously in *Call of the Wild* (1935). Sometimes billed as "Buck the Wonder Dog," his other screen credits include *Melody Trail* (1935) with Gene Autry and *Call of the Yukon* (1938) with Richard Arlen. His nemesis in *The Country Beyond* is the Great Dane Wolf, a role essayed by Prince.

Film Daily (February 26, 1936) reported that director Forde "took the *Country Beyond* company to Chatsworth for a few days' location scenes." A fan magazine item claimed that during location shooting, Hudson "had a narrow escape when a landslide went awry. Had she been injured in filming the scene, it would have cost 20th Century vast sums of money to hold up production."[25] Another mishap involved a prop weapon: "Too much realism in a make-believe film scene ... resulted in Rochelle Hudson ... being treated for a cut over her right eye. Miss Hudson was struggling with Alan Dinehart for possession of a revolver when a sight on the barrel of the weapon inflicted the cut."[26]

In the *Motion Picture Herald*'s "What the Picture Did for Me" column (September 19, 1936), a Texas exhibitor described *The Country Beyond* as "an exceptionally good outdoor ... picture that made a few of the so-called 'highbrows' admit that they could enjoy a Saturday show. Thoroughly enjoyed it here and should be [the same] anywhere if spotted right."

Rochelle, all togged up for a chilly Canadian winter, in *The Country Beyond* (1936).

A nitrate print of *The Country Beyond* is in the UCLA Film and Television Archive.

Reviews: "A melodrama of life, love and crime in the snow covered north. It's pretty much formula Northwest Mounted Police romance and drama stuff. Though the various players give convincing performances, two dogs—one a hero, the other a menace—are the real stars of the show.... Probably will appeal more to specialized action lovers and youngsters than to any other class of audience." *Motion Picture Herald*, April 11, 1936

"A fair program melodrama. The plot ... is routine; but it has enough exciting situations to hold the attention of the average picture-goer. It should appeal particularly to lovers of the outdoors because of the excellent scenic background of the snowy mountain country.... The closing scenes ... are the most exciting.... The affair between [Kent and Hudson] progresses pleasantly from animosity to love. Buck, the famous dog of *Call of the Wild*, again displays remarkable intelligence." *Harrison's Reports*, April 18, 1936

Poppy (1936)

W.C. Fields (*Prof. Eustace P. McGargle*), Rochelle Hudson (*Poppy McGargle*), Richard Cromwell (*Billy Farnsworth*), Catharine [Catherine] Doucet (*Countess Maggi Tubbs DePuizzi*), Lynne Overman (*Eddie G. Whiffen*), Granville Bates (*Mayor Farnsworth*), Maude Eburne (*Sarah Tucker*), Bill Wolfe (*Egmont*), Adrian Morris (*Constable Bowman*), Rosalind Keith (*Frances Parker*), Ralph Remley (*Carnival Manager*), Dewey Robinson (*Calliope Driver*), Tammany Young (*Joe*), Tom Kennedy (*Hot Dog Stand Proprietor*), Wade Boteler (*Bartender*), Charles McMurray (*Constable*), Helen Holmes (*Dowager*), Dick Rush, Malcolm Wait (*Deputy Sheriffs*)

Director: A. Edward Sutherland. *Producer*: William LeBaron. *Associate Producer*: Paul M. Jones. *Screenplay*: Waldemar Young, Virginia Van Upp. *Based on a Play by* Dorothy Donnelly. *Photographer:* William C. Mellor. *Art Directors*: Hans Dreier, Bernard Herzbrun. *Editor*: Stuart Heisler. *Recordists*: Earl Hayman, John Cope. *Music Director*: Boris Morros. *Music and Lyrics*: Ralph Rainger, Leo Robin, Sam Coslow, Frederick Hollander. *Costume Designer*: Edith Head. *Interior Decorator*: A.E. Freudeman.

Paramount; released June 19, 1936. 73 minutes.

It's 1883, and Eustace P. McGargle and his beautiful young daughter Poppy live a nomadic life, traveling from town to town as McGargle earns a living by his wits. En route to the town of Green Meadows, Poppy is knocked from a bridge when two young men race by on horseback. One of them stops to help fish her out of the creek and takes an obvious interest in her, but she's too angry to reciprocate.

In Green Meadows, McGargle finagles a booth at the town's carnival, where he sells dubious bottles of sarsaparilla and Poppy sings. The man from the bridge—Billy Farnsworth, son of the town's mayor—visits Poppy backstage and introduces himself. McGargle, meanwhile, is intrigued by the widowed Countess DePuizzi, a woman who married well and is worth a fortune. While he pursues a relationship with her, Poppy spends time with Billy, though his family snubs her. Kindly Sarah Tucker gives her a good meal and listens to Poppy's dreams of having her own home and a settled life.

From attorney E.G. Whiffen, McGargle learns that the countess' income is held in a trust because of a missing heir, Katherine Putnam, who ran away 20 years ago and had a baby daughter. McGargle promptly fills out a phony marriage certificate showing that he was wed to Putnam, planning to pass off Poppy as their daughter. Mayor Farnsworth, trustee of the estate, is dubious until he's shown the faked certificate.

Poppy is thrilled when Billy proposes, but they're interrupted when Sarah summons her to hear the news that she's now a wealthy young lady. McGargle is pleased to take over the countess' lavish home. The countess' snooty friends make Poppy feel ill at ease in her new surroundings, and she decides it's best to break off her engagement and leave town.

Now broke, the countess is tempted when Whiffen asks for her hand in marriage, assuring her he has a surefire way to get her money back. He proceeds to call McGargle and Poppy thieves, humiliating the latter. As they prepare to leave the town in disgrace, Sarah steps up with information that may change everything.

Rochelle played the title character in *Poppy* (1936) opposite W.C. Fields.

Rochelle plays the title character but *Poppy* is first and foremost a vehicle for W.C. Fields (1880–1946), one of the great comedians of the 20th century. Though overall the film is somewhat spotty, there are enough good set pieces and moments to make it worth a look. It's a film version of a musical comedy in which Fields starred on Broadway to great success in 1923 and '24. *Poppy* had previously been adapted to film in the silent comedy *Sally of the Sawdust* (1925), in which Fields also played the lead. According to his biographer, Fields was in shaky health when *Poppy* was filmed—"tottery on his feet, quiet and morose when on the sidelines"—but managed with difficulty to rise to the occasion when some of his best bits were shot.[27] The use of a double for him is apparent in several scenes, such as the one in which he's thrown off a carnival float.

Fields gets laughs both visual and verbal, as when McGargle improvises the tragic story of his late wife's passing: "The poor dear was killed in Upper Sandusky. Run over by a pie wagon. A hit and galloping away driver. One of the horses…" At that point, his listener decides to cut short the recitation, which was made doubly amusing by Fields' unique comic delivery.

Paramount agreed to pay $750 a week to borrow Rochelle from Fox, with a four-week guarantee. The contract stipulated that only Fields' name could appear in larger type than hers in *Poppy* advertising and publicity. Although a Fields film can sometimes seem like a one-man show, second-billed Rochelle has substantial screen time and a few good opportunities. She elicits audience sympathy with her character's wistful longing for a settled, everyday life, as opposed to the hand-to-mouth existence she shares with McGargle.

As in *Life Begins at 40*, she and love interest Richard Cromwell match up well. She's charming when she urges him not to hurt the fish he caught. He assures her that fish don't have feelings, and is startled when his catch seems to answer, "That's what you think!" She laughs with delight when he falls for the ventriloquist tricks Pop taught her.

Writing for her fan club members in March 1936, Rochelle noted, "My picture *Poppy* is going along nicely but very slowly as Mr. Fields has been very ill and has to be careful not to overdo. I recorded my song last week and it was what they wanted so that made me happy. I may be a singer yet." With Fields in less than optimal condition, retakes were often necessary, as when Poppy and her dad scarf down food at a hot dog stand. As set visitor Sidney Skolsky (March 26, 1936) observed, director A. Edward Sutherland wasn't satisfied with the first take; more food was consumed as the actors did it again. Slightly bloated, Rochelle said, "You would have to make this scene right after lunch."

Lynne Overman (1887–1943) has some good moments as attorney Whiffen. A highlight finds the larcenous lawyer standing behind Mayor Farnsworth as the skeptical trustee questions McGargle about his late wife. Asked how tall Miss Putnam was, McGargle sees Whiffen hold up five fingers on one hand, and three on the other. The lawyer blanches when McGargle does the math and says confidently, "Eight feet!"

Catherine Doucet (1875–1958) capably handles the role of the small-town woman turned nobility, one that, with some modification, could have been a Margaret Dumont character in a Marx Brothers film. Bill Wolfe (1894–1975), with his face made for character roles, is at the center of a running gag as the customer swindled by McGargle at the carnival; he turns up again as the countess' gardener, determined to get his money back. Maude Eburne (1875–1960), more sympathetically cast than she often was, offers a pleasing performance as Sarah, mostly a good soul but also capable of telling the countess, "Do you want me to slap that giggling mouth of yours?"

Reviews: "[W.C. Fields] could get laughs with Hamlet's soliloquy, which is just about what he's doing in *Poppy*. Amid the 19th century melodramatics and the considerable sob stuff that goes with it, Fields manages to shake off the ill effects and get his laughs…. The juvenile romance … is just a series of interruptions between the Fields comedy business…. Miss Hudson is pleasant as the [*sic*] McGargle's young ward, but they asked for too much in requesting her to sing a verse and a chorus while her heart is breaking." *Variety*, June 24, 1936

"This is a laughfest, which will please the Fields fans and make new ones for the comedian…. Rochelle Hudson is excellent in the title role and she and Richard Cromwell supply the love interest…. A. Edward Sutherland's direction is of the best." *Film Daily*, June 9, 1936

Reunion (1936)

Jean Hersholt (*Dr. John Luke*), The Dionne Quintuplets [Yvonne, Cecile, Marie, Annette, Emelie] (*The Wyatt Quintuplets*), Rochelle Hudson (*Nurse Mary MacKenzie*), Helen Vinson (*Gloria Sheridan*), Slim Summerville (*Constable Jim Ogden*), Robert Kent (*Dr. Tony Luke*), John Qualen (*Asa Wyatt*), Dorothy Peterson (*Nurse Katherine Kennedy*), Alan Dinehart (*Phillip Crandall*), J. Edward Bromberg (*Charles Renard*), Sara Haden (*Ellie*), Montagu Love (*Sir Basil Crawford*), George Ernest (*Rusty*), Tom Moore (*Dr. Richard Sheridan*), Esther Ralston (*Janet Fair*), Katharine Alexander (*Martha Crandall*), Julius Tannen (*Sam Fisher*), George Chandler (*Harry*), Edward McWade (*Gazette Editor*), Maude Eburne (*Mrs. Barton*), Claudia Coleman (*Mrs. Simms*), Hank Mann (*Jake*), Hattie McDaniel (*Sadie*), Eddie Dunn (*Gardener*), Mary MacLaren (*Mrs. Ogden*), Grace Hayle (*Mrs. Williams*), Jim Toney (*Workman*)

Director: Norman Taurog. *Executive Producer*: Darryl F. Zanuck. *Screenplay*: Sam Hellman, Gladys Lehman, Sonya Levien. *Story*: Bruce Gould. *Photographer*: Daniel B. Clark. *Art Director*: Mark-Lee Kirk. *Set Decorator*: Thomas Little. *Assistant Director*: Ed O'Fearna. *Editor*: Jack Murray. *Costumes*: Royer. *Sound*: W.D. Flick, Roger Heman.

20th Century–Fox; released November 20, 1936. 80 minutes.

Dr. John Luke of Moosetown, Canada, is honored by the Chamber of Commerce with a celebration commemorating his delivery of 3000 babies, among them the Wyatt quintuplets. Present at the occasion are Governor and Mrs. Phillip Crandall (he being the first infant the doctor ever delivered), movie actress Janet Fair (still known to locals as Mamie Hawkins) and even a bank robber who broke out of jail to take part.

Dr. Luke carries on his work with the help of loyal nurse Mary MacKenzie. Mary is in love with his nephew Dr. Tony Luke. Tony has quit a job in Toronto in order to join his uncle's practice. Ever since Asa Wyatt and his wife had quintuplets, other Moosetown residents hope the same may happen for them. Constable

Jim Ogden is disappointed when his wife gives birth to only one baby, rather than the six he anticipated.

Janet Fair, whose acting career has come to a virtual halt, is delighted to be offered the lead in a New York show, and with some difficulty she scrapes together the train fare to get her and her maid Sadie there. She's happy to find that Moosetown residents remember her and eagerly seek her autograph. Governor Crandall knows that his wife Martha would dearly like to be a mother herself, but he's opposed to the idea of adoption, telling her that it could be used against him politically.

Unexpectedly turning up at the celebration, Gloria Sheridan tells Tony that she intends to get a divorce so they can be together. Mary is jealous when it appears that Tony has another woman in his life, but he clearly still loves Mary. Dr. Luke takes it upon himself to help Tony choose the right mate, solve the Crandalls' problems, look after 11-year-old foundling Rusty, and find a happy ending for Janet, who resorts to desperate measures when she's notified that she's lost her comeback role.

Americans in the 1930s were fascinated by the story of the Dionne girls, the first documented case of quintuplets who survived infancy and grew to adulthood. Born in 1934, they were first seen by movie audiences in *The Country Doctor* (1936), released about eight months prior to *Reunion*. Jean Hersholt played Dr. John Luke in both features, his role based on the real-life obstetrician Dr. Allan R. Dafoe who delivered the Dionne babies.

Sonya Levien, writer of *The Country Doctor*, did two draft scripts of *Reunion* which failed to satisfy executive producer Darryl F. Zanuck. Sam Hellman and Gladys Lehman did revisions, but Zanuck still felt that the story "lacks emotional conflict. There is no excitement or suspense."[28] Not until August was a draft script found satisfactory.

Some moviegoers and reviewers were surprised that the quints don't play a more sizable role in *Reunion*. After a brief sequence early in the film, they don't return until past the one-hour mark, when we see several minutes of footage shot without sound, showing the toddlers at play. According to the opening titles, their scenes were shot "under the technical supervision" of Dr. Dafoe. Cinematographer Daniel B. Clark reported, "The task of filming the quints is a real technical problem, due to the unavoidable restrictions which safeguard the babies," which included limiting the shoot to no more than one hour per day and using less intense lighting than was normal on a studio soundstage.[29]

With the five babies only incidentally present, most of *Reunion*'s running time is devoted to interlocking stories about the other attendees at Dr. Luke's celebration, and the ways in which he plays not only a doctor but a Dear Abby–style adviser to the lovelorn of his town. The role is something of a warmup for what will become Hersholt's signature role, that of Dr. Christian in an RKO B-movie series that lasted six entries between 1939 and 1941 (and spawned a successful radio series). The result is an entertaining programmer that carries few, if any, surprises, but passes the time pleasantly and delivers solid entertainment.

Rochelle and Robert Kent make an appealing couple despite a story that has them estranged for most of the film. At one point, Dr. Luke chides them for "backing away from each other like a couple of strange Airedales." She's charming as the nurse who's in love, but shows that she's not to be taken for granted, telling him when he vacillates between her and Gloria that she can't fall in love with someone who turns his emotions on and off. Rochelle and her leading man are stepping into roles that were originated by others in *The Country Doctor*, where June Lang played Mary and Michael Whalen was Tony. A publicity item quoted Rochelle as saying, "If you think one child can get into mischief, you should see five up to their tricks at one time. I'm positively exhausted." She claimed to have been particularly fond of Annette Dionne, "possibly because she seemed to pay me more attention than did the others.... I'm not particularly maternal, you know, but I would have liked to have brought Annette home with me."[30]

Veteran character actors John Qualen (1899–1987) and Slim Summerville (1892–1946) play effectively off one another as, respectively, the father of the Wyatt quintuplets, and a father who hopes to outshine him with *six* babies of his own. Like Hersholt, they are reprising roles they created in *The Country Doctor*.

Esther Ralston (1902–1994), though still in her thirties, plays a character who, like herself, enjoyed her peak of popularity in the silent era. While her character is despondent over her fall from stardom, fan magazines depicted Miss Ralston putting on hold her life as a "lady of leisure" solely to please her young daughter, who had never seen her on a movie screen. Appearing in only a couple of brief scenes is Hattie McDaniel, Janet's maid, unimpressed by the sight of Moosetown: "These small country towns don't give me nothin'. I'm a big city gal, and I gotta have scope!"

In the *Motion Picture Herald*'s "What the Picture Did for Me" column (June 19, 1937), a small-town theater owner in South Dakota wrote, "A fair show but you expect to see more of the 5 kiddies really, but they just show up for the opening and the finish and the rest of the show is just built in by a good cast, so all is OK." The Dionne Quintuplets turned up two years later for one final feature, *Five of a Kind* (1938), with Hersholt, Qualen and Summerville, and they were also seen in several shorts and newsreels. Two are still living as of this writing.

Reviews: "Story, production and player values are skillfully blended ... to make a desirable attraction for exhibitors and audiences... [W]arm in human interest in which rich, homely humor, appealing pathos-tinged drama and intriguing topical incidents are intelligently combined... [It] seems geared for box office-excitement." *Motion Picture Daily*, November 11, 1936

"The cute and tricky Quintuplets highlight this comedy-drama. With those five tiny stars, the picture should hit strongly at the box-office.... Many a good gag makes for plenty of laughter, and with the doctor straightening out the lives of a few of the visitors, things are always interesting.... The large cast is very capable, with Esther Ralston, Helen Vinson, Alan Dinehart, Robert Kent and Rochelle Hudson doing very well.... Norman Taurog's direction gives the piece a lively pace and blends the comedy with the dramatic in a most entertaining manner." *Film Daily*, November 13, 1936

Woman-Wise (1937)

Rochelle Hudson (*Alice Fuller*), Michael Whalen (*Tracey Browne*), Thomas Beck (*Clint De Witt*), Alan Dinehart (*Richards*), Douglas Fowley (*Stevens*), George Hassell (*John De Witt*), Astrid Allwyn (*"Bubbles" Carson*), Chick Chandler (*Bob Benton*), Pat Flaherty (*Duke Fuller*), Lynn Bari (*Secretary*), Ward Bond (*Kramer*), Myra Marsh (*Mrs. Fuller*), Francis McDonald (*Charley*), Douglas Haig (*Oscar*), Charles C. Wilson (*Commissioner*), Lynn Bari (*Secretary*), Ward Bond (*Kramer*), George Turner (*Lasker*), Bob Perry (*Referee*), George Chandler (*Clerk*), Tom McGuire (*Bartender*)

Director: Allan Dwan. *Producer*: Sol M. Wurtzel. *Original Screenplay*: Ben Markson. *Photographer*: Robert Planck. *Editor*: Al de Gaetano. *Art Director*: Lewis Creber. *Music Director*: Samuel Kaylin. *Production Designer*: Lewis H. Creber. *Costume Designer*: Herschel. *Sound*: Harry M. Leonard, George Leverett. *Assistant Director*: Samuel Schneider.

20th Century–Fox; released January 22, 1937. 62 minutes.

Tracey Browne, sports editor of the *Evening Globe*, is disturbed to see that promoter "Gumshoes" Richards is training a washed-up boxer, Duke Fuller, for a comeback. A rival publication challenges Tracey to take on Fuller in a fight, with the winner to receive $2000 from Richards. Tracey easily knocks out the older man. Fuller's daughter Alice angrily says that her father needs the money he can earn prizefighting.

Alice takes a job at the *Globe*, where she is made assistant to the boss' spoiled son Clint De Witt, who's being given a chance to show he can do something besides enjoy nightclub life. Alice seems to be a good influence on Clint, and Tracey believes they are becoming romantically involved.

Richards lures Clint into incurring a large gambling debt. When Clint demands a loan from the promoter, Richards gives it to him, but uses the canceled check to get Clint into trouble with his dad. Tracey tries to protect Clint, but this results in his being fired by the elder De Witt.

According to *Film Daily* (December 3, 1936), the film's working title was *Peach Edition* until the month prior to its release. Early reports indicated that Sonja Henie would play a role, but this didn't pan out.

Rochelle is directed for the first time by the prolific Allan Dwan (1885–1981), who also helmed her next picture, *That I May Live*. Playing a clever, feisty young lady, Rochelle gets the chance to punch out Astrid Allwyn's character, "Bubbles" Carson.

The combative relationship between Alice and Tracey also resulted in fisticuffs, and an injury for Rochelle, per one newspaper item. "The next time Rochelle Hudson hits a gentleman, she is going to choose one with a softer chin than that of Michael Whalen…. Swinging a heavy punch that tottered the six-foot Irish actor, Rochelle came to the set the next morning with a sprained wrist." A follow-up scene in which she took a poke at actor Thomas Beck had to be postponed for a few days, until her wrist healed.[31]

Studio publicity described *Woman-Wise* as "the laugh-provoking tale of a boss who thought he knew all about women, and of a little spitfire who outwitted and outsocked him," as well as "the moving story of a sports writer's crusade to clean up a fixed-fight gang, and how his pretty newspaper assistant outsmarts them all by using women's wit and men's tactics." Among the taglines used in poster art was, "Woman-Wise? Phooey! She had to close both his eyes to open them to love!"

A nitrate print of *Woman-Wise* is held in the collections of the UCLA Film and Television Archive.

Reviews: "*Woman-Wise* is important mainly because it sets up Michael Whalen as an actor of A-1 appeal and reveals Rochelle Hudson as a pert, accomplished young lady who cannot be overlooked in future.... Humorous version of prize-fight ring with sports scribe-newspaper background rings true because of nice writing by Ben Markson, adept direction by Alan [sic] Dwan and uniformly trim performances.... Rochelle Hudson is splendid as the impetuous prize-fighter's daughter. She has grasped the changing moods with the ease of a veteran." *Variety*, January 20, 1937

"This pix [sic] offers a good romantic team in Rochelle Hudson and Michael Whalen.... The story is light and breezy, moves fast, and is well splattered with comedy bits to offset the thrills and tension which build to a battling finish." *Film Daily*, January 16, 1937

That I May Live (1937)

Rochelle Hudson (*Irene Howard*), Robert Kent (*Dick Mannion*), J. Edward Bromberg (*Tex Shapiro*), Jack La Rue (*Charlie*), Frank Conroy (*Pop*), Fred Kelsey (*Abner Jenkins*), George Cooper (*Mack*), DeWitt Jennings (*Chief of Police*), Russell Simpson (*Bish Plivens*), William Benedict (*Kurt Plivens*), Mary Gordon (*Mrs. Healy*), Eily Malyon (*Cally Plivens*)

Director: Allan Dwan. *Producer*: Sol M. Wurtzel. *Original Screenplay*: Ben Markson, William Conselman. *Story*: David Lambert. *Art Director*: Lewis H. Creber. *Photographer*: Robert Planck. *Editor*: Louis Loeffler. *Costume Designer*: Herschel. *Music Director*: Samuel Kaylin. *Sound*: Harry M. Leonard, George Leverett. *Assistant Director*: Aaron Rosenberg.

20th Century–Fox; released April 30, 1937. 70 minutes.

Fresh out of prison, Dick Mannion intends to stay on the straight and narrow, but his former cohorts strong-arm him into using his safecracking skills on their heist at a small-town bank. Forced to go along on the job, Dick refuses to open the safe. Cold-hearted Charlie proceeds to kill the night watchman and kayo Dick, leaving him with the incriminating gun.

Badly needing food, Dick tries to hold up a lunch wagon, eliciting the sympathy of pretty waitress Irene Howard. She gets him to give up his weapon (a wrench) and persuades her boss Tom to put him to work as a dishwasher. Dick and Irene fall in love, which Tom resents. Dick plans to leave Irene behind, but she accompanies him as he attempts to hitchhike to a new start.

On the road, they meet salesman Tex Shapiro, who invites the couple to share his bus. They stop at an auto camp, peddling Tex's wares. Tex urges Dick to propose to Irene, saying, "If you're married and ain't got a job, at least you got a wife." But Dick is hesitant, thinking it unfair given that he's a wanted man. With a little help from Tex, the proposal is made. Irene, who has seen Dick's face on a WANTED poster, weds him, saying she doesn't care about his past. The young couple soon welcomes a baby daughter.

Tex persuades Dick to turn himself in to the police. Irene and Dick conspire to gather evidence from the members of his former gang, which results in her pretending to join their forces.

20th Century–Fox acquired the rights to David Lambert's original story in 1936. *Motion Picture Daily* (June 27, 1936) reported that Lewis Seiler had been chosen to direct and that Robert Ellis and Helen Logan were now working with him on the screenplay. Instead, the directorial assignment went to Allan Dwan, who was later quoted as saying, "Rochelle Hudson emerges from this picture as one of the most physically appealing actresses on the screen and it is this quality which she is forced to employ to gain her end against the forces opposing her man and herself."[32]

Character actor J. Edward Bromberg (1903–1951), seen in the key supporting role of Tex Shapiro, provides most of the film's comedy relief. This is the second of three pictures in which he and Rochelle are castmates. Bromberg found his Hollywood career in ruins after refusing to testify before the House Committee on Un-American Activities in 1951. He died of a heart attack later that year. Featured player Jack La Rue (1902–1984) shared the screen with Rochelle a second time in *Bush Pilot* ten years later.

In the *Motion Picture Herald*'s "What the Picture Did for Me" column (September 25, 1937), an Oklahoma theater manager praised *That I May Live*: "Extra good program picture. Pleased about 100 percent better than average. Ran this one on Bargain Nites."

A nitrate print of *That I May Live* is held in the collection of the UCLA Film and Television Archive.

Reviews: "Has sufficient melodrama and suspense to satisfy the less discriminating action fans and the production is worthy of better story material. In most spots it will serve only as the lower half of dual bills, but action houses should get fair returns with it single-billed.... Miss Hudson and Kent make an agreeable romantic team, but neither boasts much acting ability and they fail to convince at times. Allan Dwan's direction is only fair.'" *Film Bulletin*, March 6, 1937

"Although the situation on which the photoplay is premised is not new, the theme has been carried out in intelligent fashion.... All characterizations are forceful and convincing.... Dialogue, action and situations are intelligently blended to erect the proper dramatic atmosphere.... Not a big picture, it nevertheless should hold the attention of average audiences." *Motion Picture Herald*, March 6, 1937

Ex-con Dick (Robert Kent) faces the future with the help of kindly Irene (Rochelle Hudson) in *That I May Live* (1937).

Born Reckless (1937)

Rochelle Hudson (*Sybil Roberts*), Brian Donlevy (*Bob "Hurry" Kane*), Barton MacLane (*Jim Barnes*), Robert Kent (*Lee Martin*), Harry Carey (*Dad Martin*), Pauline Moore (*Dorothy Collins*), Chick Chandler (*Windy Bowman*), William Pawley (*Mac*), Francis McDonald (*Louie*), George Wolcott [Walcott] (*Danny Horton*), Joseph Crehan (*District Attorney*), Stanley Andrews (*Police Commissioner*), Douglas Wood (*Mayor*), Joyce Compton (*Dora*), Gloria Roy (*Claire*), Charles Lane (*Barnes' Lawyer*), Richard Terry (*Gimp*), Ivan Miller (*Garage Owner*), Eddie Dunn (*Garage Foreman*), Sam McDaniel (*Train Porter*), Emmett Vogan (*Radio Announcer*), Henry Otho (*Detective*), Lon Chaney, Jr. (*Garage Mechanic*), Jimmie Dundee (*Martin's Mechanic*), Mary MacLaren (*Nurse*), Frank Marlowe (*Mobster*), Chick Collins, Oscar "Dutch" Hendrian, Billy Wayne (*Cab Drivers*)

Director: Malcolm St. Clair. *Associate Producer*: Milton H. Feld. *Screenplay*: John Patrick, Robert Ellis, Helen Logan. *Story*: Jack Andrews. *Photographer*: Daniel B. Clark. *Art Director*: Chester Gore. *Assistant Director*: Samuel Schneider. *Editor*: Alex Troffey. *Costumes*: Herschel. *Sound*: S.C. Chapman, Harry M. Leonard. *Music Director*: Samuel Kaylin.

20th Century–Fox; released July 9, 1937. 59 minutes.

Racecar driver Bob Kane, known as "Hurry" Kane, has plans to live it up after winning a $25,000 purse. Hailing a cab after disembarking from a train voyage, he and his driver, Windy Bowman, are in for a rough ride. An intense rivalry has broken out among local taxi drivers, causing even a short trip to be interrupted by intentional fender-benders, dangerous cutoffs by other drivers, and ultimately an incident in which a collision is narrowly avoided.

After a melee with the offending driver, Bob takes the wheel of Windy's cab, offering a ride to a beautiful young woman left stranded by the other cab. She asks him to take her to the county jail, but rebuffs his friendly advances, declining even to furnish her name.

Arriving for a visit with his pal Lee Martin, who with his father operates the Martin Cab Company, Bob learns that the business is suffering because they have refused to pay protection being demanded by racketeer Jim Barnes, owner of the rival Excelsior Cab Company. Bob offers to join the Martin Company's fleet of drivers, and soon shows Barnes he can give back as good as he gets. Bob, offered a better-paying job by Barnes, is surprised to recognize the racketeer's lady friend as the woman he drove to the jail. Barnes shows off an armored taxicab he had constructed specially, and invites Bob to try it out. Bob smashes it into several of his rival's cabs while a furious Barnes watches. Barnes' lady friend, Sybil Roberts, offers to lure the upstart Bob over to their side, and it's clear there's an attraction on both their parts. Meanwhile, Barnes gets revenge against the Martins and Bob by using the armored car to mow down Windy.

When the senior Mr. Martin takes his case to the district attorney, Bob, who witnessed the attack on Windy, is called upon to testify, but surprisingly changes his story in a way that causes the case against Barnes to be dropped. Barnes enlists Sybil to offer Bob $1000 to leave town, but he has another plan in mind.

Unsure where Sybil's loyalties lie, Bob works to frame his rival, while Barnes does likewise. A deadly confrontation threatens to settle matters once and for all, when Barnes catches his lady friend in the act of stealing documents from his safe. Bob races the clock to save himself and Sybil, get the goods on Barnes, and prevent an act of sabotage the racketeer has ordered against the Martin family.

Born Reckless gets off to a unpromising start, with Bob's racing career depicted almost entirely through grain-flecked stock footage and rear projection. But the film ultimately provides plenty to satisfy action fans, generally good performances, and palpable chemistry between Rochelle and her leading man Brian Donlevy. Running just under an hour, it's an enjoyable programmer with a suspenseful conclusion. 20th Century–Fox purchased an original story, "Armored Taxi," that was adapted by a trio of screenwriters. Early announcements had that title attached to the forthcoming film, but it was renamed before release. Newspaper ads proclaimed, "He fights crime for the fun of it! He'd rather court danger than a beautiful stranger—till he meets a girl who loves to flirt—with sudden death!"

Rochelle, billed over Donlevy though he's playing the lead, gives a strong performance as the enigmatic Sybil, whose motives are never entirely clear. (At one point, Donlevy's character asks, understandably, "Are you for me, or against me?") As the film unspools, clues about her emerge, including her strong reaction to the mention of the name Danny Horton, and the revelation that all Barnes is getting out of their relationship is "a good-night kiss at the door." We also learn, in the climactic scenes, that she can handle a gat quite capably. Reliable supporting players Harry Carey and Chick Chandler are effective in featured roles, and a young, still dark-haired Charles Lane (1905–2007) is nonetheless instantly recognizable as a lawyer. Warners contract player Barton MacLane (1902–1969) was borrowed for the main villainous role.

Studio publicity said, "In a role radically different from anything she has attempted before, this lovely star [Hudson] flirts with the hazards that Donlevy courts, and the romance that grows between these two flowers behind bullet-proof glass." Shortly after this film's release, the studio announced that Hudson and Donlevy would reteam for a follow-up feature, *Island in the Sky*. But when that picture was released in April 1938, neither was in the cast.

Reviews: "This taxi war affair which involves racketeering is aimed at the audiences that want he-man action and thrills. It is slam-bang material with auto crashes of all sorts. Because of its better name players and major studio production it can rate the top houses using this kind of fare. The cast members all perform very well." *Film Daily*, June 22, 1937

"For a clientele that goes in for plenty of action and excitement, this picture fills the bill. There is everything from a big time auto race to a taxi war, along with gangsters and crooked politicians.... There is some good slapstick comedy, a slight romantic interest and several good story twists. ...Brian Donlevy, Rochelle Hudson and Barton MacLane ... acquit themselves admirably under the expert direction of Malcolm St. Clair, who deserves credit for keeping the story moving at its rapid pace." *Hollywood Motion Picture Review*, June 19, 1937

She Had to Eat (1937)

Jack Haley (*Danny Decker*), Rochelle Hudson (*Ann Garrison*), Arthur Treacher (*Carter*), Eugene Pallette (*Raymond Quincy Nash*), Douglas Fowley (*Duke Stacey*), John Qualen (*Sleepy*), Maurice Cass (*Fingerprint Expert*), Wallis Clark (*Ralph Wilkinson*), Lelah Tyler (*Mrs. Cue*), Tom Kennedy (*Pete*), Tom Dugan (*Rusty*), Franklin Pangborn (*Mr. Phoecian-Wylie*), Spencer Charters (*Ralph Franklin*), Helen Lowell (*Melinda Franklin*), Syd Saylor (*Shorty*), Paul McVey (*Captain McBurn*), Harold Miller (*Desk Clerk*), Edward McWade (*Stationmaster Tucker*), Robert McClung (*Newsboy*), Fred Kelsey (*Officer Tracey*), Harrison Greene (*Harry Eckelhart*), Florence Gill (*Miss Peabody*), Hal K. Dawson (*Mr. McIntire*), Joseph E. Bernard (*Railroad Man*), Sidney Bracey (*Waiter*), J.P. McGowan (*Police Sergeant*), John Hamilton (*Police Captain*), Russ Clark (*Engineer*), Ferdinand Munier (*Williamson*), Larry Steers (*Country Club Diner*), Ruth Peterson (*Waitress*), George Magrill (*G-Man*)

Director: Malcolm St. Clair. *Screenplay*: Samuel G. Engel. *Based on Stories by* M.M. Musselman, James Edward Grant. *Associate Producer*: Samuel G. Engel. *Music and Lyrics*: Sidney Clare, Harry Akst. *Photographer:* Barney McGill. *Art Director*: Lewis Creber. *Assistant Director*: Jasper Blystone. *Production Manager*: Ed Ebele. *Editor*: Louis Loeffler. *Costumes*: Herschel. *Sound*: Alfred Bruzlin, Harry M. Leonard. *Music Director*: Samuel Kaylin.

20th Century–Fox; released July 2, 1937. 74 minutes.

Wealthy oddball Raymond Quincy Nash, accompanied by his faithful gentleman's gentleman, charters a train along a route said to offer good game hunting, but is disappointed with what he sees. On a stopover in Nebula, Arizona, he meets young Danny Decker, who with his mother owns a small gas station. When the boozy Nash tries to show off his skeet-shooting skills, Danny easily bests him. Nash offers him the chance to compete in a tournament in North Carolina.

Aboard the train the following morning, Nash, sobered up, no longer remembers the events of the night before, and he ejects Danny in a town called New City. Stopping to wire his mother for money, Danny is mistaken for his lookalike, killer Mike "Babyface" Burns, who just escaped from a nearby prison. Outside the telegraph office, Danny meets charming young Ann Garrison, who flips a bottle cap down a grate in the street and convinced him he caused her to lose her last quarter. He shares the last of his money with her, but before they can get better acquainted, he's picked up by the police. A fingerprint analysis proves that Danny is not Mike Burns, and he's released.

Danny sees Ann pulling the bottle cap trick on another man. Over coffee, she tells him she's an unemployed song plugger, surviving by her wits after a hospital stay depleted her funds. Expecting money from his mother, Danny tells Ann he will give her some. Ann tells him she employs various tricks to get by, explaining it requires only "nerve and noodle" to do so.

At a luxury car dealership, Ann charms the proprietor, Mr. Phoecian-Wylie, into letting them take one of his vehicles for a test drive, affording them a pleasant trip through the countryside. Danny is spotted by a couple of gangsters who report to their boss, Duke Stacey.

Danny and Ann once again cross paths with Nash and his butler, who needs help getting his soused employer back to the train. Duke and his boys assume that Danny is Mike Burns, and take him and his companions hostage. Luckily for Danny, the always-resourceful Ann has another trick or two up her sleeve that may prevent her man from being delivered for a $100,000 reward.

She Had to Eat is a strange film that strands some very fine actors in a weak script, counting on the players to punch up a screwball comedy offering precious few laughs. Various "zany" elements have been tossed in. Though the film gets slightly better after a mostly dull first half, it ultimately achieves little more than mediocrity.

Jack Haley (1897–1979) plays along gamely as Danny, amiable and at least not as dopey as some of his screen characters. A running gag that mostly falls flat finds Haley's character repeatedly told by the police, and by gangsters, to drop his pants, to determine whether or not he has a scar on his thigh like Mike Burns does. Director Malcolm St. Clair invariably blocks the scene so that we (and Ann) are spared a look at Danny's undergarments, but the hoped-for laughs never materialize.

Some top-notch character actors do their best with what they've been handed. Eugene Pallette (1889–1954) is saddled with a character who's more annoying than funny, with his loyal butler (Arthur Treacher) explaining that he suffers from "a pseudo-variety of dementia precox, bordering on paranoia." Franklin Pangborn (1889–1958) shows that a gifted comic actor can be amusing just getting wet in a rainstorm, but otherwise is left to mine for laughs as best he can, given a supposedly funny name that he keeps having to correct when others mispronounce it. Every time he says "Phoecian-Wylie," Haley dutifully repeats, "It's hyphenated," but the bit doesn't get any funnier with repetition.

Rochelle gives verve and charm to the part of his leading lady, Ann (described in studio publicity as "a sweet little girl with a permanent hunger—for thrills"). But her material isn't much better than anyone else's. She's allowed to sing two numbers, the latter a rousing song that she performs for the slightly shocked president of a Percy Bysshe Shelley literacy society that was expecting her to recite poetry. She gives snappy readings to a couple of wisecracks, as when bad guy Duke sarcastically promises to leave her something in his will; she retorts, "I hope it won't be too long." When a mug tired of Danny's chatter complains, "Ah, pipe down. I can't think," she says, "Is that his fault?"

In the *Motion Picture Herald*'s "What the Picture Did for Me" column (September 11, 1937) a Maine theater owner reported glumly, "Did not please and will not please."

Reviews: "Just average program entertainment. The story is silly to the point of boredom; it lacks human appeal and fails to hold one's attention. Arthur Treacher and Eugene Pallette, both good comedians, are able to make some of the lines sound comical, but they are handicapped by poor material. The few songs do not help matters much." *Harrison's Reports*, June 26, 1937

"Rochelle Hudson is charming. Pallette and Treacher do ace work and score the chuckles along with Haley." *Film Daily*, July 23, 1937

Rascals (1938)

Jane Withers (*Gypsy*), Rochelle Hudson (*Margaret Adams*), Robert Wilcox (*Tony*), Borrah Minevitch (*Gino*), Steffi Duna (*Stella*), Katharine Alexander (*Agatha Adams*), Chester Clute (*Roger Adams*), José Crespo (*Baron Von Brun*), Paul Stanton (*Dr. Cecil Carter*), Frank Reicher (*Dr. C.M. Garvey*), Edward Cooper (*Grayson*), Kathleen Burke (*Dr. Carter's Nurse*), Myra Marsh (*Hospital Nurse*), Frank Puglia (*Florist*), Robert Gleckler (*Police Lieutenant*), Eddie Dunn (*Dugan*), Howard C. Hickman (*Judge*), Wilfred Lucas (*Café Proprietor*), Jack Baxley (*Storekeeper*), Phyllis Coghlan (*Evelyn*), Hope Emerson (*Miss Gordon*), Jerry Mandy (*Electrician*), Abe Diamond, Leo Diamond, Harry Feinberg, Louis Feldman, Al Furbish, Harry Hier, Ernie Morris, Alex Novelle (*Harmonica Rascals*), Bert Roach, John Sheehan (*Townsmen*), Edward Gargan, Ivan Miller (*Police Officers*), Si Jenks, Ivan Miller, Russ Powell (*Picknickers*), Phillips Smalley, Mary Treen (*Waiting Room Patients*)

Director: H. Bruce Humberstone. *Original Screenplay*: Robert Ellis, Helen Logan. *Associate Producer*: John Stone. *Music and Lyrics*: Sidney Clare, Harry Akst. *Dance Stager*: Nick Castle. *Photographer*: Edward Cronjager. *Art Directors*: Bernard Herzbrun, Haldane Douglas. *Costumes*: Helen A. Myron. *Sound*: E. Clayton Ward, William H. Anderson. *Music Director*: Samuel Kaylin.

20th Century–Fox; released May 20, 1938. 77 minutes.

A caravan of traveling gypsies, moving from one town to the next, are surprised when a disheveled-looking but beautiful woman comes upon their campsite and promptly faints. Gypsy, a little girl, and her pal, handsome young Tony, take care of the stranger. She tells them she doesn't remember her identity, but adds, "I don't want to go back there." Meanwhile, a well-to-do society couple, Mr. and Mrs. Adams, meets with the police about their missing daughter Margaret, who vanished shortly before her scheduled wedding to Baron Von Brun, who seems eager to exchange his title for their money.

At Gypsy's suggestion, the young stranger is given the stage name Rawnie ("Gypsy for lady," we're told) and undergoes coaching to do a fortunetelling act as part of the traveling show. This arouses the jealousy of troupe member Stella, whose work in that capacity was deemed unsatisfactory, and who believes the newcomer shares her fondness for Tony. The newly christened "Rawnie" does well as a fortuneteller, but not quite so well with Tony, whom she impulsively bites after he breaks up a fight between her and Stella. Angry, he tells her, "You're just a dizzy society dame out looking for a thrill."

Quarantined due to an outbreak of mumps, the campers are growing hungry, so Gypsy and Rawnie go into town to raise some money. Caught telling fortunes, they're forced to flee so quickly that Rawnie dashes out into the street and is hit by a laundry truck. The doctor who examines her tells Gypsy that her friend had a previous head injury that can be treated, but the operation's effects on her memory are unpredictable. The caravan members raise the needed funds, though Rawnie is hesitant. Gypsy is heartbroken to see that, following the surgery, her friend no longer remembers her. Tony recommends that they leave the former Rawnie to sort out her new life, but Gypsy refuses to give up so easily.

Rascals offers viewers a satisfactory helping of music, dance, comedy and romance, though it works both sides of the street in terms of the way gypsies are presented. The script falls back on the commonly held stereotypes of its era, among them the gypsies' alleged propensity for pickpocketing and shoplifting. (Late in the film, when trying to persuade Tony to rescue Margaret, Gypsy says, "You know what a gypsy'd do, don't you? He'd go right up to that house and steal the girl he loved!") However, the members of the traveling troupe are, for the most part, sympathetically portrayed, their life presented as more enjoyable than the Adamses' stuffy world of society connections. In general, the audience is encouraged to view Gypsy and her friends favorably and see their way of living as fun and largely carefree. The screenwriters do go out of their way, nonetheless, to establish that neither of our romantic couple is actually of Romany stock.

Jane Withers (1926–2021) had her big break as an eight-year-old featured player in the Shirley Temple vehicle *Bright Eyes*. Her antics as a bratty kid, almost the anti–Temple, went over so well with moviegoers that she was signed to a seven-year contract and was cast in her own starring features. She's her usual likable, energetic self in *Rascals*, showing what made her a big favorite of younger moviegoers in the 1930s.

In Withers' world, no one seems to blink an eye at an 11 or 12-year-old girl taking charge of things, and the absence of any parents goes unexplained.

Having already supported Fox's biggest juvenile star in *Curly Top*, Rochelle does the honors for Withers this time around, and even gets some moments of her own in the spotlight. About a year earlier, Rochelle had been scheduled to appear in Withers' film *Angel's Holiday*, but when she was re-assigned to *She Had to Eat*, that role was filled by Sally Blane. In *Rascals*, she's second-billed as a romantic lead opposite Robert Wilcox, with whom she makes quite a sexy couple. Hudson's dazzling smile gets a bit more of a workout here than it does in some of her films, though she also plunges into a vigorous girl fight with featured player Steffi Duna. Like several of her other leading men, Wilcox was reported to be romantically involved with Rochelle, as when columnist Ed Sullivan (January 10, 1938) claimed, "The Joy Hodges-Robert Wilcox engagement was wrecked by Rochelle Hudson." The leading man (1910–1955) died of a heart attack, having been married not to either Hudson or Hodges, but to actresses Florence Rice and Diana Barrymore.

Borrah Minevitch and His Gang were a well-known band, seen in movie musicals as well as heard in recordings. Frequently billed as "The Harmonica Rascals," denoting their most frequently used instrument, they comprise the bulk of the gypsy troupe seen here, along with Withers, Wilcox, Duna and a few others. Minevitch

Rawnie (Rochelle Hudson) isn't quite sure what to make of the eccentric Gino (Borrah Minevitch, left) in *Rascals* **(1938). Also pictured: Robert Wilcox as Tony.**

demonstrates a flair for physical and visual comedy, with a comic's expressive face. His best scene comes when Gino runs amok in a doctor's office, determined to prove to a nurse and patients that his brain function is badly in need of immediate attention.

Katharine Alexander (1898–1977) exudes dignity and snobbery as Margaret's domineering mother ("that pie-faced old dame," Gypsy says in a moment of frustration), while Chester Clute (1891–1956) has an amusing moment or two as her spouse. The henpecked Mr. Adams, so timid that he even apologizes for things someone else has said, takes cover behind his notably taller wife, or underneath a nearby piano, when trouble seems to be brewing.

Director H. Bruce Humberstone (1901–1984) was perhaps best-known for being at the helm of numerous Charlie Chan films. His long career extended from silent films to television of the late 1960s.

Reviews: "A very enjoyable picture ... one of the better of the Jane Withers vehicles.... Rochelle Hudson and Robert Wilcox handle the romantic interest nicely.... H. Bruce Humberstone directed the affair with a lot of snap and throughout maintains a delightful happy mood." *Film Daily*, April 7, 1938

"They threw away the juvenile picture patterns when they set out to rig up this vehicle for the irrepressible Jane Withers, and almost succeeded in repressing her ... [Borrah] Minevitch receives almost as much camera attention as the star and musical exhibitions repeatedly impede the swift flow of incidents commonly expected of a Withers romp.... Miss Withers pulls the loose ends together whenever they point the camera in her direction and it may turn out that this is often enough, after all, to satisfy her following." *Motion Picture Daily*, April 5, 1938

Mr. Moto Takes a Chance (1938)

Peter Lorre (*Mr. Moto*), Rochelle Hudson (*Victoria Mason*), Robert Kent (*Marty Weston*), J. Edward Bromberg (*Rajah Ali*), Chick Chandler (*Chick Davis*), George Regas (*Bokor*), Fredrik Vogeding (*Captain Zimmerman*), Gloria Roy (*Keema*), Victor Sen Yung (*Khmer Soldier*), Al Kikume (*Yao*), H.W. Fim (*Ali's Retainer*), James B. Leong (*Native*)

Director: Norman Foster. *Executive Producer*: Sol M. Wurtzel. *Screenplay*: Lou Breslow, John Patrick. *Original Story*: Willis Cooper, Norman Foster. *Based on the Character Created by* J.P. Marquand. *Photographer*: Virgil Miller. *Art Director*: Albert Hogsett. *Editor*: Nick DeMaggio. *Costumes*: Herschel. *Sound*: Bernard Freericks, Harry M. Leonard. *Music Director*: Samuel Kaylin.

20th Century–Fox; released June 24, 1938. 63 minutes.

Airplane pilot Victoria Mason, having embarked on a trip around the world, makes a crash landing in Tong Moi, a small principality near Cambodia. She meets two Americans, newsreel photographer Marty Weston and his assistant Chick, as well as the redoubtable detective Mr. Moto. Moto tells them he is an archaeologist excavating ancient ruins, but it does not escape his attention that Vicki staged her supposed engine fire using a flare.

The Rajah Ali invites Vicki to stay on as his guest, promising to later have guides see her through the jungle to safety. Marty's insistence on filming the rajah and his people displeases Bokor the high priest, who insists that being photographed will bring down a curse. When the rajah's pretty young wife Keema abruptly drops dead, Marty and Chick are charged with murder.

After a quick trial, Bokor insists the gods have found the men guilty and prepares to execute them. A mysterious old man makes a sudden appearance and convinces the natives that he is a wise elder. This saves the guys' necks—for the time being.

Moto asks Marty and Chick to photography an ancient temple nearby, promising that the museum for which he works will pay handsomely. Moto's actual goal is to locate a supply of smuggled munitions, which he finds after going through a trap door in the temple floor. He also shows the Americans the poison dart that was actually the source of Keema's death.

Moto has been sending updates on his progress to his client via carrier pigeon. By intercepting one of them, the rajah learns of Moto's discovery at the temple. At an elaborate dinner, the rajah announces that Vicki has agreed to become his new wife. Marty is incredulous. As it turns out, the rajah and Bokor are engaged in rival attempts to seize power over Tong Moi. Vicki and the two Americans are taken hostage. The reappearance of the mysterious elder, who is Moto in disguise, may save Vicki and her friends from sacrificial death.

As film historian Ken Hanke pointed out, 20th Century–Fox had enjoyed great success with its Charlie Chan series, making it more or less inevitable that they "would attempt to repeat the process with a similar product. In fact, it is far more surprising that it took them as long as they did to come up with something."[33] The creation of author J.P. Marquand (1893–1960), Moto was originally featured in *Saturday Evening Post* stories. *Mr. Moto Takes a Chance* is the fourth entry in the Moto series, which had begun in 1937. The series petered out in 1939, as American moviegoers were becoming disinclined to embrace Japanese heroes on-screen.

Like Chan, Peter Lorre (1904–1964) plays a soft-spoken, polite gentleman of Asian ancestry. Mr. Moto was more action-oriented than Inspector Chan, allowing Lorre (or his double, more often) to display his skills in martial arts and show himself physically able to dominate his enemies. Moto is supposedly a master of disguises, though it's unlikely most viewers paying more than slight attention failed to identify Lorre in his mystic elder getup. After making Moto's acquaintance, Chick comments, "If I was casting a horror picture, I'd have him play the murderer!" According to his biographer, Stephen D. Youngkin, Lorre was struggling with drug addiction during these years, and later disliked being reminded of the Moto series.

Unlike the typical Chan film, there's little real detection here, and anyone who tuned in midway through the film could be forgiven for expecting Johnny Weissmuller to swing into frame on a vine at any moment. As several film critics pointed out, *Mr. Moto Takes a Chance* was better suited to a Saturday afternoon kids' matinee than an adult audience, offering a hour's worth of angry natives, fights, fires, poison darts, tiger pits and assorted jungle thrills. Production began in July 1937 under the working title *Look Out, Mr. Moto*. The story was an original by studio screenwriters rather than an adaptation of any specific work by Marquand.

Rochelle, making the first of her two films with Lorre, speaks the film's first line of dialogue as aviatrix Victoria Mason. Her character is one of numerous female pilots turning up in films of the late 1930s, when Amelia Earhart's exploits and tragic disappearance were frequently front-page news. Like at least half the film's characters, Vicki is keeping a secret, one that explains her decision to have "engine trouble." Once her parachute has carried her to safety, her aviation skills play no part in the narrative. Instead, she becomes a fairly standard female lead and love interest, though a more self-reliant and capable one than some of that era. Male viewers over the age of ten doubtless took notice of the scene in which she is tied to a stake by a villain, her blouse fetchingly torn as she is threatened with torture. Cinematographer Virgil Miller captures a few close-ups of the actress that show off her beauty and expressive eyes.

The film reunited Rochelle with two of her *Born Reckless* castmates. Robert Kent competently plays good guy Marty while Chick Chandler gives a light touch to the comic relief role of his buddy, who introduces himself as Chick Davis, "formerly of Actors' Equity." During one jungle trek, Chandler has an amusing moment when he grows irritated with the nervous chatter of monkeys and finally calls out, "*Qui-et!*" He's as surprised as anyone by the ensuing hush. Fox contract player J. Edward Bromberg handles with aplomb the role of the foolish Rajah Ali, who like Vicki isn't exactly what he seems.

This was Rochelle's last picture for Fox: When her studio contract expired, it was not renewed.

Reviews: "This latest in the Moto series is good juvenile fare, but adults will not be able to take it seriously for the story is wild and over-melodramatic. But, as said, the juveniles will have a good time; they probably will not pay attention to the plot defects for the action is exciting enough to hold them in suspense throughout." *Harrison's Reports*, June 18, 1938

"For some reason, the producers of the Mr. Moto series have gone into lurid meller on this one, and it is not good meller at that. It is all wildly exciting and very unbelievable stuff ... but will afford little entertainment for mature minds.... The entire cast does commendable work." *Film Daily*, June 16, 1938

Storm Over Bengal (1938)

Patric Knowles (*Captain Jeffrey Allison*), Richard Cromwell (*Lt. Neil Allison*), Rochelle Hudson (*Joan Lattimore*), Douglass Dumbrille (*Ramin Khan*), Colin Tapley (*Hallett*), Gilbert Emery (*Col. Torrance*), Douglas Walton (*Terry*), Halliwell Hobbes (*Sir John Galt*), John Burton (*Sir Austin Carter*), Pedro de Cordoba (*Abdul Mir*), Clyde Cook (*Alf*), Claude Allister (*Redding*), Edward Van Sloan (*Maharajah of Lhanapur*), Dorothy Tree (*Mrs. Massarene*), John Davidson (*Khan's Aide*), Lal

Chand Mehra (*Abdul Mir's Aide*), Guy Bellis, Ralph Dunn, Bob Reeves (*Soldiers*), Yakima Canutt, Guy D'Ennery, Frank Ellis, Bud Wolfe (*Tribesmen*)

Director: Sidney Salkow. *Original Screenplay*: Dudley Waters. *Associate Producer*: Armand Schaefer. *Production Manager*: Al Wilson. *Photographer*: Ernest Miller. *Supervising Editor*: Murray Seldeen. *Editor*: William Morgan. *Art Director*: John Victor Mackay. *Music Director*: Cy Feuer. *Costumes*: Irene Saltern. *Special Effects*: Howard Lydecker.

Republic; released November 14, 1938. 65 minutes.

At Simla, Sir John Galt, viceroy of India, listens to rogue shortwave radio broadcasts from rebel Ramin Khan, who aspires to seize control of the country. Captain Jeffrey Allison of the British Army, a highly respected leader, prepares for action just as his fiancée, Joan Lattimore, arrives from England. Another recent arrival is Lt. Neil Allison, Jeffrey's brother, who on short acquaintance tells Joan he is in love with her. (She protests, "We've only known each other three days.") Neil resents the esteem in which others hold his successful brother, whom he calls "the white-haired boy of India." He does not believe that Jeffrey deserves Joan's devotion, claiming he has not made her a priority in his life. Joan tries to let Neil down gently, hoping they can remain friends.

Notified that the elderly maharajah of Lhanapur is seriously ill, Sir John dispatches an emissary to obtain his signature on a treaty that will allow British troops to protect the Indian people against the infidels. But a Khan loyalist intercepts the message and sends Khan a warning. Knowing that Jeffrey is integral to the Army's plan, Khan places a 50,000 rupee price on his head.

After infiltrating the rebels' hideaway, Jeffrey warns his fellow troops of an imminent attack. Deciding it is no longer safe for Joan to remain, he wants to marry her immediately and then send her to safety. But before this can take place, the British soldiers are instructed to march on Khan's hideout.

Flown to see the maharajah, Jeffrey succeeds at getting the old man's signature. But Khan pulls a gun on him and holds him captive. Though seriously wounded, Jeffrey's colleague and pilot Hallett escapes and tips off the Army that an ambush is planned at a ravine they must traverse. Neil hasn't completed his training as a pilot but he offers to take a message to the troops via plane. While Jeffrey stands tough against the Khan's threats, refusing to send a phony message to his superiors, Neil takes on a dangerous mission that could show him, once and for all, why a Britisher's devotion to his country is critical.

Storm Over Bengal is a moderately entertaining action film, well-mounted, with generally good performances. Despite the exotic setting, it's not that far removed from a cowboys-and-Indians adventure, action being its chief asset. Patric Knowles (1911–1995) makes a more than adequate hero. Richard Cromwell shares the screen with Rochelle for the third time.

Rochelle, appearing in only a handful of scenes, is given little time to develop a characterization. Both leading men try to shield her amidst danger, but at one point she impatiently tells Cromwell's Neil, "How did you expect to find me—in a mid-Victorian swoon?"

Reviews: "One of the better pictures to come from Republic, *Storm Over Bengal*, by virtue of its commercial and artistic value, justifies the increased budget. Its 65 minutes are filled with action, suspense and romance set against the background of Northwest India.... Sidney Salkow, virtual newcomer to direction ... turned out a well balanced film." *Motion Picture Daily*, November 17, 1938

"One of the most ambitious efforts of Republic, this picture should be a strong box office attraction as it offers all ingredients demanded by audiences. The cast is fine, headed by the handsome and extremely able Patric Knowles.... Rochelle Hudson makes an attractive and capable female lead.... Production value is good and the direction is smooth." *Film Daily*, November 17, 1938

Pride of the Navy (1939)

James Dunn (*"Speed" Brennan*), Rochelle Hudson (*Gloria Tyler*), Gordon Oliver (*Jerry Richards*), Horace McMahon (*"Gloomy" Kelly*), Gordon Jones (*Joe Falcon*), Charlotte Wynters (*Ethel Falcon*), Joseph Crehan (*Brad Foster*), Charles Trowbridge (*Captain Tyler*), Mary Treen (*Nurse*)

Director: Charles Lamont. *Screenplay*: Ben Markson, Saul Elkins. *Original Story*: James Webb, Joseph Hoffman. *Associate Producer*: Herman Schlom. *Production Manager*: Al Wilson. *Photographer*: Jack Marta. *Editor*: Edward Mann. *Supervising Editor*: Murray Seldeen. *Music Director*: Cy Feuer. *Art Director*: John Victor Mackay. *Costumes*: Irene Saltern.

Republic; released January 23, 1939. 65 minutes.

U.S. Navy Lt. Jerry Richards is in charge of a high-priority project at the Naval Experimentation Station at Pacific Bay. His team was granted funds to develop a small, fast vessel that can carry torpedoes. With time running out, Jerry appeals to his one-time Annapolis roommate "Speed" Brennan, who's now living a glamorous life on the speedboat racing circuit.

Still resentful that he was drummed out of the Navy years earlier due to his lack of discipline, Speed initially says no, but he reconsiders after meeting Jerry's attractive lady friend Gloria Tyler, a captain's daughter. Gloria tells him coolly that her father "said they kicked you out of Annapolis because they couldn't find a hat big enough to fit you."

The fun-loving Speed does his best to get better acquainted with Gloria, but he cannot repress his practical-joker side. Finally, when only one week remains before Navy officials are due onsite to either see results or drop the project, Speed settles down and gives the work his full attention. Inspired by the sight of two boys playing with toy boats in a department store, Speed and Jerry tackle a model that involves a pair of smaller ships linked.

After Speed and Jerry fight over Gloria at a dressy reception for visiting dignitaries, Captain Tyler tells Speed to leave the premises—and the project. The test of the newest model goes on without him and it is a disaster, ending in a crash that lands both Jerry and his mechanic Gloomy in the hospital. Reproaching himself, Speed reaches out to Gloomy, who rebuffs him.

Suddenly realizing what is needed to make Jerry's invention workable, Speed persuades Gloomy to help put on another demonstration for the Navy brass. Roping in his fellow pilot Joe Falcon, Speed puts everything at risk to prove the boat's viability and win Gloria's hand.

Programmers about heroic guys who come to the rescue of military operations were a dime a dozen in the late 1930s and early 1940s, but *Pride of the Navy* received better-than-average responses from reviewers. It hardly has time to wear out its welcome, running just over an hour, but viewed decades later it's harder to see qualities that make it stand out from other B movies of the period. The action sequences and comic scenes sometimes mix uneasily.

James Dunn (1901–1967) seems a bit long in the tooth for the role of the irrepressible Speed Brennan. Many of Brennan's actions in the first half of the film make the character slightly off-putting, as when he spikes the iced tea at Gloria's bridge party for a laugh (while also neglecting the work he's agreed to do). The screenwriters attempt to balance this with actions such as Speed's handing over his racing prize money to a colleague with a sick child, but the character just isn't very likable. Six years later, Dunn won a Best Supporting Actor Academy Award for his performance in *A Tree Grows in Brooklyn* (1945). He went on to co-star in the early TV sitcom *It's a Great Life*.

At the risk of being unkind to her co-star, Rochelle just doesn't look right paired with a leading man who sports a receding hairline and an incipient double chin. Gordon Oliver (1910–1995) seems a better match for her, but the scriptwriters aren't on his side. It's hard not to agree with her when she tells the persistent Speed, "You better let me decide about the man I'm going to marry." Her beauty is as apparent as ever, and her screen time is adequate, but her role here doesn't give her much opportunity to shine.

Horace McMahon (1906–1971) has a few good moments as Speed's lugubrious mechanic, gamely taking a spurt of oil in the face and playing second banana to his pet monkey. Charles Trowbridge (1882–1967) is fine as Gloria's father, a typical military leader who says the expected things, like, "It's definitely contrary to all regulations!" Mary Treen (1907–1989) is seen briefly as Gloomy's hospital nurse.

Director Charles Lamont (1895–1993), experienced with action films, turned his talents to comedy in later years, working with Abbott and Costello, Ma and Pa Kettle, Judy Canova, among others. He injects notes of fun wherever he can in *Pride of the Navy*, and insures that the film moves along at a steady clip.

Reviews: "Republic has a winner in this smart comedy-drama of the Navy. The shrewdly developed story is a combination of sound motion picture elements which will thoroughly entertain the average filmgoer. Production is first rate, as are the direction and the performances.... Charles Lamont's direction is smooth and fluid. He blends the comedy, dramatic and action elements expertly.... Miss Hudson is charming." *Film Bulletin*, February 11, 1939

"Republic has a darn good piece of entertainment in *Pride of the Navy*. It will

satisfy any audience that you garner to view it.... It has a light and lilting pace, the result of neat direction by Charles Lamont and personable performances by Jimmy Dunn and Rochelle Hudson.... And it all works up to a corking physical climax."
Box Office Digest, January 24, 1939

Pirates of the Skies (1939)

Kent Taylor (*Nick Conden*), Rochelle Hudson (*Barbara Whitney*), Regis Toomey (*Bill Lambert*), Marion Martin (*Kitty*), Samuel S. Hinds (*Police Commissioner*), Ray Walker (*Hal Weston*), Lucien Littlefield (*Dr. Amos Pettingill*), Stanley Andrews (*Major Smith*), Guy Usher (*Captain Higgins*), Frank Puglia (*Jerry Petri*), Horace McMahon (*Artie*), Eddy Chandler (*Slug*), Henry Brandon (*Gang Pilot*), Frances Robinson (*Smith's Secretary*), Jack Gardner (*Air Patrol Radioman*), Hooper Atchley (*Kidnaped Jeweler*), Harry Harvey (*Carnival Barker*), Fern Emmett (*Customer*), Roy Brent (*Orderly*), Frank O'Connor (*Doorman*)

Director: Joseph McDonough. *Screenplay*: Ben G. Kohn. *Story*, "Sky Police": Lester Cole. *Associate Producer*: Barney A. Sarecky. *Photographer*: Jerome Ash. *Editor*: Charles Maynard. *Art Director*: Jack Otterson. *Set Decorator*: R.A. Gausman. *Music Director*: Charles Previn.

Universal; released February 3, 1939.

Flier Nick Conden, who has a wide independent streak, is hired by the State Air Police. His estranged wife Barbara, now working as a waitress, doubts that he can toe the line in such an operation. His officer pal Bill Lambert is similarly skeptical.

The police investigate a gang of thieves who use an airplane to make fast getaways. The café where Barbara works has been bugged by owner Jerry Petri, who records the conversations of pilots to get advance notice of flights carrying valuable cargo or bank payrolls. Assigned to pick up the governor from an event, Nick spots from the air what looks to be the thieves. But engine trouble forces him to make an emergency landing at Dr. Amos Pettingill's pigeon farm and health spa. As it happens, Dr. Pettingill is the leader of the gang, receiving information from Petri by carrier pigeon and housing the robbers, who pose as patients. Nick takes notice of the canisters of fuel at the spa.

Having disobeyed orders in his pursuit of the thieves, Nick is dismissed from the Air Force. He is nevertheless determined to track down the bad guys, a task which becomes more urgent when Barbara vanishes from the café. When Nick's clues lead to Dr. Pettingill's farm, Bill Lambert is dispatched on behalf of the Air Police, but his plane is shot down. Nick must come to the rescue if he is to prove his merit, and rescue Barbara, showing her that he is worthy of her love and respect.

Kent Taylor (1907–1987) racked up numerous B movie credits in the 1930s and beyond, often cast as a charming, roguish type. He ultimately made more than 100 films. *Pirates of the Skies* was the only time he and Hudson crossed paths on-screen. Regis Toomey (1898–1991), seen as Nick's more serious buddy, is another veteran film and television actor. Always busy, Toomey appeared in a dozen films in 1939 alone; in the 1960s, he had a featured role in TV's *Burke's Law*.

Pirates of the Skies publicity promised moviegoers "fast action played against a unique background, a novel love story and more than the ordinary quantity of thrills and suspense." In the *Motion Picture Herald*'s "What the Picture Did for Me" column (May 13, 1939), an exhibitor from Rochelle's home state of Oklahoma reported that the film "paid its way by a small margin" during the theater's "off season." *Boxoffice* (March 23, 1940) reported that censor complaints, citing "gangster criminal details, enacted in airplane," necessitated cuts to the film.

Reviews: "A fair program melodrama.... Although the story is familiar, it holds one in fair suspense, because of the exciting action.... Occasionally the action is slowed up because of too much dialogue and of the interjection of comedy that is not particularly effective." *Harrison's Reports*, January 21, 1939

"Unimportant and unpretentious action film with slight novelty angle to differentiate it from hundreds of similar productions. Such a consummate gang of thieves was never seen.... Kent Taylor and Rochelle Hudson strive hard to lift story out of mediocrity.... Hudson has a minor role and doesn't shine any too well in it.... Plot is preposterous." *Variety*, April 12, 1939

Missing Daughters (1939)

Richard Arlen (*Wally King*), Rochelle Hudson (*Kay Roberts*), Marian Marsh (*Josie Lamont*), Isabel Jewell (*Peggy*), Edward Raquello (*Lucky Rogers*), Dick Wessel (*Brick McGurk*), Eddie Kane (*Nick*), Wade Boteler (*Captain McGraw*), Don Beddoe (*Al Farrow*), Claire Rochelle (*Doris*), Byron Foulger (*Bert Ford*), Jane Eberling (*Blanche*), Floyd Criswell (*Mugg*), Esther Howard (*Mother Hawks*)

Director: C.C. Coleman, Jr. *Original Screenplay*: Michael L. Simmons, George Bricker. *Photographer*: Henry Freulich. *Editor*: Gene Havlick. *Music Director*: M.W. Stoloff. *Sound*: George Cooper.

Columbia; released May 22, 1939. 62 minutes.

Young Josie Lamont, one of the latest women to come to New York in search of stage stardom, is recruited by Lucky Rogers, owner of a so-called talent agency, who puts her to work as a hostess in his nightclub, the Club Naturelle. Realizing that her boss is luring women like herself into white slavery, Josie quits, intending to go to the police. Instead, her body is soon dragged from a river. The coroner's verdict is suicide.

Radio host Wally King laments the police failure to clear up a series of murders of nightclub hostesses. Josie's sister Kay Roberts, refusing to accept that her death was a suicide, shows him a letter she received, indicating that foul play was afoot. Wally sends several chorus girls he knows to apply for jobs with Rogers; they are hired as hostesses, while Kay becomes the club's hat check girl. She learns that one of Rogers' young employees is recuperating from a beating she received, and urges her to help expose her former boss. With evidence in hand, Wally is ready to bring in the police—if Lucky doesn't eliminate him first.

This was at least the third go-around for the title *Missing Daughters*, with previous films released in 1924 and 1933. This version was labeled by at least one reviewer as a bargain-basement imitation of *Marked Woman* (1937), Warners' drama starring

Bette Davis and Humphrey Bogart. The two films shared a common featured player, the always-watchable Isabel Jewell. Some reviewers found Lucky Rogers a fictional counterpart to Lucky Luciano, while Richard Arlen's character was compared with Gotham columnist-broadcaster Walter Winchell.

Leading man Arlen (1899–1976) was a longtime favorite of B movie producers, always capable of giving an adequate performance on a compact shooting schedule, especially in action-oriented roles. This was his only film with Rochelle. The *New York Daily News*' Kate Cameron (June 11, 1939) lamented, "[Hudson's] appearances on the screen are becoming less frequent lately." One columnist noted that Hudson "displays some shapely limbs when the occasion requires."

Director C.C. Coleman, Jr. (1900–1972), helmed some 18 films in the 1930s, but his directorial credits are far exceeded by his work as an assistant director, working alongside the likes of Billy Wilder and George Cukor in a career that lasted from the late 1920s through the mid–1960s.

Posters teased, "Learn how run-away girls get the Broadway run-around!" while studio publicity promised moviegoers that *Missing Daughters* would reveal to them "the inner workings of the Bureau of Missing Persons, that colorful and efficient section of the metropolitan police department," resulting in what was described as "a tensely dramatic revelation which transforms cold statistics into gripping romantic melodrama."

In the *Motion Picture Herald*'s "What the Picture Did for Me" column (July 29, 1939), a Maine theater owner enthused, "Here's a good little programmer that will please all the way. Enjoyed by all and a get 'em title." In Oklahoma (September 2, 1939), an exhibitor proclaimed, "The picture should be seen by all girls who are intent on making their own way around."

Reviews: "This looks very much like a rehash of the notorious 'Lucky' Luciano vice case in New York several years ago. Despite the exploitable title and rather sensational, if cheap, story, the picture does not develop the punch expected. Seems that the producer skirted censor codes too carefully to justify the actions of some of the characters.... The performances are adequate." *Film Bulletin*, June 3, 1939

"A highly colored and lurid meller that can only get by in the small houses catering to the drop-in trade.... The cast is far superior to the meller material that is hoked up for the thrill fans.... The girls are ahead of their parts, good work being done by Isabel Jewell, Marian Marsh and Rochelle Hudson. Selling angles: the title, and the names of the three girls." *Variety*, June 20, 1939

Smuggled Cargo (1939)

Barry MacKay (*Gerry Clayton*), Rochelle Hudson (*Marian Franklin*), George Barbier (*C.P. Franklin*), Ralph Morgan (*John Clayton*), Cliff Edwards (*Professor*), John Wray (*Chris Hays*), Arthur Loft (*Masterson*), Wallis Clark (*Dr. Hamilton*), Robert Homans (*Kincaid*), Kenneth MacDonald (*Radio Announcer*), Emmett Vogan (*Parker*), Lane Chandler (*Orange Grower*)

Director–Associate Producer: John H. Auer. *Original Screenplay*: Michael

Jacoby. *Additional Dialogue*: Earl Felton. *Production Manager*: Al Wilson. *Photographer*: Jack Marta. *Supervising Editor*: Murray Seldeen. *Assistant Director*: George Blair. *Editor*: Ernest Nims. *Art Director*: John Victor Mackay. *Music Director*: Cy Feuer. *Costumes*: Adele Palmer.

Republic; released August 21, 1939. 62 minutes.

Frost warnings have members of California's Orange Growers Association fearful that their crops will be ruined. President John Clayton enlists his son Gerry to take his high-speed racing car out in search of needed fuel for smudge pots. When the fuel goes up in an explosion, Gerry appeals to his father's rival, Masterson, for help. Masterson refuses to come to the rescue unless he's allowed to buy the other farmers' crops at cut-rate prices. With the help of his mechanic, Professor, Gerry locks Masterson in a storage shed and makes off with the fuel.

Traveling along the same highway as Gerry and his pal are magnate C.P. Franklin and his daughter Marian. Having come to sunny California for his health, Franklin is disgusted by the chilly temperatures, but Marian insists that he needs "fresh air, exercise and lots of orange juice." When Gerry has car trouble, he flags down the Franklins and commandeers their vehicle, unaware that C.P. was on his way to sign a lucrative contract with the orange growers. The Franklins are abandoned alongside Gerry's racing car, which had just attracted the attention of motorcycle cops who throw them in jail for speeding.

Masterson shows up to get the Franklins out of jail, shortly before the Claytons do likewise. Grouchy C.P., angry about Gerry swiping his car, listens to Masterson's sales pitch for getting his business. Marian meets up again with Gerry, who apologizes to her for his rash actions. From her, he learns that Masterson has swooped in to undercut the other growers. Returning home, Gerry's just in time to hear Masterson offer the association members an even lower price for their crops. When they refuse, Masterson schemes to find the produce he needs elsewhere, but Gerry and Professor are on the trail as he plots to smuggle his bounty out of the region by railway. When the illegal shipment passes a cursory inspection at the state line, stowaways Gerry and his pal start a small fire to attract attention. Though they believe Masterson and his cohort have been arrested, the inspectors were in fact phonies, paid by the dishonest grower.

Knowing the growers have lost faith in him, John Clayton offers his resignation as association president. Visiting Masterson's office, he makes one last, unsuccessful attempt to cut a reasonable deal. When Masterson refuses, the elder Clayton pulls a gun and threatens to kill him. As the two men struggle, Masterson's cohort Chris Hays, watching through a window, seizes the opportunity to eliminate Masterson. Gerry's father is charged with murder. Professor alerts Gerry that a mob is on its way to the jailhouse, convinced that John Clayton will be let off the hook by his friend, the sheriff. With the clock ticking, Gerry must intercept the Franklins, on their way out of town by train, and come to his father's rescue.

Though the action comes at regular intervals, *Smuggled Cargo* is only intermittently intriguing, and seems longer than its brief running time. It comes to life mostly in its last 15 minutes, as the story reaches a dramatic climax. An early announcement in *Film Bulletin* (July 1, 1939), naming Rochelle and other actors cast, referred to the picture under its working title *Mob Fury*.

Rochelle is cast as half of the film's romantic pair, opposite top-billed Barry MacKay (1906–1985), whose British accent in a California orange grove goes unexplained. Director John H. Auer (1906–1975) communicates what we can expect when their first meeting is captured in matching close-ups, as Gerry and Miss Franklin look each other over with obvious appreciation. She dubs him "Robin Hood" after he takes her father's car in an emergency, and he responds by christening her "Lady Marian," unaware that her first name happens to match the beautiful heroine of Sherwood Forest. She's off-screen for too much of the film, in a role that asks little of her. MacKay was making his American film debut as the hero. Active in British film since the early 1930s, his previous credits included Alexander Korda's *The Private Life of Don Juan* (1934) and Edwin L. Marin's classic *A Christmas Carol* (1938).

Cliff Edwards (1895–1971), whose nickname "Ukulele Ike" is included in the film's opening credits, was one year away from his career-defining role as Jiminy Cricket in Disney's *Pinocchio* (1940). His comedy relief antics as Gerry's mechanic

Marian (Rochelle Hudson) meets her "Robin Hood," Gerry (Barry MacKay) in *Smuggled Cargo* (1939).

are no more than mildly funny; he and his ukulele are allowed a quick song in the film's closing moments. Ralph Morgan and George Barbier are old pros who make the most of their roles as the elder Mr. Clayton and the irritable Mr. Franklin.

Reviews: "A capable cast and well paced story make it O.K. entertainment for the nabe houses.... George Barbier is amusing as the chain store orange drink mogul and Rochelle Hudson is capable and attractive as his daughter. A seasoned cast of troupers support the principals." *Film Daily*, August 23, 1939

"There is fast action in this melodrama, but it is not always pleasurable.... The story lacks novelty both in plot and development. As an entertainment, its appeal should be directed mostly to those who demand action above anything else." *Harrison's Reports*, September 16, 1939

Konga the Wild Stallion (1939)

>Fred Stone (*Yance Calhoun*), Rochelle Hudson (*Judith Hadley*), Richard Fiske (*Steve Calhoun*), Eddy Waller (*Gloomy*), Robert Warwick (*Jordan Hadley*), Don Beddoe (*Fred Martin*), Carl Stockdale (*Mason*), George Cleveland (*Tabor*), Burr Caruth (*Breckenridge*), Harry Bernard (*Jury Foreman*), Edmund Elton (*Governor*), John Dilson (*Judge*), Herbert Heywood (*Sheriff*), Sam Ash (*Fisher*), Lee Millar (*Randall*), John Tyrrell (*Pilot*), James Craig (*Ed*), Tom London (*Cowhand*), Harry Bernard (*Jury Foreman*), Chuck Hamilton (*Workman*)
>*Director:* Sam Nelson. *Producer:* Wallace MacDonald. *Original Screenplay:* Harold Shumate. *Photographer:* Benjamin H. Kline. *Editor:* Charles Nelson.
>Columbia; released August 30, 1939. 65 minutes.

Longtime horse breeder Yance Calhoun objects when his neighbor Jordan Hadley, a wheat grower, installs barbed wire fencing around his property. When Yance's best stallion Konga is injured by the barbed wire, Hadley refuses to pay damages. The younger generation, Calhoun's son Steve and Hadley's daughter Judith, enjoy friendlier relations, especially after she helps him with the wounded Konga. Judith tries to solve the dilemma by offering to buy Konga and let him live on *her* ranch, but Yance refuses to sell.

Unable to pay his debts, Yance is in danger of losing his property. Konga runs off into the hills. Hadley traps the horses that wander onto his property, and Yance learns from his heartless neighbor that Konga was shot. A bitter argument between the two men results in Hadley being fatally shot. Yance is sent to prison.

Several years later, Yance returns home to find that the ranch has prospered under Steve's management. There's a second happy surprise concerning his beloved Konga, and Judith's efforts on behalf of both the horse and his owner.

Publicity for *Konga the Wild Stallion* promised moviegoers "thundering thrills ... with fear-frenzied wild horses on a mad stampede through the hills; a thousand wild horses, led by Konga, fleeing in panic before the terror of an airplane; guns and bloody range war as Konga's master goes to the rescue of his pet."

Top-billed Fred Stone (1873–1959) was a former circus and vaudeville performer whose film credits include the role of Katharine Hepburn's father in *Alice Adams*

The leading players in *Konga, the Wild Stallion* (1939): center foreground, left to right, Fred Stone, Rochelle Hudson and Richard Fiske

(1935). He shared with Rochelle the distinction of having worked frequently with the late Will Rogers.

Romantically, Rochelle is paired with Richard Fiske (1915–1944), who played minor roles in two of her previous films, and later a supporting character in *The Officer and the Lady*. Serving in World War II, Fiske was killed in action in 1944, not yet 30 years old. Their characters were described in studio notices as "a modern Romeo and Juliet."

In the *Motion Picture Herald*'s "What the Picture Did for Me" column (January 13, 1940), a Colorado exhibitor reported, "Not a big picture but a good action show that grossed slightly over average business. Well worth playing."

Reviews: "Beautifully photographed in outdoor settings, this sentimental yarn about a horse should appeal to the juvenile trade. It should serve nicely as a second offering on dual bills for the nabe trade.... Rochelle Hudson is decorative." *Film Daily*, April 10, 1940

"This is just a dualler, with some possibilities in spots where the horse angle can be sold.... There are some good horse scenes in this picture, and a deal [*sic*] of comedy by the supporting players." *The Exhibitor*, September 20, 1939

A Woman Is the Judge (1939)

Frieda Inescort (*Mary Cabot*), Otto Kruger (*Steven Graham*), Rochelle Hudson (*Justine West*), Mayo Methot (*Gertie*), Gordon Oliver (*Robert Langley*), Arthur Loft (*Tim Ryan*), Walter Fenner (*Harper*), John Dilson (*Ramsey*), Ben Hewlett (*Wolf*), Beryl Mercer (*Mrs. Butler*), Charles R. Moore (*Elevator Operator*), Ann Doran (*Luella*), Sibyl Harris (*Landlady*), William Lally (*Bailiff*), Edward LeSaint (*Judge*), Byron Foulger (*Ballistics Expert*), Cy Schindell (*Mickey*), Sherry Hall (*Court Clerk*), Robert Dudley (*Prosecutor*), Betty Roadman (*Matron*), Beatrice Curtis (*Waitress*), George Anderson, James Craig (*Detectives*), Eddie Coke, Guy Kingsford, Walter Sande, Robert Sterling (*Reporters*)

Director: Nick Grindé. *Producer*: Ralph Cohn. *Original Screenplay*: Karl Brown. *Photographer*: Benjamin Kline. *Editor*: Byron Robinson. *Music Director*: M.W. Stoloff. *Sound Engineer*: Jack Goodrich. *Assistant Director*: Milton Carter.

Columbia; released October 3, 1939. 61 minutes.

Judge Mary Cabot, assigned to juvenile court, has a reputation for being softhearted with defendants, as when she dismisses the charges against a young woman with a baby who stole a coat to provide for her child. Mary has a "good friends" relationship with prosecutor Steven Graham, whose marriage proposals she has repeatedly turned down. He tells her she's being transferred to criminal court, which may put the two of them at odds in trials.

Once a year, Mary has a birthday cake to commemorate the life of her daughter Virginia, whom she has not seen in 17 years. Her housekeeper, Mrs. Butler, urges her to give up on the hope that she will be reunited with her daughter, and socialize more, especially with Steven.

Racketeer "Big Tim" Ryan goes on trial with Steven prosecuting the case and Mary presiding. Ryan knows that one of his employees, a 20-year-old known as Justine West, is actually Judge Cabot's daughter. Raised by her criminal father, whom Ryan says was "one of my best men," Justine has never known anything but a dishonest life. When Steven makes an impassioned declaration in court of Ryan's guilt, his attorney promptly argues for a mistrial. Ryan wants Justine to blackmail her mother into granting a mistrial, offering her $5000 to do so.

Feeling that her mother represents the only decent element in her life, Justine refuses to carry out Ryan's plan, even though she and roommate Gertie are broke. When Justine shows up at Ryan's apartment that evening, he shows her her original birth certificate and a family photo. Allowing him to believe she will comply with his demand, Justine seizes an opportunity while Ryan is on the phone and throws the evidence into the fireplace. Ryan threatens her with a fireplace poker, and in the ensuing struggle a gun goes off, killing him.

Justine is arrested with what appears to be an airtight case against her for murder. Disgusted with her life, and seeing no way out, she resigns herself to the inevitable and refuses to help her court-appointed attorney Robert Langley. Cleaning out the apartment they shared, Gertie finds a locket with a picture of a younger Judge Cabot and an inscription, "To Baby from Mother with Love." Gertie bursts into the judge's chambers and reveals the truth. Without hesitation, Mary Cabot submits her resignation from the bench and asks if she can help Langley defend her daughter.

Unabashedly melodramatic, *A Woman Is the Judge* is a sort of inverted *Madame X* that makes for compelling entertainment. (It also shares a few story points with Rochelle's *Notorious but Nice*.) The film offers Rochelle one of her best roles, one that allows her to contrast her baby-faced loveliness with a harder edge. Learning that her boss Ryan will be tried in Mary's court, she says cynically, "Funny how things work out. Ryan uses women to do his dirty work, and now he's being judged by a woman." Rochelle's face is an impassive yet resolute mask as she listens to the police building a case against her character, knowing that her neck is being fitted for a noose but refusing nonetheless to disclose what she knows. She later says of her relationship with Mary Cabot, "It's my secret and it's going to the grave with me."

Despite Rochelle's fine performance, this is no one-woman show; instead, she is one of a triumvirate of actresses who make this tautly paced programmer hum along with great energy. Scottish-born Frieda Inescort (1901–1976) has a somewhat theatrical yet not overdone aura that makes any of her characters a force to reckon with, and compels the viewer to keep watching. She and Rochelle make a believable

Gertie (Mayo Methot, left) pays a social call on her incarcerated pal Justine (Rochelle Hudson) in *A Woman Is the Judge* (1939).

mother-daughter team, though Inescort was only the older of the two by about 15 years. Both are flatteringly photographed by cinematographer Benjamin Kline.

Mayo Methot (1904–1951) is better known for her tempestuous marriage to Humphrey Bogart than for her own acting accomplishments. Justine sees her own future when she looks at Gertie, played by Miss Methot, and diagnoses her harshly but not inaccurately as "a miserable cheap wreck of a woman who doesn't dare open her eyes long enough to realize that every day she lives, she sinks that much deeper in the mud." Gertie has some of the best lines of dialogue, which Methot delivers with gusto, as when she first meets Justine's young lawyer and protests, "Throw this one back and fish again! The game warden don't let you keep 'em this young." Fond of the bottle and hardened by life experience, Gertie visits Justine in the slammer and remarks off-handedly to the matron, "Seems kinda screwy to be in here socially."

Otto Kruger (1885–1974) gives a low-key, naturalistic performance as Mary's gentleman friend, while Beryl Mercer has a few nice moments as Mary's loyal housekeeper. Gordon Oliver, previously seen with Rochelle in *Pride of the Navy*, plays another handsome young man destined *not* to find a love connection.

Nick Grindé (1893–1979) was in the director's chair for three of Rochelle's Columbia films.

Reviews: "Sentimental fans in general and femmes in particular will probably like this one. The story is dramatic and it is effectively played. Film, aimed at the program market, fits nicely." *Film Daily*, October 3, 1939

"Benefits from Nick Grindé's strong direction and several strong supporting performances. Picture looks destined to get the most coin from dual setups, and is trimmed to fit into such combos. It's red-corpuscled fare for the double-bill spots…. Rochelle Hudson looks pert and seems to have absorbed additional thespian talent." *Variety*, October 4, 1939

Convicted Woman (1940)

Rochelle Hudson (*Betty Andrews*), Frieda Inescort (*Mary Ellis*), June Lang (*Georgia "The Duchess" Ellis*), Lola Lane (*Hazel Wren*), Glenn Ford (*Jim Brent*), Iris Meredith (*Nita Lavore*), Lorna Gray (*Frankie Mason*), Esther Dale (*Miss Brackett*), William Farnum (*Commissioner McNeil*), Mary Field (*Gracie Dunn*), Beatrice Blinn (*May Sorenson*), June Gittelson (*Tubby*), Dorothy Appleby (*Daisy*), Frank Jaquet (*Department Store Manager*), Stanley Andrews (*Prosecutor*), Milburn Morante (*Man on Park Bench*), Marie Pope (*Martha Charter*), Edward LeSaint (*Judge*), Eddie Laughton (*Jack Pendy*), Dorothy Fay (*Frances*), Harry A. Bailey (*Court Clerk*), E. Alyn Warren (*Mailman*), Don Beddoe (*Hank*), Sibyl Harris (*Mrs. Newley*), Lucie Kaye (*Cleo Pilsky*), William Lally (*Prison Guard*), Gene Stone (*Waiter*), Charles Sullivan (*Mugg*), John Tyrrell (*Bart*), Gertrude Sutton (*Miss Thompson*), Maxine Leslie (*Julie*), Hal Price (*Detective*), Ralph Peters (*Truck Driver*), Helen Dickson, Evelyn Dockson, Blanche Payson, Marin Sais (*Matrons*), James Millican, Dick Rush (*Cops*), Willis Clare, Jay Eaton, Carl M. Leviness (*Floorwalkers*), Bruce Bennett, Lynton Brent, Roger Haliday (*Reporters*)

Director: Nick Grindé. *Screenplay*: Joseph Carole. *Story*: Martin Mooney, Alex Gottlieb. *Photographer*: Benjamin Kline. *Editor*: James Sweeney. *Music Director*: M.W. Stoloff.

Columbia; released January 31, 1940. 65 minutes.

Down-on-her-luck Betty Andrews is weary from applying for jobs when she tries Boyle's Department Store. While filling out her application, she's approached by a young woman who resembles her slightly and is wearing the same dress, which they both found on the store's bargain rack. Her quick-thinking new acquaintance takes advantage of the situation to steal cash from a customer; Betty is blamed and hauled in by the police, who believe she is the "Lady Raffles" they've been seeking. Sympathetic reporter Jim Brent of the *Times* tries to befriend Betty, but she brushes him off as only interested in a sensational story. Awaiting sentencing, Betty is told by her cellmate about do-gooder attorney Mary Ellis, a social crusader who sometimes takes on worthy clients *pro bono.*

Miss Ellis' passionate defense fails to save Betty from a year-long stretch at the notorious Curtiss House of Correction. Under the firm rule of chief matron Miss Brackett, the convicts are treated miserably: long hours working in the laundry, poor food and unrelenting discipline. The punishing environment is too much for inmate Gracie Dunn, who commits suicide; Miss Brackett calmly lies about the tragedy. Plotting an escape, Betty makes the mistake of enlisting the help of double-crosser Georgia Ellis. Known as "The Duchess," Georgia arranges for Betty to hide on an outgoing laundry truck, but also rats her out to Miss Brackett. Furious, Betty tells the heartless matron, "I'll get out somehow, and when I do, I'll expose your whole rotten system!"

Managing to sneak a phone call, Betty summons Jim Brent, who arrives for an appointment posing as her attorney. Based on a note she slips him, Jim publishes a front-page story exposing the corruption at Curtiss and the cover-up of Gracie's suicide. In the ensuing investigation, the prison commissioner offers Miss Ellis a chance to run the troubled institution herself. Brackett is demoted to being her assistant.

Realizing that the present system only hardens and embitters the inmates, Miss Ellis promptly unveils sweeping changes, starting with renaming the facility the Curtiss Home for Girls. The cons get better meals, job training and a system of self-government. Still skeptical of Miss Ellis, Betty is nonplused to find her amenable to whatever the prisoners demand, including a dance. A reward system is devised to allow ten inmates to be given a parole at Thanksgiving, with Betty among the ones selected. Miss Brackett, conniving with the unscrupulous Duchess, schemes to insure that the plan will go awry, discrediting Miss Ellis' liberal views and kindhearted oversight of Curtiss.

Just over an hour long, *Convicted Woman* is a briskly paced and entertaining programmer, wasting not a minute in telling its story. Director Nick Grindé keeps things constantly on the move, rarely allowing viewers a spare moment to reflect on any implausibility in the story or ask any questions. (Does Betty have no family?

Two girls in stir: "The Duchess" (June Lang, left) and Betty (Rochelle Hudson) in *Convicted Woman* (1940).

What evidence does Jim gather before publishing his expose?) Benjamin Kline's crisp cinematography demonstrates care taken to compose and capture striking shots despite a short shooting schedule.

Films about women in prison always seem to be on the verge of falling into either exploitation or camp, but *Convicted Woman* mostly skirts these traps. It edges perhaps nearer to the latter with its depiction of Curtiss' overnight transition from hellhole to live-in vocational school, where inmates transform themselves with makeup and pretty dresses they somehow make by hand. Trade and newspaper reviewers often landed on it with a ferocity that it didn't really merit, failing to acknowledge the entertaining qualities that made it an unpretentious good time for moviegoers. Studio publicists did their best to make it sound raw and uncompromising, as if Linda Blair or Sybil Danning would turn up topless for a shower room brawl any minute. "Caged women! What would they do if they were turned loose for a day?"

Some scribes acknowledged the strong cast that delivered pleasing results, giving their performances a dose of sincerity. Rochelle skillfully depicts Betty as a fresh-faced, likable young woman, charming as she plays with a dog in the city park, as well as her rapid descent when incarceration and unjust treatment begin to toughen her. She develops a harder edge, but remains a character for whom viewers will root.

The often-forceful Frieda Inescort displays unwavering camera presence, her natural intensity somewhat sheathed as the crusader who gets one look at the Curtiss House of Correction and exclaims, "Everything I've seen is revolting!" A young and slightly geeky Glenn Ford (1916–2006) plays the *Times* reporter who takes more than a professional interest in lovely Betty. Of his three-time leading lady, Ford later told his son, "Rochelle was a great girl. She was fun to work with and very professional. It's too bad we made such lousy pictures together."[34]

Good supporting performances come from June Lang and Lola Lane, among others. Esther Dale's hard-bitten matron comes across somewhat one-note compared to Inescort's performance. Often cast in comedy bits, Mary Field tackles a more dramatic role here, as the ill-fated Gracie, and handles it well. Bruce Bennett (1906–2007) is quite noticeable in an uncredited appearance as a reporter. Among the bit players seen as inmates are Dorothy Malone and Dorothy Comingore.

Reviews: "I don't like to make a liar out of Columbia, but [the studio's] lurid description of the film hardly fits in with the facts disclosed…. When the stiff-necked Miss Brackett is replaced by a young woman lawyer … the place takes on the complexion of a very fancy finishing school…. It's a silly and unbelievable story that is propelled along its melodramatic way by a cast that is better than the film deserves." Kate Cameron, *New York Daily News*, February 25, 1940

"Not only is the plot of this melodrama trite, but some of the situations are so far-fetched that they are ridiculous. It is typical program stuff, patterned along familiar lines, offering little that is novel in the way of plot development." *Harrison's Reports*, March 2, 1940

Men Without Souls (1940)

John Litel (*Rev. Thomas Storm*), Barton MacLane (*Blackie Drew*), Rochelle Hudson (*Suzan Leonard*), Glenn Ford (*Johnny Adams*), Don Beddoe (*Warden Schafer*), Cy Kendall (*Captain White*), Eddie Laughton (*Lefty*), Dick Curtis (*Duke*), Richard Fiske (*Crowley*), Walter Soderling (*Old Mack*), Alfred Hall (*Governor*), Harry Strang (*Evans*), Edmund Cobb (*Harmon*), Cy Schindell (*Harry*), John Tyrrell (*Chuck*), Frank Mills (*Pete*), Joe Palma (*Charles*), Harry Lash (*Carter*), Frank Bruno (*Paul*), Al Rhein (*Bill*), Walter Long (*Fireman*), Harry Depp (*Secretary*), Donald Kerr (*Photographer*), Walter Sande, Ralph Peters (*Reporters*), Sam Ash, Stanley Brown, Chuck Hamilton, William Lally (*Guards*)

Director: Nick Grindé. *Screenplay*: Robert D. Andrews, Joseph Carole. *Photographer*: Benjamin Kline. *Editor*: James Sweeney. *Music Director*: M.W. Stoloff.

Columbia; released May 20, 1940. 62 minutes.

Summoned to a meeting at the governor's office, Warden Schafer is none too pleased to meet the man just appointed to serve as his institution's new chaplain, the Rev. Thomas Storm. Schafer resents the minister's previous statements that he (Schafer) runs "the worst penitentiary in the country." Storm feels the harsh discipline and miserable conditions spoil any chance of rehabilitation for the men there: "They come out of prison hopeless, filled with hatred, wanting revenge on society…. We have made them men without souls."

A prison riot breaks out in Schafer's absence. Hurrying back with the Reverend Storm in tow, Schafer finds that the prisoners have taken two of his guards hostage. Schafer's deputy, Captain White, is a sadist who believes that brutality is the only solution. Storm walks into the standoff, telling the prisoners' leader, Blackie Drew, that he's there to help. Cynical Blackie has no use for the chaplain, but Storm's efforts do help prevent fatalities.

The chaplain meets "a new crop of fish" arriving to begin their sentences, among them young Johnny Adams. Captain White assigns Johnny to share Blackie's cell, seeking to employ him as a stool pigeon to keep an eye on the hardened man. But Johnny has a purpose of his own which he doesn't immediately reveal. Blackie is suspicious when his new cellmate asks him about Andrew Lloyd, an older prisoner who died there.

Storm summons Johnny to his office and reveals that he knows the newcomer's background: Johnny is the son of Andrew Lloyd, changing his name and stealing a car in order to be sentenced to the prison and investigate his father's death. The chaplain brings in Johnny's girlfriend Suzan Leonard, who pleads with him to reconsider his dangerous plan. She promises to be loyal while he serves his time.

Back in their cell, Johnny tells Blackie about his father. Blackie confides that he's planning a prison break, and that weapons are due to arrive shortly. Patrolling the laundry room after hearing rumors about the guns, Captain White is stabbed with a file belonging to Johnny. Johnny protests his innocence, but even the chaplain is uncertain, aware of his desire to avenge his father's death. Johnny is convicted of murder and sentenced to death. With his execution imminent, Storm refuses to give up on Johnny, and appeals to the conscience he believes that Blackie still has. But Johnny has his own plan where his cellmate is concerned.

Only a few months after the release of *Convicted Woman*, Rochelle, Glenn Ford and director Nick Grindé reunited for another look at prison life, this time with Ford the inmate and Hudson the sympathetic love interest. Rochelle, playing the film's sole female character, shows up for her one and only scene just past its half-hour mark, just as she had done in *Hell's Highway*. Embodying Johnny's best reason to persevere in those few moments, she even utters the classic line, "I'll wait for you."

Ford continued to improve as a film actor with experience. Director Nick Grindé effectively contrasts his rangy physique and modest height with his burlier co-stars, to enhance a sense of Johnny's vulnerability. Barton MacLane, previously seen opposite Rochelle in *Born Reckless*, gives an energetic performance as Blackie, though he could probably have played this type of character in his sleep after more than a decade in the movies. Borrowed from Warners, John Litel (1892–1972) was always convincing as a man of erudition and distinction; he capably plays Reverend Storm, who can argue for sympathetic treatment of the prisoners, and also throw a punch when it's needed. Cy Kendall (1898–1953), cast as the brutal Captain White, was a busy character actor who might have racked up as many credits as the prolific

Litel had he lived as long. According to a *Boxoffice* item (January 6, 1940), the film's original title was *Man Without a Country*.

The film is mostly effective, though it teeters momentarily on the edge of camp when Reverend Storm brings in music, and has the prisoners engaged in a singalong to "My Bonnie Lies Over the Ocean."

Reviews: "A minor program offering. It is a rehash of the typical prison story.... Women will find very little in it to entertain them, for there is just a hint at a romance.... The plot is so familiar that it is doubtful if the average picture-goer will have the patience to sit through the entire picture. Two attempted prison breaks are the only exciting occurrences." *Harrison's Reports*, May 25, 1940

"Prison meller has plenty of action ... and picture should serve okay as lesser half of dual programs.... John Litel is well cast as a prison chaplain. Rochelle Hudson provides an attractive female atmosphere for the picture and the remainder of the cast of adequate.... Nick Grindé directs the picture with a good pace." *Film Daily*, May 20, 1940

Island of Doomed Men (1940)

Peter Lorre (*Stephen Danel*), Rochelle Hudson (*Lorraine Danel*), Robert Wilcox (*Mark Sheldon*), Don Beddoe (*Brand*), George E. Stone (*Siggy*), Kenneth MacDonald (*Doctor*), Charles Middleton (*Captain Cort*), Stanley Brown (*Eddie*), Earl Gunn (*Mitchell*), Sam Ash (*Ames*), Eddie Laughton (*Borgo*), John Tyrrell (*Durkin*), Bruce Bennett (*Hazen*), Forbes Murray (*Parole Board Chairman*), Lee Prather (*Warden*), Howard Hickman (*Judge*), Trevor Bardette (*District Attorney*), Al Hill (*Clinton*), Richard Fiske (*Hale*), Donald Douglas (*Department of Justice Official*), Bernie Breakston (*Townsend*), Raymond Bailey (*Killer*), William Gould, Edmund Mortimer (*Parole Board Members*)

Director: Charles Barton. *Original Screenplay*: Robert D. Andrews. *Photographer*: Benjamin Kline. *Editor*: James Sweeney. *Art Director*: Lionel Banks. *Gowns*: Kalloch. *Music Director*: M.W. Stoloff. Sound: Lodge Cunningham.

Columbia; released May 20, 1940. 68 minutes.

Mark Sheldon reports to the Department of Justice in Washington, D.C., to accept his first assignment as undercover agent #64. He's cautioned that, should he run into trouble, the agency will deny knowledge of his activities.

Sheldon is dispatched to a business office where he meets Agent #46. The second agent, going by the name Jackson, tells Sheldon that they will be working to "smash the dirtiest racket ever invented." Jackson describes the small, remote Dead Man's Island, where Stephen Danel uses convict labor to carry out his evil schemes. Before Sheldon can learn more, Jackson is shot and killed through the open office window. Police and onlookers quickly arrive, and Sheldon is taken into custody and accused of murder. Refusing to give his true name, he goes through the justice system as "John Smith" and is convicted. Danel, who kept an office in the same building, takes an interest in the mysterious Mr. Smith.

On Dead Man's Island, the convicts do hard labor and endure brutal treatment at the hands of Captain Cort, with lashings in store for anyone who disobeys. Danel occupies a lavishly appointed cottage which he shares with his wife Lorraine. Lorraine, who has been living there for the past three years, is miserable despite her husband's attempts to bribe her with jewelry and a comfortable lifestyle. "I can't stand staying here!" she complains. "I'm a prisoner." Danel makes it clear he will never let her leave, nor give her any real freedom.

When Sheldon applies for parole, Danel selects him and four other convicts to join his island workforce. Though Danel says the men under his watch are destined for "decent jobs in pleasant surroundings," the reality is quite different, as the newcomers learn when a would-be escapee is shot and killed before their eyes.

Danel is angered when his wife and Sheldon seem to have eyes for one another, and he resolves to make his new prisoner tell what he learned from the late Jackson. Sheldon refuses to cooperate, despite the beating he's given. Lorraine tells her servant Siggy to get word to Sheldon that she wants to talk to him. Overpowering the island's doctor, Sheldon takes away his gun and meets Lorraine at the electrically wired fence surrounding the Danels' cottage. She pledges to cooperate with him. Running loose on the island, Sheldon allows Captain Cort to recapture him, lying that he is a jewel thief and that the two, working together, can become rich.

Island of Doomed Men (1940): Even at his grubbiest, undercover agent Mark (Robert Wilcox, right) is a far more appealing prospect for Lorraine (Rochelle Hudson) than her cruel husband Stephen (Peter Lorre, left)

Sheldon tells Lorraine that is it imperative that she snatch her husband's keys and find the guns he has hidden in their cottage. Though she succeeds in getting the keys while she thinks Danel is asleep, he wakens in time to find his wife and Sheldon outside the electrified fence, with Cort in tow. Cort is stripped of his responsibilities, and both men return to the labor camp. But Sheldon has another plan to overthrow Danel and take control of the island.

Island of Doomed Men is an action-packed melodrama, anchored by the quietly menacing performance of Peter Lorre as the malevolent Danel. Under the capable direction of Charles Barton (1902–1981), the film is quite suspenseful and holds the attention throughout. Barton never allows the performers to go over the top. According to Lorre's biographer Stephen D. Youngkin, Barton gave the actor quite a bit of freedom in developing his characterization, allowing him to rewrite dialogue to better suit his singular style, but reined him in by calling for a retake if the actor's playing was too broad.

Rochelle has rarely, if ever, been more beautifully costumed, lit and photographed than she is here, thanks to cinematographer Benjamin Kline and designer Robert Kalloch (1893–1947). She matches Lorre's underplaying with an icy reserve of her own, making it clear that Lorraine is the walking embodiment of "marry in haste, repent at leisure." A former actress who wed him for security, she now loathes him, and he knows it. When she tries to be nicer to him than usual, hoping for a chance at freedom, he is unimpressed. With a trace of sadness, he tells her, "I remember when I saw you the first time on the stage. You were beautiful—very beautiful—but your acting was always unconvincing to me." She soon makes her feelings clear, snapping, "I hate the very sight of you!" Undaunted, he warns her, "What I own, I keep!"

Robert Wilcox, previously Rochelle's leading man in *Rascals*, makes a fine square-jawed hero here, while Charles Middleton enacts the subtly menacing Cort. Character actor George E. Stone (1903–1967) has a few effective moments as Danel's downtrodden servant, ultimately playing a satisfying role in his nasty boss' final outcome. Kenneth MacDonald (1901–1972) is seen as the doctor who tries in vain to reach Danel with reason. Stone and MacDonald later found frequent employment on TV's *Perry Mason*, with the aging Stone appearing as the largely silent court clerk while MacDonald presided over the judge's bench in numerous episodes.

According to *Boxoffice* (June 1, 1940), censors in Boston found a scene of a convict being whipped offensive and "ordered [it] cut to a flash."

Reviews: "An interesting story provides plenty of excitement and action.... Exhibitors should find this one easy to sell as it is a first-class criminal thriller, and the people who like this type of film will go for it in a big way. Peter Lorre is fine as a cold-blooded killer.... Robert Wilcox does a nice job as an FBI agent. ...Charles Barton directs the picture with a good pace and sense of timing." *Film Daily*, June 13, 1940

"The latest of Columbia's crime melodramas has a somewhat different and unusual plot.... Rochelle Hudson lends the only feminine interest to the picture....

The picture's innate appeal will be to men. Romance is not stressed...." *Motion Picture Herald*, June 15, 1940

Babies for Sale (1940)

    Rochelle Hudson (*Ruth Williams*), Glenn Ford (*Steve Burton*), Miles Mander (*Dr. Wallace Rankin*), Joseph Stefani (*Dr. John Gaines*), Georgia Caine (*Miss Talbot*), Isabel Jewell (*Edith Drake*), Eva Hyde (*Gerda Bonaker*), Selmer Jackson (*Arthur Kingsley*), Mary Currier (*Thelma Kingsley*), Edwin Stanley (*Mr. Edwards*), Douglas Wood (*Dr. Aleshire*), John Qualen (*Howard Anderson*), Helen Brown (*Mrs. Anderson*), Ben Taggart (*Sgt. Mike Burke*), Bruce Bennett (*Policeman*), Lew Kelly (*Gardener*), Dorothy Adams (*Mother*), John Beck (*Charity Worker*)
    Director: Charles Barton. *Screenplay*: Robert D. Andrews. *Story*: Robert Chapin, Joseph Carole. *Photographer:* Benjamin Kline. *Editor*: Charles Nelson. *Assistant Director*: Thomas Flood. *Sound*: Lodge Cunningham.
    Columbia; released June 14, 1940. 65 minutes.

    The film opens with a disclaimer, asserting that 95 percent of adoption agencies are "honest and worthy of all support," but that those wanting to adopt should know about others, "where babies are sold for cash, where helpless mothers are victimized, and where foster parents may find lifelong tragedy instead of happiness.... What happens in this story could happen to you."

    Star-Dispatch reporter Steve Burton visits the office of Dr. John Gaines, who speaks out about illegal adoptions: "Babies are sold every day—and I mean sold, like so much merchandise, for as little as $50, or as much as $10,000." Steve's front-page article based on Dr. Gaines' account outrages leaders of the city's social service agencies, who pressure his editor to print a retraction. Steve asks for time to uncover more details; when his request is denied, he tenders his resignation.

    Recently widowed Ruth Williams turns up at the Mercy Shelter with $87, anticipating the arrival of a baby. Dr. Rankin says that the shelter can assist her, but she balks at the idea of giving up her baby for adoption. The doctor argues the point with her, but allows her to stay without signing the usual contract. Shortly afterwards, he's visited by Mr. and Mrs. Anderson, the grieving parents of a seriously ill baby they adopted for $1000 from the Mercy Shelter. When they find Dr. Rankin coolly unsympathetic to their plight, Mrs. Anderson throws herself and the infant in front of a subway train.

    Reading newspaper accounts of the tragedy, Steve implores the widower to tell him where the baby was adopted. Steve pays a visit to the Mercy Shelter, using a fake name and posing as a magazine writer wanting to write a flattering story about the institution. He gets a tour from Dr. Rankin's assistant, Miss Talbot, but Rankin recognizes him from a newspaper office meeting.

    Another expectant mother, Edith, warns Ruth that the agency is not as charitable as it seems, pointing out that some residents work 12 hours a day and are pressured into giving up their babies to pay their expenses. Of Dr. Rankin and Miss Talbot, Edith says bitterly, "They're in this for what they can get out of it, and believe me, they get plenty."

Dr. Rankin indeed plans to get plenty from the well-to-do Kingsleys, a couple he believes will pay handsomely for a baby of good health and bloodlines—like Ruth's. With the wealthy client concerned about a child's reaction to being adopted, Dr. Rankin suggests that Mrs. Kingsley be enrolled as a patient at the clinic, and a birth certificate falsified to show that she, not Ruth, gave birth.

When Ruth still refuses to relinquish her rights as a mother, Dr. Rankin callously tells her that her baby died. Refusing to believe him, Ruth escapes from the shelter. Outside, she encounters Steve, who promises to help her. He asks Dr. Gaines to demand Ruth's medical files, which include a death certificate for her daughter. Teaming up, Steve, Ruth and Edith follow up on every baby born in the city during the same month. When Steve visits the Kingsley residence, he immediately recognizes the couple from their visit to Mercy. Now Ruth and her friends must find a way to prove that the baby is hers, and bring it safely home.

Babies for Sale is a satisfying melodrama, elevated by good performances. Rochelle anchors the film with her sensitive portrayal of Ruth. Deglamorized somewhat to suit the character she's playing, Rochelle is still strikingly beautiful, and moves the viewer with her sorrow, frustration and determination to win back what is hers, against the odds. She's surrounded by a very capable cast, working well under Charles Barton's direction. Nearly stealing the show with her supporting performance as the cynical but good-hearted Edith is Isabel Jewell, especially poignant in the scene where her eyes glimmer with tears as she steadfastly refuses to see her own baby, having determined to give it up. Miles Mander (1888–1946), enjoying a larger role than he often played in films of the period, exudes suave villainy as the unscrupulous doctor, who remarks at one point, "I sometimes feel that legal technicalities can be ignored."

Georgia Caine (1876–1964) does well as his assistant Miss Talbot, who seems to have the patients' best interest at heart, but as Edith notes, "That's her racket, being nice." Character actors John Qualen and Helen Brown (1915–1994) give good performances in their scene as Mr. and Mrs. Anderson; Brown's career lasted nearly 60 years, culminating with a 1994 appearance on TV's *E.R.* Bruce Bennett plays another bit part as an officer of the law, good practice for his upcoming role in *The Officer and the Lady*.

In the *Motion Picture Herald*'s "What the Picture Did for Me" column (August 3, 1940), an exhibitor from small-town Indiana commented, "Played this picture on Bank Night to better than average business. The title seemed to draw them in and everyone seemed well pleased with this picture."

Reviews: "This offering should interest the women and provide a good companion feature in the neighborhood houses. Although there aren't any names in the cast, the acting is quite satisfactory." *The Exhibitor*, May 29, 1940

"As an expose, this is good stuff, but as entertainment it ranks low. There is no comic relief whatever and the eventual ending of the plot is well-evident from its beginning.... The acting is good throughout, however, and the direction is competent." *Showmen's Trade Review*, May 18, 1940

Miss Talbot (Georgia Caine, left) and Edith (Isabel Jewell) welcome expectant mother Ruth (Rochelle Hudson) to the Mercy Shelter in *Babies for Sale* (1940).

Girls Under 21 (1940)

Bruce Cabot (*Smiley Ryan*), Rochelle Hudson (*Frances White*), Paul Kelly (*Johnny Cane*), Tina Thayer (*Jennie White*), Roberta Smith (*Sloppy Krupnik*), Lois Verner (*Fatso Cheruzzi*), Beryl Vaughan (*Marge Dolan*), Joanne Tree (*Gertie Dolan*), Dellie Ellis [Joan Lorring] (*Tessa Mangione*), William Edmunds (*Tony Mangione*), John Dilson (*Albert Carter*), John Tyrrell (*Rusty*), Gisela Werbisek (*Mrs. Krupnick*), Selmer Jackson (*Judge Frank P. Wallace*), Russell Huestis (*Store Owner*), Eddie Lee (*Waiter at Chinese Restaurant*), George McKay (*Eddie*), Ruth Robinson (*Mrs. White*), Leila Romer (*Mrs. Charuzzi*), Blanche Rose (*Mrs. McCarthy*), June Pickerell (*Mrs. Dolan*), Ben Taggart (*Police Chief*), Frank Yaconelli (*Mr. Papadakus*), Edward Peil, Sr. (*Doctor*), Wright Kramer (*Mr. Johnson*), Al Mathews (*Charlie*), Armand Wright (*Peddler*), Lee Phelps, Ralph Sanford (*Detectives*)

Director: Max Nosseck. *Producer*: Ralph Cohn. *Original Story and Screenplay*: Jay Dratler, Fanya Foss. *Photographer*: Barney McGill. *Editor*: Charles Nelson. *Music Director*: M.W. Stoloff. *Sound*: Lodge Cunningham.

Columbia; released November 15, 1940. 64 minutes.

Hoodlum Smiley Ryan is acquitted and released from prison after a three-month stay. Though he told his underlings to see that his lady friend Frances lacked for nothing in his absence, she has decided to leave him. Returning to the slum neighborhood on Yancey Street where she grew up, Frances is ostracized by most of her adult neighbors. She tells Smiley that she was humiliated by the newspaper coverage and police attention that their association brought her. She intends to again walk the straight and narrow, even though it means giving up money and a life of luxury. Neighborhood schoolteacher Johnny Cane, widely admired in the community, is supportive of her resolution.

Francie, as she is known in her old neighborhood, is troubled to see that the local teenagers, including her younger sister Jennie, think her way of escaping poverty was completely understandable and smart. Johnny, who teaches Jennie and her pals, works to interest them in self-improvement and "teach them to live decently." He looks out for their interests even when he knows they're lying to him—as when they shoplift from a drugstore. He cautions Francie that she has set a bad example for them, and they band together to change the dangerous path down which the teenagers are headed. One girl in particular, Tessa Mangione, doesn't belong in Jennie's gang but is determined to fit in.

Angered by Johnny's attentions to Francie, Smiley orders him followed. When Smiley tries to intimidate his rival with force, Johnny's friends from the neighborhood step up to defend him. Meanwhile, Francie tries to start over with a job at Thompson's Department Store. Jennie and her gang plot to steal clothes from the store, but they are forced to make a hasty escape. Tessa loses her glasses and wanders into the street, where she's hit by an oncoming car.

Suspecting that Francie can identify the young thieves, the police pick her up and charge her as a material witness. With Francie in jail, and Tessa dying of her injuries, Johnny tries to persuade the girls in Jennie's gang to give themselves up voluntarily. Members of his school's Parents' League complain about his methods, and he offers to submit his resignation if his faith in his young pupils proves unfounded.

Originally announced under the title *The Little Professor*, *Girls Under 21* is a modestly entertaining programmer that can only make so much hay out of the drama of girls who shoplift cosmetics, and are warned they wear too much makeup for decent society. It teeters between sincere drama and camp, with some sharp dialogue interspersed with an occasional howler. The screenplay's basic message is elucidated early on, when Jennie tells her older sister, "All the girls in the street are talking about you. They all got sisters working for $12 a week, taking stenography and guff from the boss." On the flip side, when Smiley assigns his flunky Rusty to Francie, the boss tells him to keep an eye on her erstwhile boyfriend as well, adding somewhat inscrutably, "If he gets gay, give him a little rubdown with a baseball bat." Johnny's idea of shaming the girls into confessing finds him scrawling in big letters on the blackboard, "Honesty is the Best Policy."

Though synopses of this film, as well as some published reviews at the time of its release, state that Francie is giving up her life as Smiley's wife, rather than just his mistress, this isn't brought out clearly in the film itself, where multiple characters call her Miss White or "the White girl."

The three leads all give capable performances. Once again, Rochelle demonstrates that she can take care of herself when handed a sizable role in a hastily made

Crusading schoolteacher Johnny (Paul Kelly) has eyes for reformed bad girl Francie (Rochelle Hudson) in *Girls Under 21* (1940).

low-budget film, even if the script and direction are not up to the highest standards. She is believable as the woman who has lost pride in herself ("Don't you think I curl up inside every time I look at myself in a mirror?"). Always worth watching, Paul Kelly (1899–1956) gives the heroic character of Johnny a believable street edge that may have come from his own Brooklyn upbringing. He could easily have traded roles with Bruce Cabot (1904–1972), though the latter acquits himself adequately as tough Smiley. All three characters have purportedly known each other since childhood; when Johnny reminds Smiley that he used to attract the attention of truant officers, the hoodlum proudly notes, "Yeah, I got promoted. The D.A.'s after me now."

Supporting performances are somewhat uneven. The actresses cast as the juvenile delinquents seem to have been directed to play their roles like the Bowery Boys in drag. Their one-note characterizations don't help; Lois Verner (1926–2003), cast as "Fatso," is hit with a barrage of insults about her weight. The teenage player billed as "Dellie Ellis," who has a few nice moments as the shy doormat Tessa, would a few years later become an important Warners contract player with the screen name "Joan Lorring." Lorring (1926–2014) received a Best Supporting Actress Oscar nomination for *The Corn Is Green* (1945).

Rochelle had a complaint to register about the film, according to a wire service story: "Why is it that movie companies insist on making winter pictures in the summer, and summer films in the winter?" Supposedly, in performing the tenement scenes, she was expected to "troupe under a blazing sun while loaded down with mufflers, an overcoat, galoshes and heavy stockings."[35]

Reviews: "Regeneration of juvenile delinquents is a noble idea and a great work, but it fails to hold much entertainment value the way it is presented in this new Columbia release. It's a drab picture of slum life, and has definite limitations. Bruce Cabot, Rochelle Hudson and Paul Kelly offer some marquee value, and their performances are adequate." *Film Daily*, November 15, 1940

"Dialogue is crude and often oversteps the bounds of decency, and while the direction is good and the acting spirited, such emphasis is placed on the excitement of law-breaking that one has very little faith in the reform of these hard little delinquents." *Motion Picture Reviews*, November 1940

Meet Boston Blackie (1941)

Chester Morris (*Boston Blackie*), Rochelle Hudson (*Cecelia Bradley*), Richard Lane (*Inspector Faraday*), Charles Wagenheim (*The Runt*), Constance Worth (*Marilyn Howard*), Jack O'Malley (*Monk*), George Magrill (*Georgie*), Michael Rand [James Seay] (*Mechanical Man*), Nestor Paiva (*Martin Vestrik*), Harry Anderson (*Dart Game Barker*), Byron Foulger (*"Blind" Man*), Lee Shumway (*Immigration Officer*), John Tyrrell (*Freak Show Doorman*), Ed Wolff (*Giant*), Walter Sande (*Officer at Carnival*), George McKay (*Baseball Barker*), William Lally (*Officer McCarthy*), Jack Gardner (*Tunnel of Horror Barker*), Stanley Brown (*Max*), Sam Bernard (*Telescope Man*), Harry Bowen (*Hot Dog Vendor*),

Director: Robert Florey. *Executive Producer*: Irving Briskin. *Producer*: Ralph Cohn. *Story and Screenplay*: Jay Dratler. *Based Upon the Boston Blackie Character Created by* Jack Boyle. *Photographer*: Franz F. Planer. *Editor*: James Sweeney. *Sound*: George Cooper. *Assistant Director*: Milton Carter.

Columbia; released February 20, 1941. 60 minutes.

The reformed safecracker known as Boston Blackie, arriving in New York by steamship, provides a gentlemanly assist to pretty Marilyn Howard when she's pestered by a man. Moments later, Blackie renews an old acquaintance with Police Inspector Faraday, who thinks he committed a recent robbery of pearls. To the surprise of his sidekick, known as "The Runt," Blackie agrees to let the inspector take him in and fulfill the officer's longtime desire to get Blackie's fingerprints.

Allowed to go back to his stateroom to pack, Blackie is startled to find the dead body of the man he saw with Marilyn, whose wallet shows him to be Martin Vestrik. Knowing he's been set up as a fall guy for the murder, Blackie escapes through the porthole, leaving behind his gun to confuse the issue.

Blackie tails Marilyn to a boardwalk carnival and freak show, where she protests her innocence and accompanies him on a ride through the Tunnel of Horror. They're followed by two thugs, one of whom kills Marilyn with a poison dart. Marilyn's dying words involve a guy who plays a "Mechanical Man" at the freak show.

Investigating, Blackie is jumped by thugs. On the lam, Blackie commandeers the vehicle of a beautiful young woman, Cecelia Bradley, explaining, "At the moment, I'm a fugitive from an autopsy." After a high-speed chase, Blackie drives the car onto a railroad boxcar shortly before the train gets rolling.

Initially angry at his presumptuous behavior, Cecelia can't help being intrigued by this charming daredevil. A radio broadcast tells them that Marilyn was an international spy. Arranging a meeting with Inspector Faraday, Blackie wins him a temporary reprieve when his fingerprints don't match the ones on the murder gun or the deadly dart.

After squaring things with the law, Blackie races against time to clear his name and prevent a threat involving enemy agents and a Navy bombsight.

Chester Morris (1901–1970) always excelled at playing roguish, incautious fellows who nonetheless could be counted on in times of crisis, and the part of Boston Blackie provided him with one of his signature roles. Active in films since the late 1920s, he spent much of the 1940s alternating Boston Blackies (the series ultimately ran to 14 installments) and starring roles in Pine-Thomas' B-grade action-adventures. In *Meet Boston Blackie*, the degree of the character's criminality is left vague; tellingly, he comments to Cecelia at one point, "I've never committed a *violent* crime." Though Blackie isn't husband material, Morris apparently was, having recently married second wife Lillian Kenton Barker, to whom he would remain wed until his death in 1970.

Rochelle, who arrives on the scene about 18 minutes into the film, has a sizable role as Blackie's love interest, one who after her initial shock gamely tags along on a completely unexpected adventure and quickly becomes the staunch ally of the guy who carjacked her. Though she's in most scenes from that point forward, we ultimately learn little about Cecelia. As will often be the case in this series, Blackie loves 'em and leaves 'em, not without some regret.

> CECILIA: You thrive on this sort of excitement, don't you? ... Couldn't anyone ever make you live like other people do?
> BLACKIE: You mean a normal life, with a Social Security number and a bankbook? I'm afraid not.

The final fadeout finds her gazing wistfully after him as he heads off to face a possible jail stint if the inspector can indeed prove he stole the missing jewels.

Meet Boston Blackie went before Columbia cameras in December 1940 under the early title *The Return of Boston Blackie*. With a snappy script by Jay Dratler and the efficient direction of Robert Florey, what resulted was an enjoyable programmer that told quite a bit of story in just an hour. It inspired enough ticket sales to insure that additional Boston Blackie films would follow.

The film introduced two supporting characters who would continue to turn up through the series. Actor Richard Lane (1899–1982) was cast as Blackie's friendly adversary Inspector Faraday (spelled "Farraday" in later entries), who says of Blackie, "He's a pretty swell guy—for a heel." Lane skillfully depicts a man who seems outwardly tough, but actually likes Blackie more than he'd care to admit. The part of "The Runt" went to actor Charles Wagenheim (1896–1979), this first time out, and was assumed by George E. Stone in later installments.

Lovely Australian-born Constance Worth (1913–1963), seen as the mysterious blonde Marilyn, was under contract to Columbia after a brief stint at RKO. Byron Foulger (1899–1970) has a minor role as a carnival performer who collects spare change pretending to be blind, and whose identity Blackie momentarily borrows.

At least one columnist reported that Rochelle would be appearing in another "Blackie" installment, but this didn't pan out.

Reviews: "The factors that save this mystery programmer and lift it above 'B' mediocrity are smart direction by Robert Florey, which starts off mighty fast and never slackens speed till the final fade-out, the novelty of the carnival setting, and above average performances by the entire cast.... The story ... is none too plausible and a bit fantastic.... Fortunately, it all moves fast enough to prevent the spectator's brain from asking any questions!" *Film Bulletin*, March 8, 1941

"Here is unsubtle, action-plus entertainment for the regular run of film fans who like their screen fare with a dash of ginger and excitement, and without too much to think about.... Chester Morris is highly satisfactory in the role of Boston Blackie, combining a smooth handling of his task with just enough of the bravado the part requires." *Motion Picture Daily*, February 26, 1941

The Stork Pays Off (1941)

"Slapsie" Maxie Rosenbloom (*"Brains" Moran*), Victor Jory (*"Deak" Foster*), Rochelle Hudson (*Irene Perry*), Horace MacMahon [McMahon] (*"Ear-to-the-Ground" Hinkle*), George McKay (*"Photofinish" Farris*), Ralf Harolde (*"Stud" Rocco*), Danny Mummert (*Herkemer*), Bonnie Irma Dane (*Bonnie*), Arthur Loft (*Barney*), Fern Emmett (*Herkemer's Mother*), Vinton Hayworth (*Todd Perry*), Byron Foulger (*Teacher*), Harry Hayden (*District Attorney*), John Dilson (*Judge*), Bobby Larson (*Billy*), John Tyrrell (*Lefty*), Harry Depp (*Mr. Kearn*), Netta Packer (*Mrs. Cornwall*), Edythe Elliott (*Mrs. Gadsby*), Harry C. Bradley (*Mr. Dennison*), Sam Ash (*Cigar Store Owner*), Eddie Lee (*Chinese Man*), Zacharias Yaconelli (*Fruit Stand Owner*), Harry Strang (*Joe Hoyt*), Harry A. Bailey, Cyril Ring (*Fathers*), Charles Miller (*Mr. Vance*), Eddie Laughton (*Rudy*), Eddie Fetherston (*Heckler*), Albert Butterfield (*Little Boy*), Joe McGuinn (*Jailer*), Dink Freeman (*Kid*), Eddie Kane (*Chairman*), Bud Geary, Joe Palma (*Henchmen*), Jack Gardner (*Reporter*)

Director: Lew Landers. *Producer*: Jack Fier. *Story and Screenplay*: Fanya Foss, Aleen Leslie. *Additional Dialogue*: Ned Dandy. *Photographer*: L.W. O'Connell. *Editor*: Gene Milford. *Art Director*: Lionel Banks. *Music Director*: M.W. Stoloff.

Columbia; released October 6, 1941. 68 minutes.

"Deak" Foster is a businessman whom some refer to as a racketeer. His specialty is extending credit to underfinanced companies—laundries, clubs, barber shops—then taking them over when they cannot repay their debts. His less-than-reliable assistants in this endeavor are three mugs known as "Brains," "Ear-to-the-Ground" and the racing-obsessed "Photofinish."

Foster's latest takeover attempt involves The Storks' House, which the guys wrongly believe to be a nightclub. Sending the three mugs to collect the $1700 debt, they meet lovely young Irene Perry, the proprietor at what looks like an ordinary suburban house. Quick on the uptake, Irene talks them into giving her $100 for the enterprise and assuming her other debts. Too late, the boys realize that her business is in fact a day nursery for children, one of them the divorcee's own toddler daughter. After confessing their mistake to Deak, he orders them to find a way to make it a paying concern.

Irene is offered a salary to run the Storks' House, and her new partners hunt up a few dozen additional children from a low-income neighborhood in need of day care. When Deak stops by, Irene praises him for helping disadvantaged kids. Infatuated, Deak puts aside any plans to make it a financially viable proposition. He confesses to his new lady friend that he made good money hustling beer during Prohibition, but as he falls for her, he begins to crave respectability. He announces a run for state assemblyman, representing the neighborhood where he grew up. He also demands that his cohorts enroll in night school.

Irene is happy operating the nursery with the dubious help of Brains and his pals, but her upper-class ex-husband Todd gets wind of it and declares it an unsuitable environment for their daughter. With child welfare investigators due any moment

Victor Jory (left) and Rochelle Hudson check out the cauliflower ears of ex-boxer "Slapsie" Maxie Rosenbloom in *The Stork Pays Off* (1941).

to inspect the house, Deak's unscrupulous rival "Stud" Rocco throws a wrench into things by having the dead body of hoodlum Six Fingers Simpson hidden in Irene's kitchen closet. Meanwhile, Deak, newly elected to political office, decides it's time to make a complete turnabout and goes to see the district attorney, confessing to some capers that he got away with, and putting his future with Irene on the line.

The Stork Pays Off is a good-natured comedy that, if caught in the right mood, is quite a bit of fun, though to some reviewers it just came off as a lame-brained story where logic had been completely thrown out the window. Having dispensed with believability, the scriptwriters were free to introduce new plot elements at any turn, and they do so liberally, if nothing else keeping the story from being totally predictable.

Top-billed "Slapsie" Maxie Rosenbloom (1904–1976) gives a lively performance as the inaptly named Brains, his intentions usually good but his smarts slightly less reliable. Rosenbloom tosses about malapropisms with ease. Explaining to his boss how he punched out a client, he says, "My fist colluded with his chin." He later shows off his vocabulary to a teacher: "A flavor is when you do a guy a good turn." He's teamed up with Horace McMahon and George McKay to compose a comic trio that has occasional whiffs of the Three Stooges.

Cast as a slightly unconventional, darkly handsome leading man, Victor Jory (1902–1982) applies his considerable skill to playing a bad guy who can eventually be accepted by the audience as the right man for a good woman. He has a long list of film and television credits, including the part of Jonas Wilkerson in *Gone with the Wind* (1939).

Her character's actions not making a great deal more sense than anyone else's, Rochelle just rolls with the punches and enters into the spirit of fun. Seemingly nonchalant when Brains and the guys show up to collect a debt she can't pay, she cheerfully allows them to take over her business, and apparently sees no reason why three low-level hoods wouldn't make good child care aides. With the Production Code rules of that era imposing strictures on the ways that divorce could be depicted in scripts, her character is a bit unusual, in that she's a sympathetic heroine who separated from her husband to raise their child alone, and is not shown to be wrong for having done so. Nor is her incipient romance with a man who has a criminal past problematic, though it's clear that she will be a good influence, setting him on a better path.

Perhaps best-known to Baby Boomers as General Schaeffer on TV's *I Dream of Jeannie*, Vinton Hayworth (1906–1970) is seen briefly as Irene's stuffy ex-husband. Byron Foulger has a few amusing moments as the unlucky night schoolteacher facing the uphill battle of making scholars out of "Brains" and his pals. Child actor Danny Mummert (1934–1974) plays a brat who repeatedly kicks Brains' shins, asking, "Ain't I cute?" Mummert had a recurring role as Alvin Fuddle in Columbia's long-running *Blondie* series. Moppet Bonnie Irma Dane is cute and appealing in her small role as Irene's daughter.

Screenwriter Aleen Leslie (1908–2010) wrote often about adolescents and family life, contributing to several of Paramount's "Henry Aldrich" films. She was also one of the most prolific writers behind the radio and television comedy *A Date with Judy*.

Reviews: "*The Stork Pays Off* is a case of a highly implausible gangster yarn being made palatable through first-rate direction and deft comedy portrayals.... Result is a topflight programmer.... Entire story is studded with funny bits, humorous lines and exciting, if comical developments.... Rochelle Hudson ... furnishes the romantic angle, and her romance with the ex-gangster is amazingly sincere and down-to-earth." *Variety*, November 12, 1941

"A pleasant little tale of a reformed beer baron and his mob—three of the best-hearted gangsters one ever met [and] the charming Rochelle Hudson.... Of course the plot is so improbable that you can't take anything seriously, but there are some excellent wisecracks and a few well-built-up farcical situations. It is good to welcome Victor Jory back to suave villain roles—he has been absent from the screen too long." *Boston Globe*, December 4, 1941

The Officer and the Lady (1941)

Rochelle Hudson (*Helen Regan*), Bruce Bennett (*Bob Conlon*), Roger Pryor (*Johnny Davis*), Richard Fiske (*Ace Quinn*), Sidney Blackmer (*Blake Standish*), Tom Kennedy (*"Bumps" O'Neil*), Oscar O'Shea (*Dan Regan*), Joe McGuinn (*Frank*), Charles Wilson (*Captain Hart*), William Hall (*Dawson*), Mary Currier (*Bobby's Mother*), Paul McVey (*Bobby's Father*), Lester Dorr (*Shooting Gallery Operator*), Edmund Cobb (*Police Lieutenant*), Patti McCarty (*Secretary*), John Tyrrell (*Harry*), Dorothy Vernon (*Matron*), Jack Chefe (*Clerk*), Marjorie Kane (*Phone Operator #14*)

Director: Sam White. *Producer*: Leon Barsha. *Screenplay*: Lambert Hillyer, Joseph Hoffman. *Story*: Joseph Hoffman. *Photographer*: George Meeker. *Editor*: Richard Fantl. *Art Director*: Lionel Banks. *Music Director*: M.W. Stoloff.

Columbia; released October 12, 1941. 60 minutes.

Policeman Bob Conlon and his partner "Bumps" are among the officers in hot pursuit of four bank robbers. Trapped on a bridge by police cars, two of the suspects escape by jumping into the river below, losing the $100,000 bankroll in the process.

Bob is in love with schoolteacher Helen Regan. Her father Dan captured a notorious crime boss, Blake Standish, but in the process was permanently disabled. Helen, who believes the stress of policemen's lives led to her mother's early death, has no intention of accepting Bob's marriage proposal. She feels that his badge makes him "a walking target."

In the meantime, Helen dates banker Johnny Davis, unaware that he planned the bank robbery. The two rivals for Helen's love have known each other since boyhood; Bob suspects Davis has something to hide. When they meet at the Regan home, they trade barbs:

JOHNNY [*glancing at Bob's uniform*]: Thought you'd have stripes by this time, Bob.
BOB: That's funny. I've been thinking the same thing about you.

A news bulletin announces that Blake Standish (the crook Dan Regan put away) has broken out of prison. After a makeover, Standish visits his confederate Johnny at the bank. Johnny assures his old boss that the upcoming robbery of a jewelry store will net Standish the money he needs to skip town. Before doing that, however, Standish intends to even the score with Dan.

On the night of the robbery, Johnny (in a fireman costume) escorts Helen to a masquerade ball, to establish an alibi. While a costumed Standish distracts Helen by asking for a dance, Johnny slips out to the jewelry store. When the robbers inadvertently knock a phone off the hook, an operator overhears them and summons the police. Bob locates an abandoned taxicab that figured in their escape. Dropped in the cab by mistake is a button from Johnny's fireman costume. Bob arrests Johnny, much to the annoyance of Helen, who refuses to believe he's guilty.

Johnny is trapped by the police into revealing Blake's whereabouts. Police arrive at Blake's apartment too late, after he and his confederates have abducted Helen and her father. Now Helen, who wanted no involvement with policemen, has to rely on one to come to the rescue.

Sometimes half the fun of a B movie is anticipating the familiar story developments and plot points that surface, like a visit from an easygoing old friend. Here, it's the one about a woman who's afraid to love a policeman, along with the one about two boyhood acquaintances, one who stayed on the straight and narrow while the other didn't. If the story of *The Officer and the Lady* is overly familiar, it's engaging nonetheless, with enough car chases and gunplay to keep action fans watching. There are a couple of points an alert viewer could nitpick if he had a mind to do so— just how long was that dance Helen enjoyed with another man while Johnny slipped out to grab a ride to the jewelry store, commit the robbery and take part in a chase before returning? Her statement to the police that Johnny was with her all evening doesn't make Helen look like the brightest schoolteacher around.

Rochelle's beauty is on good display here, chic hats setting off that lovely face. She gives an appealing performance that makes her the kind of woman any fella might want for his own. Her costuming as Scarlett O'Hara for the masquerade ball sequence shows just how well she might have looked in that role, though the Southern accent she offers isn't quite as impressive. Bruce Bennett (1906–2007), seen in minor roles in several previous films with Rochelle, steps into a lead here, he and Hudson making a handsome couple. Roger Pryor (1901–1974) shows a slick surface charm and underlying menace as the unscrupulous Johnny, who remarks at one point, "Ever hear of the law of self-preservation? I wrote it." Sidney Blackmer (1895–1973) makes his few scenes as the vengeful crime boss memorable. Tom Kennedy (1885–1975), as Bob's police partner, is the comic relief: *slightly* comic, but mostly a relief when it's over.

Sam White's direction is efficient and sturdy. The film's poster art neatly lays out the heroine's dilemma, with Rochelle pictured between her two suitors. Bob is saying, "Stick with him—and you'll land in the big house!"; Johnny replies, "Stick with him—and you'll end up in the poor house!"

Reviews: "Made to order for the action-minded patrons.... Bruce Bennett and Rochelle Hudson are a personable pair who take care of their simple acting assignments capably enough. Sidney Blackmer gives a suave portrayal of the notorious gang leader and Roger Pryor is properly villainous as the loan shark...." *Film Bulletin*, September 6, 1941

"This has thrills, excitement, and suspense. The story is well-told, with the direction and acting good. Better than average cops-and-robbers stuff, it should have no trouble satisfying the action fans in the duallers." *The Exhibitor*, July 22, 1941

Rubber Racketeers (1942)

Ricardo Cortez (*Tony Gilin*), Rochelle Hudson (*Nikki*), Bill Henry (*Bill Barry*), Barbara Read (*Mary Dale*), Milburn Stone (*Angel*), Dewey Robinson (*Larkin*), John Abbott (*Dumbo*), Pat Gleason (*Curly*), Dick Rich (*Mule*), Alan Hale, Jr. (*Red*), Sam Edwards (*Freddy Dale*), Kam Tong (*Tom*), Alex Callam (*Butch*), Dick Hogan (*Bert*), Marjorie Manners (*Lila*), Lynton Brent (*Henchman*)
Director: Harold Young. *Producer*: Maurice King. *Associate Producer*: Franklin King. *Original Screenplay*: Henry Blankfort. *Cinematographer*: L. William O'Connell. *Production Manager*: Mack V. Wright. *Editor*: Jack Dennis. *Music Director*: David Chudnow. *Sound Engineer*: Glen Glenn. *Art Director*: Frank Dexter. *Set Dresser*: Vin Taylor. *Assistant Directors*: Arthur Gardner, Herman King.
Monogram; released June 26, 1942. 67 minutes.

Just released after a prison stretch, racketeer Tony Gilin rides with his girlfriend Nikki in a vehicle that narrowly avoids colliding into a car driven by munitions plant worker Bill Barry. Two flat tires leave Bill and his fiancée Mary in a predicament when Gilin's insurance company refuses to pay enough to replace the tires during the wartime rubber shortage.

When Bob visit Gilin at his apartment, Nikki persuades Gilin to give the young man a car that belonged to Gilin's Asian houseboy Tom, who just enlisted. The encounter gives Gilin the idea for a profitable new racket: buying up used car lots and selling vehicles with refurbished tires. After a few false starts, Gilin's henchmen figure out how to make tires that look like they're made of authentic rubber. (One sidekick remarks, "Like cutting the Scotch in the old days ... just put in enough of the real thing to give it flavor.")

Now that Bill has a new car, Mary's kid brother Freddy decides to sell the vehicle he and his sister owned. He unloads it at one of Gilin's used car lots, and persuades a workers there to sell him a $10 tire, which happens to be one of the test tires rejected when the scam was being launched. On his way home, Freddy's car has a blowout and he's killed in the crash. Bill enlists his fellow plant workers to help him track down the racketeers responsible. Getting wind of the situation, Gilin enlists Nikki to chat up Bill and see what she can find out. Nikki, who likes Bill, confirms that he's on Gilin's trail, but lies to her man.

Two Gilin henchmen try to discourage Bill from pursuing justice, using their fists to make their point. Mary is frightened for him. The used car lot abruptly shuts down, and Gilin instructs his goons to take care of Bill. Nikki, her loyalties divided, calls and tips off Mary to the impending danger.

Disapproving of Gilin's latest enterprise, Nikki implores him to quit, as does houseboy Tom, home on leave. The racketeer is unmoved. Matters come to a head when Bill summons his plant worker friends for an all-out frontal assault on Gilin and his gang.

Bill Henry (1914–1982) is well-cast as the all–American good guy. Henry enjoyed a long career in films and subsequently in TV, where he continued to be active into the early 1970s. He's effectively contrasted with Ricardo Cortez (1900–1977) as the suave but ruthless Gilin, who doesn't usually get his own hands dirty, but has a cabal of henchmen always ready to do his bidding. When Nikki tries to appeal to her man's patriotism, he snarls that he doesn't go in for "that flag-waving stuff."

Rochelle is seen as Tony's lady friend Nikki, who condoned some of his earlier exploits, and does have a weakness for the jewelry with which he plies her, but balks at his latest crimes and his vendetta against Bill. Using her feminine wiles on Bill to extract information, Rochelle plays those scenes with just a touch of ambiguity, letting us wonder occasionally whether she has more than a sisterly interest in the decent young man. We don't learn much about Nikki's past, but she does say of Bill and his fiancée, "They were a couple of nice kids, like I was once." Accustomed to Gilin's duplicitous ways, she accompanies him to a nightclub the evening

Rochelle and leading man Ricardo Cortez feature prominently in this *Rubber Racketeers* (1942) lobby card.

of a planned attack on Bill, saying knowingly, "Tony, you're building an alibi." She makes Nikki's rehabilitation credible, as a woman who knows her way around a gat but does have her limits. In her closing moments, we see her confidently employ a machine-gun to drill a V for victory into a caricature of Adolf Hitler.

Chinese-American Kam Tong (1906–1969) appears as Gilin's houseboy, who's proud of his military service to the U.S. alongside other dedicated soldiers, "maybe some with whiter skin, maybe some with darker skin, but all knowing what the war is about." Alan Hale, Jr. (1921–1990), still in his early twenties, has a couple of good scenes as Bill's pal Red, more than 20 years prior to his role in *Gilligan's Island*.

Reviews: "A timely crime melodrama whose contents make it worthy of extended exploitation. It is as topical as tomorrow's headlines, and has action, romance, and a message of patriotism packed together in such fashion as to deliver a terrific wallop.... Harold Young, in his direction, uses every frame of film to advantage. The fourth production of the King Brothers, Maurice and Franklin, it is by far their best." *Motion Picture Herald*, July 4, 1942

"Current activities of tire bootleggers provides [*sic*] a topical basis for this meller of gangdom, with defense plant workers in the roles of heroes. Following familiar melodramatic trails, picture is neatly set up to accent the adventurous angles, and will provide good dual support in the secondary and family bookings.... Ricardo Cortez, Bill Henry and Rochelle Hudson carry the leads along in good style, with Harold Young's direction maintaining a speedy pace throughout. Production mounting is above par for the moderate budget outlay." *Variety*, July 1, 1942

Queen of Broadway (1942)

Rochelle Hudson (*Sherry Baker*), Buster Crabbe (*Ricky Sloane*), Paul Bryar (*Mike "Rosy" Rafferty*), Emmett Lynn (*Chris*), Donald Mayo (*Jimmy Carson*), Isabel La Mal (*Mrs. Barnett*) Blanche Rose (*Mrs. Ogilvie*), Henry Hall (*Judge Morse*), John Dilson (*Bickel*), Mil [Milton] Kibbee (*Joe*), Vince Barnett (*Schultz*), Jack Mulhall (*Bookie*), Snowflake [Fred Toones] (*Mose*)

Director: Sam Newfield. *Producer*: Bert Sternbach. *Original Story*: George Wallace Sayre. *Screenplay*: Rusty McCullough, George Wallace Sayre. *Photographer:* Jack Greenhalgh. *Sound Engineer*: Hans Weeren. *Music Score*: Leo Erdody. *Music Supervisor*: David Chudnow. *Editor*: Holbrook N. Todd. *Makeup*: Maurice Seiderman. *Set Designer*: Fred Preble. *Settings*: Harry Reif. *Assistant Director*: Melville De Lay.

Producers Releasing Corporation; released November 24, 1942. 64 minutes.

Sherry Baker is an enterprising young businesswoman who runs a successful "sports service," one that specializes in predicting the outcomes of upcoming events. Though she never bets herself, her predictions are widely publicized and her betting clients depend on her for guidance. Her 95 percent success rate is based on a mathematical system originated by her late father, a college professor whom she admits wouldn't approve of her line of work. Always at her side are her two assistants, Chris (whom she jokingly calls "Cuddles") and ex-boxer "Rosy."

Sherry is besieged for tips everywhere she goes, with her office building's

Sports agent Sherry Baker (Rochelle Hudson) and her two loyal helpers Chris (Emmett Lynn, center) and ex-pugilist Rosy (Paul Bryar) are pictured on this *Queen of Broadway* (1942) lobby card.

elevator operator and cleaning woman among those eagerly seeking her advice. But not everyone approves. Her boyfriend of three years, Ricky Sloane, is furious when she forecasts a losing season for his football team, and makes her a sizable bet.

Sherry's office is visited by a six-year-old Jimmy Carson, who says his mother sent him to place a bet. After she refuses to act as a bookie on Mrs. Carson's behalf, the boy goes home, but soon returns to announce that he was unable to rouse his mother. Rosy escorts the boy back to his apartment, where they discover that the mother has died. Rosy and Chris, who take a fatherly interest in Sherry's life, urge her to take the boy home temporarily, rather than sending to an orphanage.

Reluctantly agreeing, Sherry forms a tight bond with Jimmy and announces her intention to adopt him. It's an uphill battle, given her single-woman status and an occupation that some find unsavory. The Juvenile Court investigates her and declares her unfit to adopt him.

Hoping to help his girlfriend *and* further his own interests, Ricky appeals to the judge, who finds him a more acceptable adoptive parent than Sherry. Told his only drawback is his bachelorhood, Ricky offers a solution that seems to solve everyone's problems, but he soon realizes he and Sherry are not quite on the same page when it comes to their relationship.

As author Jerry Vermilye has noted, *Queen of Broadway* is likely to have a familiar ring to anyone who has read Damon Runyon, or seen *Little Miss Marker*, adapted from his work. From the introductory crawl, it's also easy to anticipate a certain sexist tone to the story. To wit (if not much):

> Once, on a street called Broadway, in the days before the world went mad, we knew a gal who was very unusual—as if all gals aren't very unusual! This gal's name was Sherry Baker, and her racket was telling guys what to do—as if any dame's racket isn't telling guys what to do!

That being said, this is a very likable and entertaining film, and a good showcase for Rochelle, who is allowed to display a wide range of emotions. It's a better film than its Poverty Row pedigree might lead viewers to anticipate. Rochelle's beauty and engaging smile are competently photographed, despite the tight budget, and she matches up nicely with leading man Buster Crabbe (1908–1983), whose muscular bulk looks even bulkier alongside his diminutive co-star. Child actor Donald Mayo (1935–1992), whose film credits are scant, is cute and not overly cloying as Jimmy, giving a credible performance, though he occasionally seems to be glancing away from his scene partner, as if looking for direction, or reassurance, from off-screen.

The George Wallace Sayre–Rusty McCullough screenplay tells a satisfying story in just over an hour, with some good dialogue for the players. It follows the usual clichés of its era, assuming that Sherry would be happier as a wife and mother than a successful businesswoman. As her fatherly pal Chris tells her (about 90 seconds before Jimmy comes into her life), "You stand so close to these cold figures, you can't tell if you're a machine or a woman." Still, she holds her own any time she comes up against a male authority figure, as in this exchange with her lawyer, who pooh-poohs the idea of her adopting:

> LAWYER: Of all the crazy, idiotic things, this is the craziest!
> SHERRY: I didn't come here for a lecture.
> LAWYER: You'll get one and like it.
> SHERRY: After which you'll do exactly as I say. That's why I pay you a fat yearly retainer.

Rochelle makes credible the dizzying speed with which Sherry goes from considering Jimmy a nuisance to deciding she loves him and can't bear to give him up. One or two minor continuity problems turn up, among them the first name of Judge Mason, which is John on his office door and Henry in a newspaper article on the adoption hearing. The lady investigators who handle Sherry's adoption application are, predictably, acid old crones who recommend rejecting her after just a brief encounter. There are a few quick references to World War II, as when kindhearted Sherry agrees to arrange a small bet for a woman who wants to buy a gift for her son, away in the military.

Reviews: "A pleasant program entertainment; it has human appeal, comedy, and pathos.... Although the story is not novel, one's attention is held because of the sympathy Rochelle Hudson, the heroine, awakens by her love for the child." *Harrison's Reports*, December 26, 1942

"This is a good half of a double bill, with the happy and wise-guyish touch of Broadway gambling and sentimentality mixed. As a gambling Queen, Rochelle Hudson performs well, contributing an expressive and convincing personality… [The movie is] a natural for any family audience." *Showmen's Trade Review*, November 28, 1942

Bush Pilot (1947)

Rochelle Hudson (*Hilary Ward*), Jack La Rue (*Paul Girard*), Austin Willis (*Red North*), Frank Perry (*Chuck Ward*), Joe Carr (*Andy Moodie*), Florence Kennedy (*Mrs. Ward*); Gordon Adam, Michael Lambert, Louise Campbell, Charles Emerson, Robert Christie, Jerry Rowan, Eric Clavering, Jimmie Peddie, Nancy Graham, Denis Murphy, Alene Kamins

Director: Sterling Campbell. *Producer*: Larry Cromien. *Original Story and Screenplay*: W. Scott Darling. *Additional Dialogue*: Gordon Burwash. *Dialogue Director*: John Drainie. *Associate Producer*: Jack W. Ogilvie. *Musical Score and Direction*: Samuel Hershenhoren. *Photographer*: Edward Hyland. *Operative Cameraman*: Robert Martin. *Production Manager*: Arthur Hammond. *Sound*: Edward Fenton. *Hair Stylist*: Bette Young. *Makeup*: Stephen Clensos. *Editor*: Jack Ogilvie. *Flying Sequences*: Herbert May, Ray Roy, Howard Weyman, Dorila Thereaux.

Dominion Productions; released June 7, 1947. 58 minutes.

Pilot Red North flies freelance in the Canadian village of Nouvelle, using Mrs. Ward's inn as his home base. Mrs. Ward's lovely daughter, schoolteacher Hilary, enjoys the romantic attentions of both Red and a rival, Gillespie, a nice guy who wants to marry her and take her back to Toronto where they met. Good-hearted Red's business is barely turning a profit, and two planes need frequent maintenance.

Red's livelihood is threatened by the unexpected arrival of his half-brother Paul Girard, who announces his intention of setting up a competing business. The brothers' rivalry dates back to their youth. Paul is also interested in Hilary, but she and her family, including her kid brother Chuck, resent the newcomer's attempts to horn in. Chuck, who works as Red's mechanic, aspires to be a pilot.

With Paul cutting into his business, Red accepts an offer to earn $500 by transporting nitroglycerine, over Hilary's objections. Red allows her to think he turned down the gig. When the shipment arrives at the railroad office, Red is away for the day. When Paul offers to step in and take the assignment, Chuck attempts the flight himself, with tragic consequences.

Hilary blames Red for her brother's death and makes plans to marry Gil. Despondent, Red neglects his business and worries his friends with the amount of drinking he's doing. A Toronto newspaper sponsors a drive to deliver scarlet fever vaccine to a remote Canadian location. Paul is asked to make the run, but needs to be accompanied by someone who knows the territory. Hilary fits the bill and agrees to go along. After dropping off the medicine, Paul has engine trouble on the return flight. Crashing in the wilderness, a badly injured Paul admits to Hilary that he is

Hilary (Rochelle Hudson) is taken for a ride by Paul (Jack La Rue) in *Bush Pilot* (1947).

the one who goaded her brother into making his fatal flight. Paul dies and Hilary is stranded.

A modestly entertaining film that mixes aviation thrills with personal dramas, *Bush Pilot* was shot in Canada during the summer of 1946, part of a pioneering Canadian effort to make feature films that could compete successfully with Hollywood product.[36] Dominion Productions began with an initial bankroll of $300,000, announcing its intention to make B-level movies (initially on budgets of $100,000 each, with larger expenditures anticipated as the company grew). Rochelle and her co-star Jack La Rue, along with several key crew members, were recruited from the U.S. to lend their filmmaking expertise. Ultimately, *Bush Pilot* required an outlay of $200,000, with outdoor footage shot "at Rosseau in the Muskokas north of Toronto ... [and] in the Laurentian Mountains."[37] An item in the *The* [Montreal] *Gazette* (July 10, 1946) noted that photography had just been completed on *Bush Pilot*, with a scene shot at a studio facility in the city "because it was impossible to do it on the principal location set at Lake Rosseau, Ont." Director Sterling Campbell (1896–1990) was a veteran of the Royal Canadian Air Force, and had also overseen aerial stunts on Hollywood films including *The Dawn Patrol* and *Hell's Angels* (both 1930).

W. Scott Darling's script draws on some slightly shopworn story elements, among them the fate of the fellow transporting a load of dangerous explosives. Top-billed, Rochelle has a fairly well-written romantic lead to play, with character actress Florence Kennedy, as her mother, having the only other sizable female role. The men in her life are competently played, though Canadian actor Austin Willis (1917–2004), given an "introducing" credit in the opening titles, actually outshines the Hollywood-imported La Rue. Supporting performances by a cast of mostly local talent, several of them active in the Canadian radio industry, are adequate, on a par with those found in American B films of the time.

A publicity blurb claimed, "Rochelle Hudson ... made a big hit with Canadian fashion designers during the shooting of the picture.... In Toronto, Miss Hudson exclaimed over the strides Canadian fashion designers have made since the war and modeled some of the latest attire.... In fact she added a varied selection of Canadian designed costumes to her wardrobe."[38]

Picked up by Screen Guild for distribution stateside, *Bush Pilot* didn't attract much notice from Hollywood trade papers, most of which didn't even review it. But it played around the country, usually on the bottom half of a double bill with films such as Joan Crawford's *Possessed* (1947).

Reviews: "Sterling Cambell [*sic*], director, has kept the romantic complications and the air adventures in the foreground to provide the maximum in audience interest.... Fair." *Motion Picture Herald*, November 29, 1947

"A promising newcomer to screen is Austin Willis, whose performance easily overshadows those of Rochelle Hudson and Jack LaRue [*sic*]." Dorothy Masters, *New York Daily News*, July 23, 1947

Devil's Cargo (1948)

John Calvert (*Michael "The Falcon" Watling*), Rochelle Hudson (*Margo Delgado*), Roscoe Karns (*Lt. Hardy*), Lyle Talbot (*Johnny Morello*), Theodore von Eltz (*Thomas Mallon*), Michael Mark (*Salvation Army Captain*), Tom Kennedy (*Naga*), Paul Marion (*Ramon Delgado*), Paul Regan (*Bernie Horton*), Eula Guy (*Mrs. Murphy*), Christine Larson (*Nurse*), Walter Soderling (*Coroner*), John Bagni (*Officer Bob*), Jack Conrad (*Sam*), Peggy Wynne (*Nurse*), Peter Michael (*Mr. Worthington*), Carol Janis (*Mallon's Secretary*), Fred Coby (*Fred*), Dick Bush (*Police Turnkey*), Philip Morris (*Phil*), Mike Lally (*Photographer*), "Brain Trust" (*Himself*)

Director: John F. Link. *Producer*: Philip N. Krasne. *Screenplay*: Don Martin. *Original Story*: Robert Tallman, Jason James. *Based on the Character "The Falcon" Created by* Michael Arlen. *Photographer*: Walter Strenge. *Music Director*: Paul Dessau. *Production Manager*: Dick L'Estrange. *Editor*: Asa Boyd Clark. *Sound*: Glen Glenn. *Special Effects*: Ray Mercer. *Costume Supervisor*: Donald S. Wakeling. *Makeup*: Ted Larsen.

Film Classics/Falcon Productions; released April 1, 1948. 64 minutes.

A newspaper headline announces the murder of Bruce "Lucky" Conroy, described as a "well known turfman and horse breeder." As the police investigation gets underway, private detective Michael Watling, known as "The Falcon," receives a visit at his apartment from Ramon Delgado, who calmly confesses to the crime. He gives the Falcon a $500 retainer and asks him to keep a key in his possession. Delgado claims that Conroy was harassing Mrs. Delgado (which is why Delgado killed him) and says that he will be acquitted once the police confirm this. Police Lt. Hardy takes Delgado to jail, where lawyer Thomas Mallon offers to represent him *pro bono*.

The Falcon realizes he's being tailed and makes the acquaintance of not only the glamorous Margo Delgado, but others who seem to have a stake in the case, including Conroy's business partner Johnny Morello. Margo is not at all displeased that her husband has been arrested; the nature of her relationship with the murder victim is uncertain.

It develops that there is more than one key pertinent to the case. One of them fits a locker at a nearby bowling alley. The Falcon is on the scene when it's opened, setting off a deadly explosive. Although he escapes with injuries, a minor criminal who possessed the key is killed. A second key proves to match a bank safe deposit box. While Delgado awaits trial, he's fatally poisoned on a day when his only visitor in the lockup was his wife.

The Falcon puts together the pieces of the mystery a few steps ahead of his friendly rival Lt. Hardy, then finds himself (and another suspect) at gunpoint. The situation leads to a final act of violence and a resolution to the mystery.

Though undeniably made on the cheap, *Devil's Cargo* offers a reasonably entertaining hour-plus of action, suspense and a bit of comic relief. Production began in late 1947, under the working title *The Unwritten Law*. Second-billed Rochelle is prominently featured as Margo, an elegantly coiffed but enigmatic figure whom the Falcon tells, "I can see why a man might commit murder for you." Though the film's hasty production didn't allow for top-notch cinematography, she's beautiful nonetheless. Her character's motives remain intriguingly inscrutable. Rochelle holds her own with fellow players and she has a dramatic role to play in the climactic scene.

John Calvert (1911–2013) enjoyed a long life, but a fairly brief film career, accumulating just over a dozen acting credits from the mid–1940s to the early 1950s. He played the Falcon in three low-budget vehicles, of which *Devil's Cargo* was the first. An accomplished magician in real life, Calvert uses some of his tricks on-camera to enhance his portrayal of the Falcon. Usually with a cigarette in his hand, the character effortlessly charms every woman who appears on the scene, including the nurse who attends him after the explosion. Eliciting her sympathy with his supposed groans of pain, he explains, "It hurts me to think we've never met before. I like nurses. They know all the answers." At home, his Irish landlady Mrs. Murphy clearly has a soft spot for him, but his greatest affection seems to be reserved for his pet dog, known as "Brain Trust." The film comes full circle, as we first meet the Falcon stretched out comfortably in his bathtub when Delgado arrives unexpectedly; when the curtain falls, he's enjoying another soak while performing one last bit of legerdemain for yet another walk-in visitor, Lt. Hardy.

The film benefits from the participation of several old pros, among them Lyle

Talbot and Roscoe Karns (1891–1970), the latter cast as the hapless Lt. Hardy. Karns would soon take his copper act to TV, starring in *Rocky King, Detective*. Veteran character player Michael Mark (1886–1975), perhaps best-known for his small role in *Frankenstein* (1931), gets better billing than his one-scene cameo as a worker at the Salvation Army merits.

Boxoffice (May 1, 1948) reported that the film's distributor Film Classics "has lined up 20 dates for a package show consisting of the picture, *Devil's Cargo*, and a show review headed by the film's star, John Calvert." Starting in the Charlotte, North Carolina, area, the combination was to be extended to other parts of the country if sufficiently successful.

In *Motion Picture Herald*'s "What the Picture Did for Me" column (December 25, 1948), an Indiana exhibitor complained, "This series picture died for us. ...It lacks action enough to suit our patrons."

Reviews: "John Calvert ... evidently has seen several of Ronald Colman's pictures. For either by coincidence or design, he apes Mr. Colman's mannerisms, speech, intonations, etc., in a disturbing manner.... The story itself is a fairly good mystery, nicely played by Rochelle Hudson ... and others in the cast ... but it suffers badly because of poor photography. *Devil's Cargo* will do okay as supporting fare on double-bill programs." *Showmen's Trade Review*, March 20, 1948

"In a minor category this one stacks up as adequate whodunit fare with all the proper trimmings and enough in the way of story invention to sustain spectator interest.... Piece is played out with suitable performances.... It has movement pace [sic]." *Film Daily*, March 16, 1948

Sky Liner (1949)

Richard Travis (*Steve Blair*), Pamela Blake (*Carol*), Rochelle Hudson (*Amy Winthrop*), Steven Geray (*Bokejian*), Gaylord [Steve] Pendleton (*Smith*), Ralph Peters (*Joe Kirk*), Michael Whalen (*Ben Howard*), Greg McClure (*J.S. Conningsby*), Lisa Ferraday (*Mariette Le Fare*), Roy Butler (*Mr. Jennings*), Jean Clark (*Mrs. Jennings*), David Holt (*Buford*), Dodie Bauer (*Grace Ward*), William Leicester (*Captain Fairchild*), Herbert Evans (*Sir Harry Finneston*), Anna May Slaughter (*Mary Ann*), Bess Flowers (*Mother*), John McGuire (*George Eakins*), Alan Hersholt (*Courier*), Jack Mulhall (*Col. Hanson*), George Meeker (*Financier*), Jean Sorel (*Second Stewardess*), Burt Wenland (*Co-Pilot*)

Director: William Berke. *Executive Producer*: Robert Lippert. *Producer*: William Stephens. *Screenplay*: Maurice Tombragel. *Original Story*: John Wilste. *Photographer*: Carl Berger. *Special Effects*: Howard Weeks. *Editor*: Edward Mann. *Art Director*: Martin Obzina. *Set Decorator*: Ray Robinson. *Property Master*: Leigh Carson. *Assistant Director*: Melville Shyer. *Music Supervisor*: David Chudnow. *Musical Composer and Director*: Raoul Kraushaar. *Dialogue Director*: Stanley Price. *Sound*: William Randall, Frank Moran. *Stillman*: Stack Graves. *Makeup*: Earl Young.

Lippert Pictures/Screen Guild Productions; released July 28, 1949. 61 minutes.

George Eakins of the U.S. State Department, preparing for a trip from New York to Los Angeles, awaits the delivery of a set of confidential instructions. His secretary, Amy Winthrop, admits a man who seems to be the expected courier, but he hits Eakins over the head with a blackjack. Amy then goes to a telephone and reports to an accomplice.

At the airport, Amy checks in for Constellation Flight 153 and is joined by a man named Smith, who is posing as Eakins. The phony Eakins asks the ticket agent about purchasing a ticket for a friend who will join the flight in Chicago. The man in question, a Mr. Bokejian, is seemingly a diplomatic envoy from a foreign country, bargaining for oil and mineral rights. Boarding the plane, Smith tells Amy that he hit Eakins too hard and killed him.

The pilot and flight crew are alerted that there is a federal man aboard, and that they must cooperate with him. Meanwhile, various passengers think back on their own lives, including a jewel thief who killed a wealthy man during a burglary, and Ben Howard, who left an I.O.U. for $1500 he took without authorization from a finance company. Bokejian joins the flight at its Chicago stopover and chats with Sir Harry Finneston who, like Bokejian, is headed for a diplomatic conference. Smith and Bokejian meet surreptitiously in the washroom, where they haggle over a price for the documents the latter wants. Bokejian opens the sealed State Department envelope, only to find that it contains blank sheets of official letterhead.

Smith is found dead in the washroom. Federal agent Steve Blair, consulting with the pilot, arranges for the plane to set down at an army base where the body can be removed and examined. The plane resumes its flight, with Blair having set in place a plan to have it met on landing and all passengers detained. After the autopsy is complete, the doctor sends word to Blair that the dead man was injected with a fountain pen containing ink laced with curare. Blair is also informed that the real George Eakins was found dead in his office. Passengers are notified that they will be questioned when the plane lands in Burbank, which comes as unnerving news to more than one of them.

Amy admits to Steve that the dead man, Smith, was her husband. He acknowledges that she has been under investigation as an espionage agent for some time, but she refuses to disclose her reasons. Upon arrival, the plane is met by law enforcement officials, but one passenger stages a desperate getaway attempt after a violent attack on Steve.

Sky Liner is a fairly forgettable programmer that packs most of its action into the last couple of reels. Even at this brief running time, it has some dull spots, and for much of the running time the story is disjointed, with various characters doing vaguely suspicious things for reasons not entirely clear. Executive producer Robert L. Lippert (1909–1976) was a prolific and successful maker of B movies, but this is not one of his better efforts. The same could be said of director William Berke (1903–1958), a veteran of multiple Pine-Thomas films of the 1940s. He does, at least, keep the action moving as much as possible, given the talky screenplay. The film was released on DVD, somewhat misleadingly, as part of a "Forgotten Noir" package.

Trans World Airlines furnished uncredited "production assistance" to give *Sky Liner* the ambience of air travel, with documentary footage, and, as a result, some far-from-subtle product placement throughout the film. Set decorator Ray Robinson seems to have been given a budget in the low three figures, resulting in cramped, shabby-looking sets for a State Department office and the check-in counter at a New York airport, among others. An airplane washroom, which had better reason to be tiny, is the setting for several key scenes, while the scenes between the flight crew and stewardess Carol take place on a cockpit set that's better than the one in Edward D. Wood's *Plan 9 from Outer Space* (1958)—but not by a lot. At least no one talks about "balling it up in Albuquerque."

Rochelle has what could have been a juicy role as an espionage agent, but the script and production values don't really rise to the occasion. She's photographed rather poorly, and looks a bit tired and worn, though she was still only in her early thirties. Disappointingly, she doesn't figure significantly into the finale. Other performances are mostly competent. Pamela Blake (1915–2009), cast as the good-girl stewardess, already had experience with low-budget films and serials, and handles her undemanding role capably. Top-billed Richard Travis (1913–1989) makes an adequate if unremarkable hero.

The DVD release of *Sky Liner* seems to be missing some footage described in reviews at the time of the film's release, including some of Anna May Slaughter's performance as a precocious child-star-to-be, though the running time remains the same as given in *Variety*'s review. This was Rochelle's last theatrical film for six years.

Reviews: "There is excitement and suspense in this story of espionage and murder aboard a plane carrying a varied assortment of crooks and other passengers.... This picture should please as a second feature on any program.... Richard Travis, Pamela Blake and Rochelle Hudson do quite well in the leading roles.... Direction by William Berke keeps the action going." *Showmen's Trade Review*, August 6, 1949

"*Sky Liner* plots all its action aboard a west-bound transcontinental plane and proves to be an okay lowercase subject for secondary bookings.... William Berke's direction keeps the pot boiling at a good clip before bringing on the gun-blazing climax when justice is served. Travis does an expert, likable chore as the G-man [while] Rochelle Hudson and Gaylord Pendleton are the crooks." *Variety*, August 3, 1949

Roots in the Soil (1949)

Richard Travis, Michael Whalen, Rochelle Hudson, Clara Blandick
Director: Wallace Fox. *Story*: James P. Prindle.
Wilding Picture Productions; released September 12, 1949. 61 minutes.

As an article in *Business Screen* magazine (Vol. 11, No. 4, 1950) explained, Deere and Company, manufacturers of farm equipment, had been a pioneer in the use of industrial films. It regularly sponsored "John Deere Day" events in rural communities, free to attend, at which attendees could watch movies that centered on farm life, receive a free lunch and, not incidentally, get information on Deere products. *Roots in the Soil* "tells the human interest story of a small time banker." A blurb in the *Chillicothe* (Ohio) *Gazette and News-Advertiser* (March 3, 1950) elaborated:

> *Roots in the Soil* is the story of a small-town bank cashier (Richard Travis) who can't say "no" to anyone with a hard-luck story. His generosity affects the lives of his wife (Rochelle Hudson), his three children, in fact the entire community, though it sometimes backfires. You and your family will enjoy every minute of this true-to-life story plus the beautiful singing of a chorus of nearly fifty voices.

Director Wallace Fox (1895–1958) was experienced in the making of low-budget films, having toiled extensively in Poverty Row productions of the 1940s. His better-known titles include *The Corpse Vanishes* (1942) as well as several entries in the East Side Kids series.

Rebel Without a Cause (1955)

James Dean (*Jim Stark*), Natalie Wood (*Judy*), Sal Mineo (*John "Plato" Crawford*), Jim Backus (*Frank Stark*), Ann Doran (*Carol Stark*), Corey Allen (*Buzz Gunderson*), William Hopper (*Judy's Father*), Rochelle Hudson (*Judy's Mother*), Dennis Hopper (*Goon*), Edward Platt (*Ray Fremick*), Steffi Sidney (*Mil*), Marietta Canty (*Crawford Family Maid*), Virginia Brissac (*Mrs. Stark*), Beverly Long (*Helen*), Ian Wolfe (*Dr. Minton*), Frank Mazzola (*Crunch*), Robert Foulk (*Gene*), Jack Simmons (*Cookie*), Tom Bernard (*Harry*), Nick Adams (*Chick*), Jack Grinnage (*Moose*), Clifford Morris (*Cliff*), Jimmy Baird (*Beau*), Paul Birch (*Police Chief*), David McMahon (*Crunch's Father*), Dick Wessel (*Planetarium Guide*), Robert B. Williams (*Ed*), Almira Sessions (*Elderly Teacher*), Dorothy Abbott (*Nurse*), Peter Miller (*Hoodlum*), Ralph Moratz (*Schoolboy at Planetarium*), Louise Lane (*Policewoman*), Paul Bryar, Chuck Hamilton, Nelson Leigh (*Desk Sergeants*)

Director: Nicholas Ray. *Producer*: David Weisbart. *Screenplay*: Stewart Stern. *Adaptation*: Irving Shulman. *Story*: Nicholas Ray. *Photographer*: Ernest Haller. *Art Director*: Malcolm Bert. *Editor*: William Ziegler. *Sound*: Stanley Jones. *Set Decorator*: William Wallace. *Costumes*: Moss Mabry. *Makeup Supervisor*: Gordon Bau. *Dialogue Supervisor*: Dennis Stock. *Assistant Directors*: Don Page, Robert Farfan. *Music*: Leonard Rosenman.

Warner Bros.; released October 29, 1955. 111 minutes.

Teenager Jim Stark is hauled into the juvenile division of a Los Angeles police station late one evening, after being picked up for being drunk. Also being questioned by the cops that night are two other adolescents, pretty Judy and the diminutive Plato. All come from good families and live in nice homes, but seem to lack strong parental guidance. The department's Ray Fremick has sympathy for Jim, who has an ineffectual father and sharply critical mother.

Still new in the area, Jim doesn't fit in well with the other high school students, though both Judy and Plato offer him their friendship. But Buzz Gunderson and his gang of followers hassle Jim. Goaded into a knife fight with Buzz, Jim goes home with blood on his shirt, but his father can't seem to provide the parenting he needs. At Judy's house, the beautiful 16-year-old is coldly rejected by her father when she tries to be affectionate with him.

Jim agrees to participate in a "chickie run" to settle his score with Buzz, without knowing exactly what the event will be. He finds himself racing a car toward a nearby cliff, with Buzz doing the same. The first to jump free is to be declared the "chicken." At the last second, Buzz's jacket gets hung up on the door handle, preventing him from escaping, and he plunges with the car into the canyon. Jim feels he should admit his participation to the police, but his parents are less certain. His mother declares they should move again, as they have previously done when Jim was in trouble.

In danger from Buzz's friends, Plato takes his mother's gun in case the three need to defend themselves. At the vacant mansion where they're hiding out, while Jim and Judy acknowledge their love for one another. When the hoodlums break into their hiding place, Plato shoots one of them. Jim tries to manage a safe outcome with the help of his police friend, but tragedy strikes.

One of the most iconic American films of the 1950s, if not the 20th century altogether, *Rebel Without a Cause* shocked many moviegoers upon its initial release with its story of disaffected teenagers acting out against a society that seemingly has failed them. Production began in late March 1955. When principal photography began, *Rebel* was being shot in black-and-white, but studio executives approved an upgrade to color early in the production schedule. Studio publicity said it dealt with "today's most vital controversy."

The film's impact on younger Americans was heightened by the September 30, 1955, death of star James Dean, age 24, nearly a month prior to its release. Dean, Natalie Wood (1938–1981) and Sal Mineo (1939–1976) received critical acclaim for their performances. All three died at a relatively young age, with Mineo murdered and Wood drowned. Unusual for Hollywood films of the period, the latter two were both actually teenagers at the time they were cast in *Rebel*.

Dean's enormously influential performance as Jim Stark resulted from an especially close collaboration with director Nicholas Ray; Dean was given considerable leeway in depicting his character. According to authors Lawrence Frascella and Al Weisel, the adult actors cast as parents in *Rebel* found the director's working methods unsettling. "Although they all possessed long Hollywood resumes, none of them had ever experienced anything like the atmosphere of improvisation and borderline anarchy that reigned on the *Rebel* set."[39]

Although being cast as the female lead's mother might suggest a fairly prominent featured role, Rochelle's is actually a rather minor and underdeveloped character. Stewart Stern's screenplay describes her as "an attractive, brittle woman of thirty-five." Some 20 years after she played teenage girls involved with young men on the outskirts of society, Rochelle had now, just shy of 40, graduated to playing the mother of such characters. In an early scene, before we've met Judy's parents, she says sorrowfully of her father, "He calls me a dirty tramp," and she reacts strongly when she's told it's her mother, rather than her father, who will pick her up at the police station.

Rochelle makes her entrance 40 minutes into the film, when we get our first glimpse of Judy's home life. The pretty teen, coming into the dining room, tries to snuggle up to her dad as she has in the past, but he rejects her firmly, telling her she's now too old to cuddle with him. When she persists, he slaps her. Given little dialogue in this scene, Rochelle mostly acts with her eyes and facial expression, seen in medium close-ups primarily as an observer at the tense scene, when it's not being shot on the back on her head. After Judy storms out, the mother tries to console her spouse, saying, "It's just the age where nothing fits." From that point forward, we see little of Judy's parents; Rochelle is glimpsed a few times in the master bedroom, sharing with Hopper the typical twin beds commonplace for husbands and wives of that era's TV and films.

Frascella and Weisel describe Hudson's character as "something of a cardboard cutout of the typical 1950s mom, imported directly from an early sitcom."[40] In fact, like co-star Jim Backus, who had just finished a three-year run in TV's *I Married Joan* (1952–55), Rochelle came to the film after production ceased on her CBS series *That's My Boy* (1954–55). Her casting in *Rebel* was announced in March 1955. It was to be her first feature film in six years. Her on-screen husband, William Hopper, would soon make a name for himself in TV as well, spending nine seasons playing private detective Paul Drake on *Perry Mason* (1957–66). Although the casting of experienced TV performers in the parental roles may be no more than happenstance, it does somewhat suggest the notion that Jim Stark and his rebellious classmates are pushing back against the small-screen version of family life, as exemplified by the likes of Ozzie and Harriet and the Cleavers. It could also be noted that Wood was herself a veteran of a family sitcom, *The Pride of the Family*, which had a short run in 1953–54.

Not surprisingly, *Rebel Without a Cause* was subject to censorship battles, with two particular sticking points being the implication of Plato's attachment to Jim Stark, at a time when any portrayal of homosexuality was strictly taboo, and the screenplay's depiction of Judy's relationship with her father, which some interpreted as incestuous in nature.

Rebel Without a Cause was named to the National Film Registry in 1990, part of the second wave of films so honored.

Reviews: "A sharp, biting study of juvenile delinquency ... violent and realistic in all aspects—dialogue, action and suspense.... This is not light, frothy entertainment, but a heavy dramatic effort which is a penetrating inspection of emotions and motives in the lives of the characters.... The portrayals by the youngsters are effective. Others in the cast are Rochelle Hudson and William Hopper, who portray the lackadaisical parents of Miss Wood...." *Motion Picture Daily*, October 26, 1955

"An unpleasant but visually gripping juvenile delinquency melodrama.... Although it is frequently brutal and shocking in its depiction of juvenile violence, it probably will prove to be an outstanding box office attraction by reason of the fact that it stars James Dean.... All in all, it is a picture that is tense and disturbing ... but does not present the problem with powerful dramatic impact, nor does it effectively suggest how the problem might be combatted." *Harrison's Reports*, October 22, 1955

Strait-Jacket (1964)

Joan Crawford (*Lucy Harbin*), Diane Baker (*Carol Cutler*), Leif Erickson (*Bill Cutler*), Howard St. John (*Raymond Fields*), John Anthony Hayes (*Michael Fields*), Rochelle Hudson (*Emily Cutler*), George Kennedy (*Leo Krause*), Edith Atwater (*Alison Fields*), Mitchell Cox (*Dr. Anderson*), Lee Majors (*Frank Harbin*), Vicki Cos (*Young Carol*), Patricia Crest (*Stella Fulton*), Lynn Lundgren (*Beautician*), Robert Ward (*Shoe Clerk*)

Producer-Director: William Castle. *Screenplay*: Robert Bloch. *Photographer*: Arthur Arling. *Music*: Van Alexander. *Production Designer*: Boris Leven. *Editor*: Edwin Bryant. *Set Decorator*: Frank Tuttle. *Assistant Director*: Herbert Greene. *Miss Crawford's Makeup*: Monte Westmore. *Miss Crawford's Hair Styles*: Peggy Shannon. *Makeup*: Ben Lane. *Hair Stylist*: Virginia Jones. *Sound Supervisor*: Charles J. Rice. *Sound*: Lambert Day. *Special Effects*: Richard Albain.

Columbia; released January 8, 1964. 93 minutes.

Middle-aged Lucy Harbin is being released from the mental institution where she has been for some 20 years, after killing her unfaithful husband and his lover with an axe. Her daughter Carol, now a young woman, witnessed the murders as a child, but was taken cross-country to live with Lucy's brother Bill and his wife Emily on their farm. Carol tells her boyfriend, Michael Fields, about her mother's past, but he assures her it makes no difference to him.

Lucy is anxious and ill at ease when the Cutlers welcome her home, uncertain she can fit in. She is pleased to learn that Carol has a promising career as a sculptor, with a studio space at the farm. Carol encourages her mother to update her drab appearance, buying for her a wig and a dress that make her resemble the way she looked 20 years earlier.

Lucy awakens the household one night shrieking, claiming she found decapitated heads in her bed. Bill assures her it was just a nightmare, but Emily suggests that a call to Lucy's doctor would be wise. Carol insists her mother just needs rest and kindness. Although Lucy grew up on a farm, the atmosphere at the Cutlers' makes her tense, as when she sees seedy hired man Leo Krause slaughter a chicken with an axe. At the home of Michael's wealthy parents, Carol informs them that her mother, long an invalid, is now living with them. Her reticence makes the snobbish Mrs. Fields suspect there is more to the story.

Carol is eager for Lucy to meet Michael, but when she does, she's halfway drunk and acts inappropriately, flirting with her daughter's handsome man. Her mood abruptly changes when her physician, Dr. Anderson, arrives for a visit, en route to a fishing vacation. Dr. Anderson cautions Carol that, for her mother, revisiting the past is dangerous. While he's taking a look around the property, Dr. Anderson is killed by an unseen axe-wielding attacker.

When Carol returns from an outing with Michael, Lucy tells her the doctor left earlier, but his car is still there. Carol puts it in a shed, but Leo takes it out and begins to repaint it, claiming it is now his. He just laughs when Carol tries to fire him, suggesting that she can't afford to alienate him. Not long afterwards, he too falls victim to the assailant.

The Cutlers and Lucy are invited to dinner at the home of Michael's parents, but the evening goes poorly. Lucy lets it slip that the young couple is engaged, and Mrs. Fields insists a marriage can never take place. When Mrs. Fields challenges Lucy to tell the truth about her confinement, Lucy runs out in humiliation. After their guests have gone, there's violence at the Fields house. A surprise is awaiting almost everyone as to the identity of the killer.

Strait-Jacket is a campy, no-holds-barred thriller by the happy schlockmeister, William Castle (1914–1977), whose horror flicks packed 'em in during the late 1950s and early 1960s. Robert Bloch's script is rife with illogical twists and turns but director Castle is really only interested in serving up a carnival atmosphere where the patrons can shriek at regular intervals. His approach to filmmaking is perhaps best exemplified by the closing shot, in which the Columbia Pictures torch lady is headless, her head sitting at her feet.

Previously reliant on promotional gimmicks to sell tickets, Castle drew on star power for the first time with *Strait-Jacket*, casting Academy Award winner Joan Crawford (1905–1977) as Lucy Harbin. Though Crawford goes balls-to-the-wall when the scene calls for it (as when she bellows at Mrs. Fields that her time in the asylum was "20 years of pure hell!"), she adds another dimension to the rather exploitative film by giving her character a vulnerable and deeply emotional quality. Even amidst the rampant camp, some of her moments, as when she is first reunited with her daughter, are surprisingly touching.

Rochelle has a sizable featured role as Emily, Lucy's pragmatic sister-in-law, who provides the voice of reason in an enterprise where it's in short supply. Usually clothed in nondescript outfits befitting a farmer's wife, she is deglamorized but still an attractive woman in her late forties. *Strait-Jacket* was her final meaningful role in a major studio release, as her subsequent two films failed to make good use of her talents.

Given a showier role than Rochelle, Edith Atwater (1911–1986) is icily proper as Michael's wary mother, while Leif Erickson (1911–1986) and Howard St. John (1905–1974) are satisfactory in the less interesting male roles. Diane Baker (born 1938) capably handles the role of Lucy's daughter Carol. Having worked previously with Crawford, she stepped into the role at the eleventh hour, after director Castle and his star determined that the originally chosen Anne Helm was not delivering a satisfactory performance (a decision the latter blamed on Miss Crawford's desire to have Baker in the role). Lee Majors (born 1939) makes his film debut in the minor role of Lucy's husband, who is hacked to death before the opening titles roll.

Reviews: "A William Castle vehicle that serves up so many horror (and horrible) clichés with numerous disembodied noggins that the result is an unintentional comedy.... If [Crawford's character] doesn't belong in a strait-jacket, the picture does. It is wild, hard to believe and tedious to witness.... The acting may be atrocious but it's good to have Rochelle Hudson on hand even if she's not more worthily engaged." Margaret Harford, *Los Angeles Times*, January 10, 1964

"*Strait-Jacket* ought to make a fortune for producer-director William Castle.... Though the film is riddled with perforations, it nevertheless achieves its aim—it is a shocker, one of the most horrifying horror films I have seen in quite a while. This does not, let me remind you, mean that I think it is a work of art. It is not—but if horror is your kind of movie fare (and it seems to be what many are looking for) you can't go far wrong with *Strait-Jacket*.... Miss Crawford ... does some very classy acting—as though she sincerely believes an actress must do her best whatever the circumstances." Louis R. Cedrone, Jr., *Evening Sun* (Baltimore), January 17, 1964

The Night Walker (1964)

Robert Taylor (*Barry Morland*), Barbara Stanwyck (*Irene Trent*), Judith [Judi] Meredith (*Joyce Holliday*), Hayden Rorke (*Howard Trent*), Rochelle Hudson (*Hilda*), Lloyd Bochner (*The Dream*), Marjorie Bennett (*Apartment Manager*), Jess Barker (*Malone*), Tetsu Komai (*Gardener*), Kathleen Mulqueen (*Beauty Salon Customer*)

Producer-Director: William Castle. *Screenplay*: Robert Bloch. *Associate Producer*: Dona Holloway. *Photographer*: Harold E. Stine. *Art Directors*: Alexander Golitzen, Frank Arrigo. *Set Decorators*: John McCarthy, Julia Heron. *Sound*: Waldon O. Watson, David Moriarty. *Music*: Vic Mizzy. *Music Supervisor*: Joseph Gershenson. *Unit Production Manager*: Herman Webber. *Editor*: Edwin H. Bryant. *Costumes*: Helen Colvig. *Makeup*: Bud Westmore. *Hair Stylist*: Larry Germain. *Assistant Director*: Terence Nelson.

Universal; released December 30, 1964. 86 minutes.

Wealthy Howard Trent summons lawyer Barry Morland to his home. Howard, blind and disfigured, plays for Barry a recording he has made of his wife Irene talking in her sleep, and tells the attorney he thinks Irene is having an affair. Barry points out that Irene never leaves the house, but Howard makes it clear he thinks Barry is her lover.

Outside Howard's presence, Irene tells Barry that she dreams every night of a handsome young man she has never met. After Barry leaves, an angry Howard confronts Irene, demanding that she admit to her extramarital relationship. She tells him she only dreams of a better man than him, and storms off. Moments later, there is an explosion in the house.

An arson investigator tells Irene that the damage was limited to Howard's laboratory, and that her husband's body wasn't found. That night, Irene dreams that she hears the tapping of Howard's cane, then sees an explosion in the laboratory. She finds her late husband, gruesomely burned.

Irene tells Barry she can no longer live in the house. She decides to move back into the apartment behind the beauty shop she still owns. Instead of getting a good night's sleep, she's again visited by the dream man. She tells Barry she's beginning to have difficulty distinguishing between dreams and reality. When Barry asks her if she killed Howard, Irene slaps his face.

Visited by her dream man, Irene is escorted to a chapel where he tells her they are to be married. In a horrifying tableau, the minister and wedding guests are wax figures, and Howard emerges as she screams in terror. The next day, she implores

Barry to help her, and together they locate the apartment where she and the dream man drank champagne. Barry tells her that the building belongs to Irene's late husband, but the apartment is now vacant, and the manager says she has never met Irene or the dream man she describes. Barry tries to tell her she is only remembering nightmares. Irene feels vindicated when she finds the wedding ring she was given on the floor of the deserted chapel. After they leave the chapel, the dream man emerges from hiding, phones the beauty salon and tells its new young employee Joyce that their plans must change.

Visiting the Trents' former home, Barry finds a tape recorder playing a conversation between Howard and a private detective he hired; the detective assures his client that his wife is not having an affair. After nearly being hit by a dart thrown by an unseen person, Barry phones Irene, but Joyce intercepts his call. Irene's dream man enters Howard's laboratory, finding the wax figures from Irene's wedding nightmare, and a tape recording of the ceremony.

When Irene finally reaches Barry, they head out for a final meeting at the Trent house, where she will finally learn the disturbing secrets behind her terrifying dreams.

Less satisfying than *Strait-Jacket*, *The Night Walker* is an odd hybrid that seems to find Castle beginning to crave respectability. While it has its moments as a thriller, it ultimately fails to satisfy either those looking for a well-made Stanwyck-Taylor movie, or those seeking a good scare. After a while, it begins to resemble a carnival spook show, in which the horror ultimately fails to resonate because it is so patently phony.

Having learned from *Strait-Jacket* and its star Joan Crawford the benefit of using a great classic actress in his films, Castle relies on Barbara Stanwyck (1907–1990) to bring this story to life, with the added promotional gimmick of teaming her with her real-life ex-husband, Robert Taylor (1911–1969). Miss Stanwyck has an aura of rock-solid practicality and grit that initially make her seem slightly miscast as a woman who may be on the verge of a nervous breakdown. When she does give way to fright, her screams are startlingly real, seemingly ripped from her gut. This was her last feature film, though she continued acting for another two decades, concentrating her efforts on television. Though Miss Stanwyck is clearly playing the central character here, she ceded top billing to Taylor.

Screenwriter Robert Bloch (1917–1994), something of a marquee name himself after *Psycho* (1960), contributes another script for Castle that has echoes of his *Strait-Jacket* story. It has some good set pieces, but ultimately doesn't cohere. Vic Mizzy (1916–2009), who created some of 1960s TV's most memorable theme songs (*Green Acres*, *The Addams Family*), provides a musical score that occasionally seems better-suited to *The Ghost and Mr. Chicken*.

Despite fairly prominent billing, Rochelle is largely wasted in an unimportant role as Hilda, one of the beauty shop workers. She is given very little to do; her most memorable line comes at the end of a busy workday, when she says with a sigh,

"Another day, another dollar," an attitude that nicely sums up her participation in *The Night Walker*.

Hayden Rorke (1910–1987), just a few months short of being cast in his best-known role, as Dr. Bellows on TV's *I Dream of Jeannie*, successfully conveys Howard's cold menace. Veteran character actress Marjorie Bennett (1896–1982) is charmingly odd in her brief role as an apartment manager.

Strait-Jacket had been quite successful the previous year, but *The Night Walker* failed to measure up. As Castle admitted, "The picture played to almost empty theatres."[41]

Reviews: "[*The Night Walker*] lacks much of the excitement and surprise elements found in some of [Castle's] earlier shows, but it does retain the mediocre dialogue and absence of interesting characterizations.... Most of his movies are little more than vehicles for shock sequences which Castle must hire some psychotic to dream up.... ...It is really annoying to see two really talented stars in such shallow and undemanding roles, but, I guess they feel that the money is worth the humiliation." Ann Bordelon, *Austin* (Texas) *American*, January 29, 1965

"The suspense is maintained as it was in the old, equally corny thrillers like *The Cat and the Canary*, which also kept you in a constant state of apprehension.... Shock is piled upon shock by that old master of the chiller, William Castle. The film is tailored for the addicts of horror, who will gratefully overlook any defects in dialogue or logic." Kay Wahl, *Oakland Tribune*, February 11, 1965

Gallery of Horror (1967)

Lon Chaney (*Dr. Mendell*), John Carradine (*Host/Tristram Halbin*), Rochelle Hudson (*Helen Spalding*), Roger Gentry (*Bob Farrell/Mob Leader/Dr. Sevard/Jonathan Harker*), Ron Doyle (*Brenner/Dr. Charles Spalding/Dr. Cushing*), Karen Joy (*Julie Farrell/Medina*), Vic McGee (*Dr. Finchley/Desmond/Amos Duncan/The Burgermeister*), Ron Brogan (*Marsh*), Margaret Moore (*Mrs. O'Shea*), Gray Daniels (*Coachman*), Mitch Evans (*Count Alucard*), Joey Benson (*Dr. Sedgewick*)

Director: David L. Hewitt. *Producers*: David L. Hewitt, Ray Dorn. *Screenplay*: David Prentiss [David L. Hewitt], Gary R. Heacock. *Original Stories*: Russ Jones. *Associate Producer*: Gary R. Heacock. *Photographer*: Austin McKinney. *Art Director*: Ray Dorn. *Editor*: Tim Hinkle. *Lighting Director*: John McNichols. *Recordist*: Jay Hathaway. *Set Construction*: A-1 Studio Service. *Makeup*: Jean Lister [Hewitt]. *Music and Sound Effects*: Commercial Sound Recorders. *Re-recording*: United Pictures Sound Studios. *Script Supervisor*: Jean Hewitt.

American General Pictures; released April 1967. 83 minutes.

On-screen host John Carradine introduces five short horror stories: "The Witches' Clock," "King Vampire," "Spark of Life," "Count Dracula" and "Monster Raid."

The latter begins with loyal servant Desmond calling on his late, and now entombed, employer Dr. Charles Spalding. A decrepit Dr. Spalding, long in a state of suspended animation, crawls out of his coffin and heads for his former home. Flashbacks show that Dr. Spalding had been working on a formula to locate and harness the "spark of life" that animated creatures such as zombies and werewolves. His assistant James Sevard is having an affair with Spalding's wife Helen. Helen has fallen for James, but fears he may be using her as a pawn while he attempts to learn Dr. Spalding's scientific secrets. When Dr. Sevard balks at being the guinea pig for testing the formula, Dr. Spalding decides to try it on himself. Dr. Sevard injects such a powerful dose of the serum into the older doctor that he is rendered seemingly lifeless, and the lovers proceed to have him buried. With Dr. Spalding out of the way, Helen and James are free to be together—until a terrible creature invades the laboratory, seeking revenge.

Gallery of Horror went by more names than a bad-check artist. At various times, it saw release in theaters, on TV or on video as *Return from the Past*, *The Blood Suckers* and *Dr. Terror's Gallery of Horror*. It attempted to ride on the coattails of other horror anthologies that were popular in the mid–1960s, but this awesomely cheap product relies upon a weak script, minimal sets, stock footage and some highly amateurish acting.

Rochelle's last film role is a rather sad coda to her career. Though she was given an above-the-title credit, something that seldom happened in her earlier days, it would have taken far more than that to redeem *Gallery of Horror*. She acts mostly opposite Roger Gentry (1934–2013) as her duplicitous young lover, doing her best

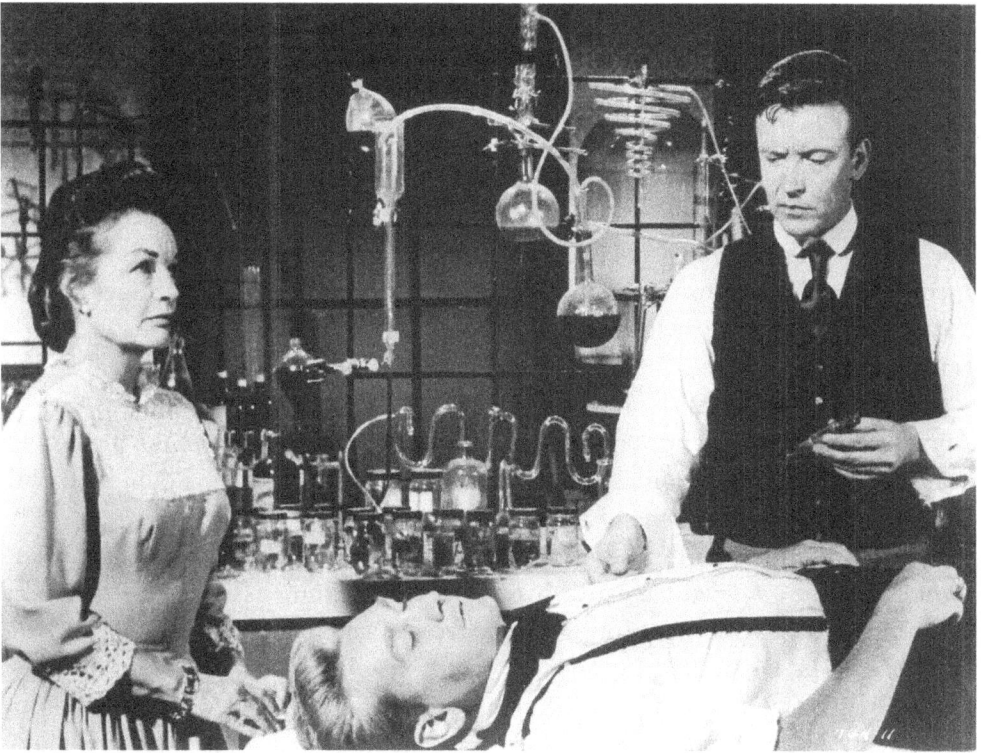

Gallery of Horrors: Helen Spalding (Rochelle Hudson) watches uncertainly as her lover, Dr. Sevard (Roger Gentry), administers a powerful drug to her husband Charles (Ron Doyle).

with the stodgy, declamatory dialogue she has to recite. ("Sometimes I wonder about your intentions, James.... I think you're just using me as a pawn, to find out everything Charles knows.") The segment is lengthened with stock footage of a figure representing Dr. Spalding racing home via horse-drawn carriage, while actor Ron Doyle (born 1934) sneers corny voiceover about "my faithful wife" and her lover.

Though several of the actors appear as different characters in different episodes, Rochelle is confined to "Monster Raid." Actor-writer Russ Jones, who wrote the original stories, didn't recall how she came to be involved in the project: "I don't know if she was looking to 'come back' or if she was simply looking just to do something. I just remember her as being very sweet."[42] He recalled that her episode ended more abruptly and unsatisfyingly than the others because she objected to the scripted denouement, which called for the monster to embrace her and sneer, "Now give your husband a great big kiss." Jones wasn't present when the scene was filmed, but he was later told, "Rochelle Hudson said she didn't want to be on-screen with the corpse."[43] It's unlikely that she was on the set for more than a single day.

Her leading man Roger Gentry gives a somewhat stiff and uncertain performance; most of the rest of his film résumé is comprised of titles like *Marsha, the Erotic Housewife* (1970) and *The Thing with Two Heads* (1972). Ron Doyle, cast as the vengeful Dr. Spalding, played minor roles in numerous episodes of TV's *The F.B.I.* In terms of quality, this film was a long way down from *Les Misérables* (1935), in which John Carradine had been seen briefly.

Director David L. Hewitt was at the helm of several low-budget horror and sci-fi films in the 1960s, including *The Wizard of Mars, The Mighty Gorga* and *Journey to the Center of Time*. Though he won few plaudits for his time in the director's chair, he was also a busy purveyor of visual and special effects, with much bigger films (*Willow, Honey, I Shrunk the Kids*) on his résumé in that capacity. Scenarist Jones was then primarily known as the creator of the horror comic book *Creepy*. Jones donned the makeup to assume the role of the monstrous Dr. Spalding in "Monster Raid"'s crypt scene.

Though an exact release date for the film is elusive, it had playdates as early as April 1967 in Arizona, and was screened through much of the summer, more often than not in drive-ins. It often appeared on the bottom half of a double bill with Hewitt's *Journey to the Center of Time*.

Reviews: "Rock-bottom low-budgeter features a sad-looking Lon Chaney and John Carradine along with a badly directed cast of unknowns appearing in several plodding horror episodes accenting cardboard sets and inadequate lighting." *Castle of Frankenstein*, Vol. 6, No. 4, 1974

"Terrible five-part horror anthology made fast and cheap.... The sets look straight out of a play put on by a rural high school. The script is completely ludicrous. In other words—total entertainment! Don't miss it!" Michael Weldon, *The Psychotronic Encyclopedia of Film*

Minor Film Roles and Short Films

Laugh and Get Rich (RKO, 1931). *Cast*: Edna May Oliver, Hugh Herbert, Dorothy Lee. *Director*: Gregory La Cava. RH as Miss Jones.

Everything's Rosie (RKO, 1931). *Cast*: Robert Woolsey, Anita Louise, John Darrow. *Director*: Clyde Bruckman. RH as Guest at Lowe Party.

The Public Defender (RKO, 1931). *Cast*: Richard Dix, Shirley Grey. *Director*: J. Walter Ruben. Rochelle has one line as a telephone operator whose co-worker hears a gunshot over an open telephone line. "You'd better report it," says Rochelle.

The Voice of Hollywood, #8 (Educational/Tiffany, 1931). Rochelle and her fellow WAMPAS Baby Stars for 1931 are introduced, with Monte Blue as emcee. *Film Daily* (November 1, 1931) said, "This should go strong with the fans, presenting as it does most of the new faces with whom the public is just learning to get acquainted."

Girl Crazy (RKO, 1932). *Cast*: Bert Wheeler, Robert Woolsey, Dorothy Lee, Eddie Quillan. *Director*: William A. Seiter. An adaptation of the successful Broadway musical which starred Ginger Rogers and was an early showcase for Ethel Merman. IMDb credits Rochelle with an unbilled appearance as one of the senoritas seen at the Hotel at San Luz, but she's difficult to spot in the DVD release issued by Warner Archive.

Is My Face Red? (RKO, 1932). *Cast*: Helen Twelvetrees, Ricardo Cortez, Jill Esmond, Robert Armstrong. *Director*: William A. Seiter. Bill Poster, author of the "Keyhole to the City" newspaper gossip column, is involved with two women as he investigates a murder. Rochelle has one line as a newlywed passenger on the S.S. *Leviathan*: When Poster combs the ship looking for a traveling socialite, he peers into a cabin where Rochelle's character is embracing her new husband, saying, "My darling!" Rochelle's groom answers, "My lovely bride!" and their unwitting voyeur says, "My mistake!"

Screen Snapshots, Series 9, #1 (Columbia, 1932). *Director*: Ralph Staub. Rochelle makes her first appearance in this long-running series of documentary shorts showing stars in their leisure activities. Also seen are Joan and Constance Bennett, Jean Harlow, Buster Keaton and Joe E. Brown.

Penguin Pool Murder (RKO, 1932). *Cast*: Edna May Oliver, Robert Armstrong, James Gleason, Mae Clarke. *Director*: George Archainbaud. This was the first of a six-movie series based on Stuart Palmer's mystery novels about spinster detective Miss Withers. Reunited with Edna May Oliver, with whom she co-starred in *Fanny Foley Herself*, Rochelle has a brief but amusing scene as the switchboard operator in suspect Gerald Parker's office. Miss Withers, walking in to see the young lady fixing her face, says, "When you've got your disguise on, I'd like to ask you a few questions. That is, if you can talk through all that makeup." Rochelle's character provides the detective with some needed information about a phone call she put through to her boss.

Secrets of the French Police (RKO, 1932). *Cast*: Gwili Andre, Gregory Ratoff, Frank Morgan. *Director*: A. Edward Sutherland. Detective Francois St. Cyr investigates the murder of Brigadier Danton, an undercover agent for the French police. His investigation leads him to General Hans Moloff's chateau and a young woman who may be Princess Anastasia, daughter of the late Russian tsar. Rochelle, despite her fairly prominent billing, has little more than a bit role as K-31, an operative of the undercover squad. She's on-screen for less than a minute. However, given that the film was cut considerably prior to release, she may well have appeared in scenes that landed on the cutting room floor.

The Past of Mary Holmes (RKO, 1933). *Cast*: Helen MacKellar, Eric Linden, Jean Arthur. *Directors*: Harlan Thompson, Slavko Vorkapich. Former opera singer Mary Holmes, now an aging eccentric known to her neighbors as "The Goose Woman," resents her son and interferes when he announces his marriage plans. Rochelle appears ninth in the cast list as Betty.

Lucky Devils (RKO, 1933). *Cast*: William Boyd, Dorothy Wilson, William Gargan. *Director*: Ralph Ince. Hollywood stuntman Skipper Clark tries to avoid involvement with women, thinking his dangerous work precludes romance, but he falls in love and marries an aspiring actress. Rochelle plays a set visitor watching, enthralled, as a violent bank robbery scene is filmed. Afterwards, she asks for an autograph from a woman who took a fall down a long staircase. She's shocked when the "woman" pulls off his wig and explains that he's a stuntman.

Scarlet River (RKO, 1933). *Cast*: Tom Keene, Dorothy Wilson, Creighton Chaney [Lon Chaney, Jr.], Betty Furness. *Director*: Otto Brower. Western star Tom Baxter, having difficulty shooting his latest film on locations too near the city, travels with his company to the Scarlet River Ranch, where he becomes a hero to the lady owner. When Tom visits the studio commissary, Rochelle makes a cameo appearance as herself: She's lunching with a group that includes Julie Haydon when Tom sits at their table. Rochelle says, "Hello, Tom," "In training?" and not much else. Other RKO players who are briefly seen: Myrna Loy, Bruce Cabot and Joel McCrea.

20th Century–Fox Promotional Film (Fox, 1936). Columnist Jimmie Fidler narrates this documentary short about the recent merger of Twentieth Century Pictures and Fox Films. A tour of the studio lot is included, along with footage of actors Alice Faye, Janet Gaynor and Myrna Loy. Rochelle and her fellow players from *Everybody's Old Man*, Irvin S. Cobb and Sara Haden, also appear.

Screen Snapshots, Series 17, #5 (Columbia, 1938). *Director*: Ralph Staub. Other stars seen at play in this installment include Bette Davis, the Three Stooges, Ann Sothern and Johnny Weissmuller. Segments show leisure activities in Palm Springs and the opening of a new nightclub.

Screen Snapshots, Series 19, #5: Art in Hollywood (Columbia, 1940). *Director*: Ralph Staub. The emphasis this time is on actors who paint, sculpt or draw. The Three Stooges return, and are accompanied by Rochelle, Fred MacMurray, Judith Anderson *et al.*

Picture People #1: Stars in Defense (RKO, 1941). Cast: Joan Carroll, James Craig, Reginald Denny, James Gleason. *Director*: M. Clay Adams. An eight-minute short depicting Hollywood's contributions to national defense. Rochelle is one of the guests at actress Sigrid Gurie's "aluminum party." Two previous Hudson co-stars, Arline Judge and Marian Marsh, are featured as well.

Animation and Voice Work

During Rochelle's peak period of movie work, exhibitors regularly offered theatergoers a full package of entertainment at each show, including newsreels, comedy shorts and cartoons. She was one of the actresses occasionally called upon to voice animated characters. Her best-known assignment came when she was handed the role of Honey, lady friend to a character known as Bosko, who was described as "a perennially cheerful little golliwog who sang and danced with his girlfriend."[44]

His creator Rudolf Ising said some 50 years after Bosko's introduction, "A lot of people thought he was supposed to be a little colored boy, but we didn't. He was just a black-and-white character with a derby hat and a Southern accent." However, author Michael Barrier notes that the application for copyright, submitted in early 1928, identified Bosko as a "Negro boy."[45]

In early 1930, Hugh Harman and Ising signed a three-year contract with Leon Schlesinger to produce Bosko cartoons under the umbrella title "Looney Tunes." Schlesinger, in turn, made a deal with Warner Brothers; the first cartoon delivered was *Sinkin' in the Bathtub*. The character came along in the early days of sound films, which necessitated technical innovations for animated films as well as live-action ones. Ising described the process that was used: "[Max] Maxwell did Bosko's voice and a young actress named Rochelle Hudson did Honey's. We shot film of them in blackface makeup when we recorded the sound tracks and studied it for the mouth movements."[46]

The series was sufficiently successful to continue for several years. As a trade paper noted in 1933, "One series of 18 musical cartoons featuring Bosko and Honey … is planned by Harman-Ising Productions, Ltd., for next season."[47] However, Harman and Ising had a falling-out with Warners' executives that same year and took their popular character to MGM, where several more entries were made under the "Happy Harmonies" banner.

Rochelle never received on-screen credit for her voice performances, which was normal for the period. This anonymity makes it more difficult to say with certainty whether any other actress was ever used to play Honey. However, she apparently continued to furnish the character's voice into the late 1930s, throughout her time as a Fox contract player.

Bosko

    Sinkin' in the Bathtub (1930)
    Hold Anything (1930)
    Big Man from the North (1931)
    The Dumb Patrol (1931)
    Yodeling Yokels (1931)
    Bosko's Holiday (1931)
    Bosko's Soda Fountain (1931)
    Bosko at the Zoo (1932)
    Battling Bosko (1932)
    Bosko's Party (1932)
    Bosko's Dog Race (1932)
    Bosko at the Beach (1932)
    Bosko's Store (1932)
    Bosko the Lumberjack (1932)
    Ride Him, Bosko! (1932)
    Bosko the Drawback (1932). "Bosko the hero [scores] a couple of sensational touchdowns.... Plenty of action and excitement that will please the kids." *Film Daily*, January 28, 1933
    Bosko's Dizzy Date (1932)
    Bosko in Dutch (1933). "Just as good as any cartoon except Mickey Mouse...." *Motion Picture Herald*, September 2, 1933
    Bosko in Person (1933). "This is one of the best turned out by the Harman-Ising studio. Bosko puts on a 'personal appearance' act with a girl partner [who] mimics Greta Garbo and others. Action is lively, the musical numbers are tuneful, and the job as a whole makes snappy entertainment of its kind." *Film Daily*, May 29, 1933.
    Bosko the Speed King (1933)
    Bosko's Knight-Mare (1933)
    Bosko the Sheep-Herder (1933)
    Beau Bosko (1933). "A take-off on *Beau Geste* ... a lively and very amusing number of its kind." *Film Daily*, September 23, 1933.
    Bosko the Musketeer (1933)
    Bosko's Picture Show (1933)
    Bosko's Parlor Pranks (1934)
    Hey-Hey Fever (1934)

The Old House (1936)
Circus Daze (1937)
Bosko's Easter Eggs (1937)
Little Ol' Bosko and the Cannibals (1937). "An excellent color cartoon continuing the 'Straight to Grandma's Here I Go' idea that was so effective when Bosko met the Pirates." *Motion Picture Herald*, December 11, 1937.

Foxy & Roxy

This short-lived series of "Merrie Melodies" was also the work of Rudolf Ising. It featured a cartoon hero who bore a strong resemblance to Mickey Mouse. His lady friend was christened Roxy in the third entry, *One More Time*.

Lady, Play Your Mandolin! (1931)
Smile, Darn Ya, Smile! (1931). "An excellent example of the song cartoon, with a good idea and synchronization." *Film Daily*, August 9, 1931
One More Time (1931)

Other

How Do I Know It's Sunday (1934). "One of the Merrie Melodies numbers, this is reasonably entertaining and an amusing cartoon subject which should be especially pleasing for the youngsters." *Motion Picture Herald*, July 28, 1934

Radio Performances

WAMPAS Baby Stars. September 11, 1931. Rochelle and a dozen other starlets were spotlighted in a Hollywood parade that included a nationwide radio hookup.

The Lux Radio Theater. "Alibi Ike." April 18, 1937. *Cast*: Joe E. Brown, Helen Chandler, William Frawley. Rochelle was announced in advance publicity as playing comedian Brown's love interest in this episode, but the air show credits Helen Chandler with the role.

Walter Winchell's Jergens Journal. NBC, June 13, 1937. Rochelle was the newspaper columnist's guest.

The Kate Smith Hour. March 31, 1938. Guest star Rochelle performed "a short dramatic sketch written especially for the broadcast."[48]

Hollywood Open House. NBC, July 3, 1943. Rochelle appeared in the premiere broadcast of this variety show hosted by Tobe Reed.

Noah Webster Says. Blue, August 10, 1943. Haven McQuarrie hosted this quiz show that tested players on their vocabularies. Rochelle was a guest on an installment featuring servicemen as contestants.

Television Performances

From television's early days, Rochelle's movies of the 1930s and 1940s were being broadcast, pleasing longtime fans and introducing her to new ones. Their popularity led to opportunities to perform in the new medium. Making her video dramatic debut in a 1951 episode of *Racket Squad*, she continued to act periodically on TV through the mid–1960s, bowing out after a cameo role in a 1965 episode of *Branded*.

That's My Boy

After several years of occasional guest appearances on TV, Rochelle's most high-profile assignment came when she was cast as the leading lady of the CBS sitcom *That's My Boy* in 1954. The half-hour comedy series was created and produced by Cy Howard, best-known for his hit show *My Friend Irma*, a radio favorite before it moved to TV. *That's My Boy* was written by Howard and Everett Freeman, with Bill Baldwin serving as announcer and Bob Finkel in the director's chair.

The series was adapted from a popular 1951 film starring Dean Martin and Jerry Lewis. Eddie Mayehoff, seen as "Jarrin' Jack" Jackson in the movie, reprised that role for the TV sitcom. Mayehoff was being given a second chance on TV after his first comedy series, *Doc Corkle*, became one of the young medium's bigger bombs in 1952. It was yanked from the schedule after just a few weeks.

Rochelle was cast as his loving wife Alice, a former Olympic swimming champion. They lived in Rossmore, Ohio, with their teenage son, Jack Jr. (Gil Stratton, Jr.). Much to his father's disappointment, Junior shows no interest in or aptitude for athletics. Though believably cast as a gawky teenager, Stratton was in fact a married man with two children. Cy Howard told columnist Erskine Johnson (April 19, 1954), "It's a thrill to give people like Eddie and Rochelle and Stratton the chance at roles that will bring out their greatness as performing performers. Hollywood is full of people like them, people who are better than the lines you give them. But you must have courage to cast people you believe in."

About the series itself, Howard said,

> This will not be a situation dramatic series, nor will it be a domestic comedy. The show will be a character comedy series concerning a family with an income of about $35,000 yearly.... That is, presenting a family that has money enough to buy a second radio set or TV receiver for the home, and to have a second car in the garage! ...My central character is a copy of a man from the Middle West, between Chicago and Milwaukee, a spot in the country I know best. He is the junior partner in a construction company. I know his type well.[49]

Recurring roles were assigned to actress Claudia Barrett, as Joyce, a love interest for Junior; John Maxwell as Joyce's father, Dr. Hunter, and Larry Blake as next-door neighbor Sam Barker. Per Donald Freeman, "Other regular members of the cast are Helen Kleeb, the housemaid who refuses to be dominated by Jack; his faithful

Junior (Gil Stratton, Jr., left) shows more of a flair for board games than athletics in *That's My Boy*. His mom (Rochelle Hudson) doesn't mind, but his dad (Eddie Mayehoff) is another story.

secretary, Miss Willoughby, played by Allene Roberts; Francis Pierlot as the waspish bookkeeper, Henry Baker; and John Smith as Henry's husky son, Bill."[50]

Variety (April 14, 1954) had a mixed reaction to the series premiere, with the reviewer finding the basic premise promising, and Mayehoff's Jarrin' Jack character "idealy [sic] suited for [his] talents." The problem, said the trade journal, was "too much evidence of pressing too hard to make up for script deficiencies." Though the focus of the comedy was clearly on Mayehoff, Rochelle, along with young Gil Stratton, Jr., were said to "slide right into their respective roles." Another critic singled her out for praise: "Miss Hudson, it's a delight to report, has gained maturity while losing little of her beauty. She seems moreover, to have identity and character, being neither the pants-wearing matriarch nor the 'yes-dear' helpmeet of popular fiction."[51]

A friendlier reaction to the show came from reviewer Ed Heath, who wrote, "*That's My Boy* has everything it takes—including a reasonably fresh storyline…. In the first go-round, 'Jarring Jack' was visited by an old college buddy, a football star of 20 years ago. Evaporating hairline and considerable overweight notwithstanding, the guest provided all the encouragement necessary to launch Mayehoff in a clever re-enactment of the old days." Heath concluded that the series "shows promise of being a TV hit.... I think you'll like it."[52]

A *TV Guide* reviewer (June 4, 1954) said, "TV writers usually have it tough building one half-hour show around a single situation. Pity the writers of *That's My Boy* ... they must concoct an entire season of half-hour programs on a solitary theme." While conceding that most of the show's laughs came from Mayehoff, the critic added that Stratton "is a near-perfect choice for the son's role. He looks the part and has learned the secret of underplaying, which makes him a fine foil for Mayehoff's bombasts."

The show initially performed well enough that *Variety* (May 26, 1954) noted that Howard was "prepping a radio version of *That's My Boy*, for summer programming on CBS ... [with] same principals used in the video version." Shortly afterwards, the trade journal reported (June 9, 1954) that the video version "will ride through the summer in the Saturday night at 10 slot. Plymouth wing of Chrysler Corp. has come through with a 13-week renewal which carries to the Oct. 2 mark."

During that first, abbreviated season, the show was broadcast live. But for the fall season, it converted to film, with George Burns' company McCadden Productions providing the production equipment and expertise.

When the series returned, it faced new competition in its Saturday time slot from NBC's *The George Gobel Show*, starring a young, crew-cutted comedian not previously widely known to audiences. Gobel's show (which also featured a spouse named Alice) became an immediate smash, and the ratings of *That's My Boy* suffered accordingly. *Broadcasting* (November 15, 1954) reported, "Plymouth ... has been unhappy with the ratings" Likewise, *Variety* (November 24, 1954) noted, "Gobel's Saturday night NBC-TV series has been murdering the rival *That's My Boy* show on CBS." *Sponsor* (December 27, 1954) added, "With a November Nielsen of 32.8, the [George] Gobel show was too strong a competitor for a new [sic] show on CBS TV, *That's My Boy*, sponsored by Chrysler at $26,500 weekly."

Howard continued to fine-tune the show. In a *TV Guide* profile (November 6, 1954), star Mayehoff explained, "Gradually, we're getting away from too much emphasis on the ex-athlete stuff and trying to build a firmer relationship between Jackson and his boy. Because, when he says, 'That's my boy,' he means it. He's not kiddin.' He loves that boy."

But the weekly ratings spoke louder than anything else, and Plymouth withdrew its sponsorship. Originally announced plans called for it to be replaced with another sitcom, *Professional Father*, also to be beamed under Plymouth's sponsorship, as of January 1955. Instead, Plymouth relinquished the time slot altogether.

In 1957, with Mayehoff winning fresh acclaim for his performance in Broadway's *Visit to a Small Planet*, someone noticed that his old series was gathering dust in the network's vaults. One report indicated, "For a couple of years now CBS has had a 26-week series of *That's My Boy* films which Mayehoff did for the network; with the enthusiastic reports on Mayehoff's [stage] performance it is offering them for syndication."⁵³ But it wasn't until two years later, in the summer of 1959, that CBS pulled out a batch of films and scheduled a series of early Sunday evening reruns. Most had aired only once during the show's initial run, thanks to the sponsor's abrupt cancellation midway through Season Two. The repeats continued into September.

Episodes

April 10, 1954. No synopsis of the debut episode was provided to newspapers or to *TV Guide* (April 9, 1954), which merely described the opener as "The story of a [*sic*] ex-collegiate athlete who refuses to forget his former gridiron fame."

April 17, 1954. "Alice informs Jack that he must get rid of his trophies, because Junior is afflicted with a psychosomatic illness whenever he comes into contact with them."⁵⁴

April 24, 1954. "Dad wants Junior to be boy's week mayor, but he is voted zoning commissioner [and] nearly ruins dad's business." *Detroit Free Press*, April 24, 1954

May 1, 1954. "Jarrin' Jack Jackson unwittingly sponsors a no-match boxing match for charity.... When the strappling [*sic*] son of Jarrin' Jack's bookkeeper is injured while training for a fight, Junior Jackson subs for him against an opponent twice his size."⁵⁵

May 8, 1954. "Jarrin' Jack Jackson learns never to judge [a] book by its cover—or a man by his biceps."⁵⁶

May 15, 1954. "Mr. Jackson suffers a crushing blow, when in the midst of preparations for a possible visit from Ed Murrow on the latter's *Person to Person* telecast, his coveted athletic trophies mysteriously disappear."⁵⁷

May 22, 1954. "Junior Jackson finds his Dad's lesson in love-making a bit old-fashioned. When he goes a-courting, the modern miss doesn't think much of his 'square' technique."⁵⁸

May 29, 1954. "Lessons in how to be a good sport are ladled out by Jarrin' Jack Jackson."⁵⁹

June 5, 1954. "Culture Will Out." "Jarrin' Jack is pleased to hear that an alumnus is giving money to the athletic department. Junior isn't quite so happy. He feels that the science department deserves the donation."⁶⁰

June 12, 1954. "Jarrin' Jack Jackson finds himself taking 'finals' he forgot to take in his college days at Rossmore."⁶¹

June 19, 1954. "In a sentimental mood, Junior Jackson shops in a sporting goods store for a Father's Day gift ... and a token of affection for his sweetheart, Stephanie. Somehow the gifts get misdirected and Jackson pere ... gets a stuffed owl intended for Junior's bird-loving girlfriend."⁶²

June 26, 1954. "Dad tries to get grid hero Bill Baker to influence his son Junior, but the opposite effect is achieved." *TV Guide* listings and other sources give this synopsis for both the June 26 and July 3 episodes.⁶³

July 3, 1954. "Determined to make a football player out of his son, 'Jarrin' Jack' Jackson hatches [a] plot to get Junior under influence of grid hero Bill Baker."⁶⁴

July 10, 1954. "When the time comes to name Rossmore's most outstanding citizen the honor quite naturally falls to Jarrin' Jack Jackson. But how to keep chesty dad from knowing about his latest accolade is a real problem for his family."[65]

July 17, 1954. "An old flame of 'Jarrin'' Jack Jackson kindles a conflagration when she descends on the Jackson household."[66]

July 24, 1954. "It's a banner day for Jarrin' Jack Jackson when he is selected to house the star players of the visiting 'pro' grid champs en route to Chicago for their big game. But overzealousness in imparting gridiron know-how to his house guests results in an injury that makes it a near bloomer day for the eager team."[67]

July 31, 1954. "When Jarring [sic] Jack Jackson discovers that his son has won a place on the school chess team instead of the baseball squad, he buys baseball uniforms for Junior and himself."[68]

August 7, 1954. "Jarrin' Jack tries to interfere with Junior's plans for a party and is angrily dismissed from the house. He sulks about town and seems certain to miss a party planned without his help—a birthday surprise at the Barkers' house."[69]

August 14, 1954. "When annual country club athletic contests roll around, 'Jarrin' Jack' plots 'demi-decathlon' win for Jackson family over the Sam Barkers."[70]

August 21, 1954. "Rossmore's prime do-gooder is to be tendered a surprise testimonial dinner by his fellow citizens. The catch is that the honoring committee wants to have Jack's trophies on hand for the event. If they disappear from the house, Jack will become suspicious. What to do?"[71]

August 28, 1954. "Jarrin' Jack finds himself top banana in an artistic fruit salad when he commissions Junior to do his portrait."[72]

September 4, 1954. "Jarrin' Jack Jackson and Junior ... find fossils become factor in business deal."[73]

September 11, 1954. First filmed episode. No synopsis available.

September 18, 1954. "A dream comes true for 'Jarrin' Jack Jackson when Junior registers for college. Jack gets upset, however, when Junior doesn't seem to appreciate the advantages of college life at dear old Rossmore."[74]

September 25, 1954. "Son Junior considers himself a budding advertising man and persuades Jarrin' Jack to advertise on television by showing old football movies…. The choice of films, however, gives Jarrin' Jack the worst 60 minutes of his life."[75]

October 2, 1954. "Junior's unpredictable activities continue to cause his father anxiety. But Jarrin' Jack, equal to any situation, dons his Sherlock Homes [sic] hat and begins his investigation."[76]

October 9, 1954. "Junior's schooling is endangered when 'Jarrin' Jack' has to purchase some expensive equipment to dredge Noonan's Swamp. The only solution Jack can think of doesn't seem to be appropriate for his son."[77]

October 16, 1954. "'Jarrin' Jack Jackson is cited for walking on the park grass and is then pressured into running for the post of Park Commissioner."[78] Repeated June 21, 1959.

October 23, 1954. "Jarrin' Jack Jackson looks forward gleefully to a vacation-time moose hunt with his colleagues until his wife insists Junior join them."[79] Repeated June 28, 1959.

October 30, 1954. "Jarrin' Jack Jackson shakes the mothballs out of his old raccoon coat and visits his old fraternity house at old Rossmore…. The reason of Jack's visit is to be sure Junior is properly launched in his old fraternity, Alpha Lambda Kappa. But … the boys don't consider Junior their type of guy."[80] Repeated July 5, 1959.

November 6, 1954, "The boss' wife vetoes Jarrin' Jack's attempts to purchase 'Holbeck Heights,' the land adjoining Noonan's Swamp. Maybe if Jack turns on that ole football-hero charm, he can win over his opponent."[81] Repeated July 12, 1959.

November 13, 1954. "It's the day of the big Rossmore College football classic and 'Jarrin' Jack' … look[s] forward enthusiastically to his annual locker-room pep talk to the Rossmore team…. However, Henrietta Patterson (Mable [sic] Albertson) has other plans for him and the old grad learns that business comes before football."[82] Repeated July 19, 1959.

November 20, 1954. "Junior wins his big 'R' … And it's a big day for Jarring [sic] Jack Jackson, even though his son didn't win the letter on the gridiron, but rather for making the Rossmore Symphony Orchestra."[83]

November 27, 1954. "Jack and the boss' wife are at it again! The topic of debate is the old familiar one—what to do with Noonan's swamp."[84] Repeated July 26, 1959.

December 4, 1954. "A feud brews hot and heavy when 'Jarrin' Jack' Jackson decides to enlarge his home and inadvertently builds the addition onto Sam Barker's (Larry Blake) property…. Sam, of course, doesn't take the land grab lying down and he and Jack begin a series of lighthearted reprisals."[85] Repeated August 2, 1959.

December 11, 1954. "'Jarrin' Jack Jackson … hoping to be selected as the honored Rossmore citizen to fire the city's ancient cannon on Founder's Day, fails to enhance his position when he plays bridge with the mayor's wife and trumps her ace."[86] Repeated August 16, 1959.

December 18, 1954. "Henrietta Patterson … the boss' wife, turns Scrooge and threatens to dispense with the annual pre–Christmas office party that 'Jarrin' Jack' Jackson … has prepared."[87] Repeated September 13, 1959.

January 1, 1955. "The Actor." "Jack is determined to play the 'lover boy' role in a local dramatic show. But the director is unimpressed by his past glory as a football hero, and Jack seems destined for bit parts only…. John Banner and John Harmon play the director and the salesman, respectively."[88]

Guest Appearances

Though a highly experienced actress used to the ways of filmmaking, Rochelle's early TV parts came largely in lesser shows.

Treasure Quest. ABC, Summer 1949. *Variety* (July 27, 1949) indicated that Rochelle, along with actress Brenda Forbes, made an appearance on this game show hosted by John Weigel. The series was previously known as *Bon Voyage. Variety* (May 11, 1949) described it as "a geographical quizzer [that] uses stills and rhyming clues with two pre-selected teams." No episodes are known to survive.

Racket Squad. "The Diamond That Wasn't." CBS, August 9, 1951. *Teleplay*: Lee Loeb. *Director*: James Tinling. *Producers*: Hal Roach, Jr., Carroll Case. *Cast*: Reed Hadley, Rochelle Hudson, Johnny Downs, Morgan Farley, Ivan Parry. In each episode of this half-hour dramatic series, Police Captain John Braddock (Reed Hadley) tells the story of a con man and his racket. In "The Diamond That Wasn't," Rochelle plays Sue Morgan, bookkeeper-secretary at the Ideal Loan Company. Bill Andrews becomes a frequent customer, pawning overnight a valuable diamond ring in order to raise cash for gambling on horse races. He flirts with Sue and they begin dating. After multiple visits, appraiser Pop Anderson is no longer looking at it carefully and Bill obtains $1250 on it. When he doesn't return, shop owner Mr. Sloan fires Pop for lending the money on the cheap zircon that has replaced the ring they saw previously. Andrews sends in a confederate to buy the cheap copy for $15, then returns with his receipt, demanding Mr. Sloan reimburse him $3750 for the ring. Rochelle's character, a nice young woman who is angry that Bill tricked her, knocks him out cold when the police come to apprehend him. This episode reunites her with Johnny Downs, her co-star 15 years earlier in *Everybody's Old Man*.

Ring. Primrose Productions. 13 half-hour dramatic films. "Featured in the first program are Akim Tamiroff and Elena Verduga [sic] in their first TV appearances, Rochelle Hudson and Lyle Talbot."[89] Although there is no documentation that this series actually aired, Rochelle's episode was later shown on *Schlitz Playhouse of Stars* (see below).

The Unexpected. Syndicated, March 1952. *Producer*: Frederic Ziv. *Director*: Eddie Davis. *Writers*: Jerry Lawrence, Bob Lee. Rochelle guest starred in the premiere episode of this 30-minute anthology series. A press release announced, "Popular, pert screen performer Rochelle Hudson will star in the first play ... titled 'Calculated Risk' tonight.... These programs, which will be narrated by Herbert Marshall and in which he will also play various roles, will often utilize the surprise ending for purposes of dramatic impact."[90] Rochelle played the part of Diana, opposite Louis Jean Heydt in a dual role. According to *Variety* (March 12, 1952), the episode "had a story viewpoint that didn't come off too well ... had some ingenious moments, but generally showed a lot of extraneous details and evidence of stretching, that killed the inventive part of the plot."

Jukebox Jury. KNXT-TV, Los Angeles, July 11, 1952. Not yet seen nationally, disc jockey Peter Potter's show found celebrities helping to review recently released records. Rochelle was the guest on this installment.

Schlitz Playhouse of Stars. "Trouble on Pier Twelve." CBS, October 10, 1952. *Writers*: Val Lindberg, L.C. Stoumen. *Director*: Robert Florey. *Host*: Irene Dunne.

Guest Stars: Akim Tamiroff, Rochelle Hudson, John Howard, Lyle Talbot, Elena Verdugo. "Veteran screen actor Akim Tamiroff plays the role of a sea captain accused of double homicide."[91] An advertisement in the *Rock Island* (Illinois) *Argus* (October 10, 1952) said, "A two-time killer tries again in this tense, polished thriller that brings you to your seat-edge and keeps you there."

I'm the Law. "The Cowboy and the Blind Man Story." Syndicated, 1953. *Teleplay*: Jackson Gillis. *Story*: David Victor, Jackson Gillis. *Executive Producer*: Pat Costello. *Producer*: Jean Yarbrough. *Director*: George Archainbaud. *Cast*: Rochelle Hudson (*Cynthia Chase*), Gordon Jones (*Sammy McNeill*), Percy Helton (*Dick Murphy*), Larry Blake. Longtime film star George Raft starred as Lt. Kirby in this police drama, which lasted only 26 episodes. Rochelle guest starred in this episode as a performer who does a shooting act at the Club Diamond, costumed as Annie Oakley. Screen cowboy Sammy McNeill describes her: "She's got big, blue, bashful eyes, hair just as black as coal…. Her heart's just as big as the whole outdoors!" He tells the lieutenant she's being followed and needs protection. Kirby finds her doing target practice at home at the Dudley Apartments. Brazening it out, she says, "Lots of guys follow me—even guys without hair … [*fires a shot*] Do you seriously think I need someone to protect me or something?" There's a murder in the nearby apartment of Dick Murphy, a blind song plugger. When it's learned that the victim was Cynthia's husband, Kirby asks McNeill if she was blackmailing him, as it's obvious the man was killed by a skilled marksman—or markswoman. *Broadcasting* (February 16, 1953) said of Rochelle, "Her role, in a lackluster script, was that of a girl sharpshooter, most of whose appearances on camera were associated with her work. It was not a challenging assignment, but she carried it out competently, flinching only occasionally when the pistol went off."

Pulse of the City. "The Case of Captain Denning." DuMont, Fall 1953. *Producer*: Milton Simon. Rochelle made a guest appearance in this episode. An almost entirely forgotten show, *Pulse of the City* owes what little latter-day attention it attracts to the fact that it was an early directorial credit for young Robert Altman. TV historian Horace Newcomb described it as "a limited crime anthology … (broadcast via the DuMont stations in late 1953),"[92] while author Patrick McGilligan wrote that it was "a kind of poor man's *Dragnet*. It was an anthology series about ambulance-chasing and crime incidents in the big city." According to McGilligan, Altman oversaw multiple episodes, alternating with another director.[93]

Catalogers at the UCLA Film and Television Archive called it a "dramatic series centering on the efforts of public health officials as they assist people and fight communicable diseases." Other segment titles, per UCLA, included "The Case of Norman Doyle" and "The Case of Bill Huff."

Shower of Stars. "Entertainment on Wheels." CBS, November 17, 1954. *Host*: William Lundigan. *Producer*: Ralph Levy. *Director*: Seymour Berns. *Teleplay*: Milton Pascal, Morris Freedman. This variety show, sponsored by Chrysler, devoted most of the segment to promoting the manufacturer's line of 1955 models, using stars from other shows it sponsored at the time. Rochelle and her *That's My Boy* co-stars Eddie Mayehoff and Gil Stratton, Jr., were seen briefly promoting Plymouth vehicles. Said *Variety* (November 24, 1954), "As a dealer show, it was probably great—as a regularly scheduled television entry, 'Entertainment on Wheels' was somewhat on the dull side."

Jane Wyman Presents the Fireside Theatre. "The Director." NBC, September 13, 1955. *Writer*: Rod Serling. *Director*: Herschel Daugherty. *Cast*: Jack Carson, James Barton, Rochelle Hudson. "A director gives an old-time actor a chance for a comeback by starring him in a TV show. But the cast is furious because the oldster can't remember his lines."[94]

The Christmas Lane Parade. December 3, 1960. Rochelle helped anchor regional television coverage of the annual Yuletide parade in Huntington Park, California. Pat Boone served as grand marshal, while she paired with Stan Chambers to narrate.

77 Sunset Strip. "The Legend of Leckonby." ABC, March 24, 1961. *Writer*: Robert C. Dennis. *Director*: Robert Douglas. *Cast*: Roger Smith, Richard Long, Edd Byrnes. *Guest Stars*: Rochelle Hudson, Richard Carlyle, Jean Allison, Victor Buono. Private eye Jeff Spencer is hired to shadow recently paroled bank robber Stanley Leckonby and find $85,000 that was never recovered. Jeff trails the seemingly mild-mannered Stanley, who insists he lost the money gambling, although he was arrested only four days after the robbery. The search leads Jeff to Stanley's old rooming house and to a bar called the Silver Whistle that he frequented. Rochelle, top-billed among the guest cast, gives a vivid performance in the character role of Renee Lamson, proprietor of the rooming house. A slightly blowsy woman who, fifteen years earlier, ran an illegal drinking and gambling club, Renee is the type of landlady who asks Jeff, on first acquaintance, "You lookin' for a room, or a hideout?" Clearly on Stanley's side, she warns the investigator, "You're up against an authentic genius! Stanley's the kind of brain you meet once in a lifetime." Renee ultimately pays a high price for seizing the opportunity to snatch a shoebox that may contain

Publicity photograph of Rochelle and her canine companion, issued to promote her 1963 guest appearance on ABC-TV's *Day in Court*.

Alice Whitcomb (Rochelle Hudson) pleads the case of Jason McCord with her husband, Major Whitcomb (Wendell Corey), on *Branded*.

the loot. This seriocomic episode is likely Rochelle's best television guest appearance: She makes the most of a good role with her expressive face and camera presence. One scene contains an in-joke reference to co-star Richard Long's real-life wife, actress Mara Corday. Stanley keeps a list of women's names and numbers in a notebook, among them Marilyn Watts, Corday's birth name.

Day in Court. ABC, October 2, 1963. *Writer*: Kenneth M. Rosen. *Director*: Paul

Nickell. This daytime series presented dramatizations adapted from real-life court cases, mixing actual lawyers with actors playing witnesses and defendants. UCLA law faculty member Edgar Allan Jones, Jr., presided over domestic cases heard on Mondays, Wednesdays and Fridays. Rochelle appeared in this episode as Mrs. Lear, a woman seeking a divorce from her husband, an executive in an electronics firm. Having lost their ten-year-old daughter a few years earlier, Mrs. Lear now claims that her husband is preoccupied by his work and neglects her. Her divorce is granted in the finale. An incomplete copy of the episode, containing only footage of her scenes, is preserved in the Hudson Papers at the University of Wyoming.

Branded. "The Mission, Part 3." NBC, March 28, 1965. *Producer*: Andrew J. Fenady. *Teleplay*: Jameson Brewer. *Story*: Larry Cohen. *Director*: Bernard McEveety. *Cast*: Chuck Connors, Wendell Corey. The final installment of a three- episode story finds Jason McCord on a secret mission for President Ulysses S. Grant, assigned to pose as the leader of a gang raiding Army installments. Rochelle, Peter Breck and Patrick Wayne are the episode's three "Cameo Guest Stars"; she plays Alice Whitcomb, wife of Major Whitcomb (Corey), who orders McCord shot at dawn. Corey does not appear in the version of the episode subsequently released on DVD. A publicity photo issued by the network showed Rochelle in a scene from the episode and the note, "Rochelle Hudson begs her husband, played by Wendell Corey, to spare Jason McCord's life in the final episode of the three-part *Branded*."[95] This was her final television performance.

In the mid–1950s, the Grey Advertising Agency put Rochelle, Coleen Gray and Joan Vohs to work in a promotional campaign, featuring them in TV ads for deodorant. The actresses "are believable, says Gray, because of the manner in which they give the testimonial and because they obviously are users of the product themselves."[96]

Chapter Notes

Preface

1. Jeannette Meehan, "Waited Six Years for Hollywood Break," *Atlanta Constitution*, November 10, 1935.
2. Jack Stinnett, "Behind the Screen," *Daily Oklahoman*, October 30, 1932.

Biography

1. "Hudson-Goddard," *Wave-Democrat* (Enid, OK), January 13, 1910.
2. Celya Cendow, "City Dentist Collects Pictures and Autographs of Governors; Most Are 'Eager' to Cooperate," *Daily Oklahoman*, March 10, 1940.
3. "Employment Bureau Activities," *Pawnee County Journal* (Pawnee, OK), July 6, 1916.
4. "Job Seekers to Be Closely Examined," *Herald-Sentinel* (Cordell, OK), November 30, 1916.
5. Mae Hudson, untitled document, Box 7, Rochelle Hudson Papers, American Heritage Center, University of Wyoming.
6. Noel Houston, "Film Stardom Beckons to Rochelle Hudson, Oklahoma City Girl, Who Was 'On Her Toes' When Contract Arrived," *Oklahoma News* (Oklahoma City, OK), October 9, 1934.
7. Hudson, Rochelle Hudson Papers.
8. *Ibid.*
9. "Rochelle Hudson Fools Family Doctor," *Daily News* (Los Angeles, CA), January 21, 1936.
10. Madeleine Myers, "Keeping Posted at Palm Desert C.C.," *Palm Desert Post*, March 2, 1972.
11. "How You Going to Keep 'Em Down on the Farm?" *Oklahoma City Times*, June 19, 1920.
12. "No Unemployment If Bonds Carry," *Oklahoma City Times*, September 16, 1921.
13. Ruth McCarty, "Miles-Huckins Wedding Interests Society," *Oklahoma News*, May 17, 1922.
14. Ruth McCarty, "State's Quadruplets in Golden Wedding Party," *Oklahoma News*, September 26, 1922.
15. "Kappa Zeta Pi Club Gives Large Dance," *Oklahoma News*, December 3, 1922.
16. "Conditions Here Praised," *Oklahoma News*, October 3, 1924.
17. "Attended Recital by Niece at the City," *Geary* (OK) *Times-Journal*, June 19, 1924.
18. Stinnett, "Behind the Screen."
19. "Pioneer Drowns While Enroute to California," *American Guardian* (Oklahoma City, OK), August 19, 1927.
20. Ben Maddox, "Art Is the Bunk!" *Hollywood*, February 1934.
21. "Social Program Under Miss Obegi Charms Auxiliary," *Van Nuys News*, November 22, 1927.
22. "Entertainment of Aid Society a Success," *Van Nuys News*, May 3, 1929.
23. "Employment Bureau Head Bears Burden of Oil Job Seekers," *Oklahoma News*, May 1, 1929.
24. "City Building Aids Workers," *Daily Oklahoman*, October 1, 1929.
25. "School Set Members at Home Event; Little Visitor, Leaving for Home in California, Honored Guest," *Daily Oklahoman*, August 28, 1929.
26. Joseph Mitchell, "Rochelle Hudson May Still Be Very Young But She Knows the Publicity Game," *Pittsburgh Press*, March 31, 1936.
27. Houston, "Film Stardom."
28. Richard Lamparski, *Whatever Became of: Third Series* (New York: Crown, 1970), p. 135.
29. "Rachelle Hudson Awarded Five Year Contract," *Van Nuys News*, July 11, 1930.
30. Maddox, "Art Is the Bunk!"
31. Meehan, "Waited Six Years."
32. Maddox, "Art Is the Bunk!"
33. "Oklahoma Girl Signs with R.-K.-O.," *Los Angeles Times*, November 8, 1930.
34. Edward E. Gloss, "Oakie Joins Parade of Seafaring Actors," *Akron* (OH) *Beacon-Journal*, December 4, 1930.
35. Houston, "Film Stardom."
36. Maddox, "Art Is the Bunk!"
37. "Studios Train Own Juve Mob," *Variety*, September 29, 1931.
38. "Little Sidney Fox," *The New Movie Magazine*, March 1932.
39. Rosalind Shaffer, "Wampas Stars Welcomed by Cheering Crowd," *Chicago Tribune*, September 20, 1931.
40. "Little Sidney Fox."
41. "Wampas of Yesteryear," *Tacoma* (WA) *News-Tribune*, January 4, 1938.
42. M.D. Phillips, "Thirteen Girls Racing for Stardom," *The Film-Lovers' Annual* (London: Dean & Sons, 1932), p. 59.

43. Stinnett, "Behind the Screen."
44. Henry Willson, "Junior Hollywood Gossip," *New Movie Magazine*, July 1934.
45. Grace Kingsley, "Hobnobbing in Hollywood," *Los Angeles Times*, November 25, 1932.
46. Dan Thomas, "Swell Head Has Complete Cure," *Spartanburg (SC) Herald*, June 7, 1935.
47. Meehan, "Waited Six Years."
48. "Rochelle Hudson Saved from Death," *Akron (OH) Beacon-Journal*, May 5, 1933.
49. Paul Harrison, "Hollywood's Million-Dollar Mistakes," *The Spokesman-Review* (Spokane, WA), October 11, 1936.
50. Meehan, "Waited Six Years."
51. Peter C. Rollins, *Will Rogers: A Bio-Bibliography* (Westport, CT: Greenwood Press, 1984), p. 24.
52. "Child Stars Good Pupils," *Spokesman-Review* (Spokane, WA), November 29, 1936.
53. "A Coming Star Is Calm," *Kansas City Star*, April 5, 1935.
54. "The Movie Crusade Brings New Stars for Old," *Lubbock Morning Avalanche*, September 7, 1934.
55. Charles E. Davis, Jr., "Star Back into Movies After Lifelike [sic] Film," *Los Angeles Times*, February 2, 1964.
56. "Girl Who Made Good in Movies Returns to Home," *Oklahoma News*, April 29, 1934.
57. Maddox, "Art Is the Bunk!"
58. Edwin Schallert, "Stage Set for Zanuck's Return Next Week; 'Call of the Wild' Probab Opelener [sic]," *Los Angeles Times*, August 16, 1934.
59. Anne Ellis Meyers, "Rochelle Hudson Puts Up Her Hair," *Motion Picture*, November 1935.
60. Lamparski, *Whatever Became of*, p. 135.
61. "Says She's Too Busy to Talk of Love," *Evening Sun* (Baltimore, MD), December 7, 1934.
62. Don Carlson, "Flickers," *Film Bulletin*, July 3, 1935.
63. "Much More Is Expected from Women Today," *Modern Screen*, October 1935.
64. "James Acker, a Date with Rochelle Hudson," *Hollywood*, November 1935.
65. "Rochelle Hudson Is Back in Films," *Tallahassee Democrat*, October 10, 1963.
66. Acker, "A Date."
67. "Denial and Apology Sent to Claremore Sent by Rochelle Hudson," *Miami (OK) News-Record*, March 25, 1935.
68. "Claremore 'Up in Arms' Over Charge of Actress," *Springfield (MO) News-Leader*, March 25, 1935.
69. Ibid.
70. Maddox, "Art Is the Bunk!"
71. "On and Off the Set," *Picture Play*, December 1935.
72. Muriel Babcock, "Rising Star Rochelle 'Discovered,'" *San Francisco Examiner*, July 7, 1935.
73. Ibid.
74. Acker, "A Date."
75. Hubbard Keavy, "Hollywood Screen Life," *Poughkeepsie (NY) Eagle-News*, July 29, 1935.
76. Thomas, "Swell Head."
77. Joseph Mitchell, "Rochelle Hudson May Still Be Very Young But She Knows the Publicity Game," *Pittsburgh Press*, March 31, 1936.
78. Edwin Schallert, "John Boles Expected to Sing in Film," *Los Angeles Times*, October 15, 1935.
79. "Snow Slide in Picture Taking Traps Actress," *Sacramento Bee*, January 27, 1936.
80. John Terry, "Rochelle Hudson Sighs and Rests, Smiles Benignly on Waikiki," *Honolulu Star-Bulletin*, June 10, 1936.
81. Noel Houston, "Dropping In on Rochelle Hudson," *Daily Oklahoman* (Oklahoma City, OK), January 19, 1936.
82. Margaret Post Niemeyer, "Miss Rochelle Hudson," *St. Louis Post-Dispatch*, November 29, 1936.
83. Dan Van Neste, *They Coulda Been Contenders: Twelve Actors Who Should Have Become Cinematic Superstars* (Orlando: BearManor Media, 2019), p. 275.
84. Mel Gussow, *Don't Say Yes Until I Finish Talking: A Biography of Darryl F. Zanuck* (Garden City, NY: Doubleday, 1971), p. 173.
85. Betty Klingensmith, "Studios, Stars and Stooges," *The Times* (Munster, IN), June 8, 1937.
86. Monroe Lathrop, "Movie City Extra Players Talk About 'Sell Out,'" *St. Louis Globe-Democrat*, July 18, 1937.
87. Whitney Williams, "She's 21," *Silver Screen*, August 1937.
88. Paul Harrison, "Coming 'Has-Been' Days Shrouded in Doubt," *Pittsburgh Press*, June 16, 1937.
89. Hale Horton, "She's Queen of the B's!" *Hollywood*, October 1937.
90. Elmer Sunfield, "Hollywood's High Flyers," *Hollywood*, May 1938.
91. "Rochelle Hudson in Coloroto," *New York Daily News*, May 22, 1938.
92. Howard Whitman, "Joneses Coo, Rochelle Snores, Cantor Gags," *New York Daily News*, April 6, 1938.
93. "Actress, Hal Thompson Surprise Friends with Marriage," *Knoxville Journal*, August 17, 1939.
94. Frederick C. Othman, "Rochelle Hudson Plans Hunt for Lost Gold of Mayans," *Des Moines Register*, December 21, 1939.
95. Kenneth Dixon, "Hal Thompson and Wife—Rochelle Hudson—In City," *Carlsbad Current-Argus*, November 13, 1939.
96. Martha Martin, "Mother Knows Best," *New York Daily News*, November 12, 1939.
97. David Lemmo, *Tarzan, Jungle King of Popular Culture*.(Jefferson, NC: McFarland, 2017), p. 95.
98. Paul Harrison, "Rochelle Hudson, 24-Year-Old Screen Vet, Chucks Drammer [sic] Roles, Becomes Glamour Gal," *Charlotte* (NC) *News*, April 19, 1940.
99. "George Jessel Party at 'Toots' Shor's," *Motion Picture Daily*, October 10, 1940.
100. "George Jessel, 7 Hollywood Stars Arrive

for Lyric Show," *Indianapolis News*, September 20, 1940.

101. Mildred Martin, "Between Show Parties Come Back with Bang," *Philadelphia Inquirer*, October 2, 1940.

102. Charles E. Davis, Jr., "Star Back into Movies After Lifelike [sic] Film," *Los Angeles Times*, February 2, 1964.

103. "Testifies in Suit," *Chicago Tribune*, March 14, 1942.

104. "Rochelle Hudson Says Dates Were to Give Actor Publicity," *St. Louis* (MO) *Star and Times*, March 14, 1942.

105. "Gave Him Hand, Not Hug, Says Rochelle," *New York Post*, March 15, 1942.

106. Ronald L. Davis, *Mary Martin, Broadway Legend* (Norman: University of Oklahoma Press, 2014), p. 71.

107. L.L. Stevenson, "New York Highlights," *Asbury Park* (NJ) *Press*, May 11, 1943.

108. "Vallee Band and Stars Will Play Benefit Friday," *Sacramento Bee*, August 23, 1943.

109. "Winning Serviceman Is Awarded a Date with Rochelle Hudson," *Des Moines Tribune*, August 10, 1943.

110. "Rochelle Hudson Makes Brief Stop Here," *Daily Oklahoman*, November 24, 1943.

111. "Horrors! These Go on Shelf," *News-Journal* (Mansfield, OH), August 4, 1944.

112. "Indian Tribe Adopts Rochelle Hudson," *Democrat and Chronicle* (Rochester, NY), August 4, 1944.

113. "Rochelle Hudson Wins Divorce," *Los Angeles Times*, September 1, 1945.

114. *Wisconsin State Journal* (Madison, WI), September 9, 1948.

115. Ward Morehouse, "Lahr Hits Road Again and Loves It," *Indianapolis Star*, September 12, 1948.

116. Edwin Schallert, "Rochelle Hudson Would Continue in Stage Career," *Los Angeles Times*, October 17, 1948.

117. Ibid.

118. Sterling Sorensen, "Movie Reviews; Stage; Music," *Capital Times* (Madison, WI), September 9, 1948.

119. Bill Doudna, "Bert in 'Burlesque,'" *Madison* (WI) *State-Journal*, September 9, 1948.

120. John K. Sherman, "Words & Music," *Minneapolis Star*, September 14, 1948.

121. *Minneapolis Star-Tribune*, September 14, 1948.

122. Stanley Bligh, "Bert Lahr Revels in 'Burlesque,'" *Vancouver Sun*, September 25, 1948.

123. Tom Hazlitt, "Lahr Says Film Comic's Day is Done," *Vancouver Daily Province*, September 25, 1948.

124. Virg Langdon, "Bert Lahr Is Riotous," *Tacoma News-Tribune*, September 25, 1948.

125. Edwin Schallert, "'Burlesque' Bert Lahr Field Day," *Los Angeles Times*, October 19, 1948.

126. Henry Arnsten, "Bert Lahr Scores Hit as 'Burlesque' Star," *Valley Times* (North Hollywood, CA), October 20, 1948.

127. Hal Middlesworth, "On the Level," *Daily Oklahoman*, December 15, 1948.

128. Bucky Walter, "-30- for Stanford's Famed 'Tricky Dick,'" *San Francisco Examiner*, July 21, 1981.

129. Keith Monroe, "The Hottest Typewriter in Football," *Saturday Evening Post*, November 13, 1948.

130. Don Cameron, "Palm Valley," *Desert Sun* (Palm Springs, CA), December 21, 1948.

131. Cecil Smith, "Mason to Invade World of Children; Rochelle Hudson's New Career," *Los Angeles Times*, October 21, 1954.

132. Harold Heffernan, "Rochelle Hudson Returns to Her 'First Love,'" *Miami News*, September 8, 1963.

133. "Rochelle Hudson Wins Divorce from Dick Hyland," *Kansas City Times*, July 26, 1950.

134. "Wins Decree from Athlete," *Los Angeles Post-Record*, October 31, 1934.

135. "Dick Hyland Divorced by Actress Wife," *Daily News* (Los Angeles, CA), July 25, 1950.

136. Aline Mosby, "Rochelle Hudson Making TV Comeback to Fight Old Movies," *Santa Maria* (CA) *Times*, April 8, 1954.

137. G.D. Starn and Edwin M. Conder, letter to Rochelle Hudson, July 3, 1953. Box 1, Hudson Papers.

138. Mae Hudson, handwritten note, undated. Box 1, Hudson Papers.

139. John Lester, "Radio and Television," *York* (PA) *Daily Record*, April 27, 1954.

140. "TV Portraits—Rochelle Jackson," *Times-Mail* (Bedford, IN), May 8, 1954.

141. Mosby, "Rochelle Hudson Making."

142. Tom E. Danson, "News 'n' Notes Down TV's Star Lanes," *Napa Valley Register*, July 12, 1954.

143. "Mmm-MOM!" *TV Guide*, October 9, 1954

144. Wesley Hyatt, *Short-Lived Television Series, 1948–1978: Thirty Years of More Than 1,000 Flops* (Jefferson, NC: McFarland, 2003), p. 59.

145. Cecil Smith, "Mason to Invade World of Children; Rochelle Hudson's New Career," *Los Angeles Times*, October 21, 1954.

146. Hyatt, *Short-Lived Television Series*, p. 59.

147. Harold Heffernan, "Fay Wray Returns to Screen," *Birmingham* (AL) *News*, June 5, 1955.

148. "Trying Again," *Morning Call* (Allentown, PA), December 22, 1955.

149. "Rochelle Hudson and Thompson Remarried," *Ventura County Star-Free Press*, December 22, 1955.

150. "Rochelle Hudson Return to Ex-Spouse Reported," *Los Angeles Times*, December 22, 1955.

151. "Actress Weds Manufacturer," *Spokesman-Review* (Seattle, WA), October 1, 1956.

152. "Rochelle Hudson, Wed in Missouri, Arrives Home," *Los Angeles Citizen-News*, October 1, 1956.

153. "Actress Is a Bride Here," *Kansas City* (MO) *Times*, October 1, 1956.

154. Harold Heffernan, "Rochelle Hudson

Returns to Her 'First Love,'" *Miami News*, September 8, 1963.

155. "Rochelle Hudson, Film Star, and Mother Visit in City," *Bartlesville (OK) Examiner-Enterprise*, May 12, 1960.

156. Charles E. Davis, Jr., "Star Back into Movies After Lifelike [sic] Film," *Los Angeles Times*, February 2, 1964.

157. Robert E. Stevenson, letter to Rochelle Hudson, June 2, 1960. Box 2, Hudson Papers.

158. "Rochelle Hudson Back in Makeup," *Waco Tribune-Herald*, February 19, 1961.

159. Peter Bart, "Great Names from Past Return, But the Faces Have Changed," *Des Moines Register*, August 2, 1964.

160. Heffernan, "Rochelle Hudson Returns."

161. Bob Thomas, "Rochelle Hudson's Frank Comments Won Her Publicity and Condemnation," *Town Talk* (Alexandria, LA), October 10, 1963.

162. Lamparski, *Whatever Became Of*, p. 135.

163. Davis, "Star Back."

164. Eunice Field, "What's New?" *TV-Radio Mirror*, October 1963.

165. Heffernan, "Rochelle Hudson Returns."

166. Davis, "Star Back."

167. "Rochelle Hudson Has Reluctant Comeback," *Fresno Bee*, July 19, 1964.

168. "Melchior Is 'Treasurer of Nostalgia,'" *Daily Advertiser* (Lafayette, LA), February 26, 1989.

169. Rochelle Melchior Dupuie, personal interview.

170. Jack Bradford, "Hollywood Highlights," *Honolulu Star-Bulletin*, September 2, 1968.

171. Madeleine Myers, "Keeping Posted at Palm Desert C.C.," *Palm Desert Post*, September 11, 1969.

172. Adriane Scheinost, letter to author, August 24, 2021.

173. Rochelle E. McNear, telephone interview with the author, December 5, 2021. All other quotes from Ms. McNear are from this interview.

174. "Rochelle Hudson, Star of 1930s, Found Dead," *Intelligencer-Journal* (Lancaster, PA), January 20, 1972.

175. "Rochelle Hudson Found Dead; Appeared in 75 Early Pictures," *Courier-News* (Bridgewater, NJ), January 19, 1972.

176. "Rochelle Died of Pneumonia," *Desert Sun*, January 20, 1972.

177. "Melchior Is 'Treasurer of Nostalgia.'"

178. Madeleine Myers, "Keeping Posted at Palm Desert C.C.," *Palm Desert Post*, January 27, 1972.

179. Madeleine Myers, "Keeping Posted at Palm Desert C.C.," *Palm Desert Post*, May 2, 1972.

180. Evelanne Heyman, "Teenage Talent, Training, Tenacity Take Tributes," *Desert Sun*, May 22, 1973.

181. Luther Hathcock, letter to author, December 20, 2021.

182. Evelanne Heyman, "Palm Desert Country Club Calling," *Desert Sun*, November 28, 1973.

183. Evelanne Heyman, "Palm Desert Country Club Calling," *Desert Sun*, May 15, 1974.

184. Myers, "Keeping Posted," January 27, 1972.

185. Adriane Scheinost, letter to author, August 24, 2021.

Filmography

1. Eric Churchill, "Are These Our Eric Linden?" *Silver Screen*, February 1932.

2. Edith Lindeman, "Three Little Maids in Hollywood," *Times-Dispatch* (Richmond, VA), August 25, 1935.

3. Quoted in "Asides and Interludes," *Motion Picture Herald*, February 18, 1933.

4. "Girl Who Made Good in Movies Returns to Home," *Oklahoma News*, April 29, 1934.

5. Maddox, "Art Is the Bunk!"

6. Scott Eyman, *Print the Legend: The Life and Times of John Ford* (New York: Simon & Schuster, 1999), p. 145.

7. William Wellman, Jr., *Wild Bill Wellman, Hollywood Rebel* (New York: Pantheon Books, 2015), p. 301.

8. Patrick McGilligan, *Film Crazy: Interviews with Hollywood Legends* (New York: St. Martin's Press, 2000), pp. 240–241.

9. Kathleen Norris, *Walls of Gold* (New York: Triangle Books, 1941), p. 139.

10. Henry Willson, "Junior Hollywood Gossip," *New Movie Magazine*, July 1934.

11. Brooke Kroeger, *Fannie: The Amazing Rise to Fame of Author Fannie Hurst* (New York: Times Books, 1999), p. 205.

12. Marilyn Knowlden, *Little Girl in Big Pictures* (Albany, GA: BearManor Media, 2011), p. 77.

13. Gene Fowler and Bess Meredyth, *The Mighty Barnum* (New York: Garland, 1978), introduction.

14. S.R. Mook, "Studio News," *Silver Screen*, March 1935.

15. Leonard Maltin, *The Great Movie Comedians: From Charlie Chaplin to Woody Allen* (New York: Harmony Books, 1982), p. 117.

16. Shirley Temple Black, *Child Star: An Autobiography* (New York: McGraw-Hill, 1988), p. 106.

17. Leonard Maltin, *Hooked on Hollywood: Discoveries from a Lifetime of Film Fandom* (Pittsburgh: GoodKnight Books, 2018), p. 24.

18. Henry King, based on interviews by David Sheppard and Ted Parry, *Henry King, Director: From Silents to 'Scope* (Los Angeles: Directors Guild of America, 1995), p. 93.

19. "Previewing the New Pictures," *Hollywood*, October 1935.

20. Acker, "A Date."

21. "Show Them No Mercy," Motion Picture Association of America, Production Code Administration Records, 1927–1967, http://catalog.oscars.edu/vwebv/holdingsinfo?bibid.+66279.

22. Van Neste, *They Coulda Been*, p. 274.

23. Eleanor Barnes, "Cesar Romeo Is Romantic; Doesn't Want to Be 'Nice,'" *Illustrated Daily News* (Los Angeles, CA), November 15, 1935.

24. Houston, "Dropping In."

25. "When Illness Hits Hollywood," *Hollywood*, July 1936.
26. "Rochelle Hudson Hurt," *Miami News-Record*, February 13, 1936.
27. James Curtis, *W.C. Fields: A Biography* (New York: Knopf, 2003), p. 337.
28. Michael A. Hoey, *Elvis' Favorite Director: The Amazing 52-Year Career of Norman Taurog* (Duncan, OK: BearManor Media, 2014), p. 29.
29. Daniel B. Clark, "Restrictions Hedge Quints When They Are Brought Before Camera," *American Cinematographer*, August 1938.
30. Whitney Williams, "She's 21," *Silver Screen*, August 1937.
31. "Rochelle Hudson Hurts Wrist, Socking Mike," *The Courier-Post* (Camden, NJ), March 13, 1937.
32. "The Cutting Room," *Motion Picture Herald*, February 13, 1937.
33. Ken Hanke, *Charlie Chan at the Movies: History, Filmography, and Criticism* (Jefferson, NC: McFarland, 1989), p. 255.
34. Peter Ford, *Glenn Ford: A Life* (Madison: University of Wisconsin Press, 2001), p. 30.
35. "In Movies It's Warm in Winter, Cold in Summer," *Indianapolis Star*, September 8, 1940.
36. "Full-Length Canadian Movies by Dominion Productions Ltd.," *The Financial Post* (Toronto), June 8, 1946.
37. "May Create Film Studio in B.C. for Canadian Pictures," *Victoria* (B.C.) *Daily Times*, October 29, 1946.
38. "'Possessed' Features New Capitol Bill Now Playing," *Windsor* (Ontario) *Star*, December 6, 1947.
39. Lawrence Frascella and Al Weisel, *Live Fast, Die Young: The Wild Ride of Making Rebel Without a Cause* (New York: Simon & Schuster, 2005), p. 137.
40. Ibid., p. 150.
41. William Castle, *Step Right Up! I'm Gonna Scare the Pants Off America* (New York: Pharos Books, 1992), p. 182.
42. Tom Weaver, *Eye on Science Fiction: 20 Interviews with Classic SF and Horror Filmmakers* (Jefferson, NC: McFarland, 2007), p. 184.
43. Ibid., p. 186.
44. Charles Solomon, "Getting a Picture of Early Film Cartoons," *Los Angeles Times*, December 25, 1985.
45. Michael Barrier, *Hollywood Cartoons: American Animation in Its Golden Age* (New York: Oxford University Press, 1999), p. 155.
46. Solomon, "Getting a Picture."
47. "Harman-Ising to Make 18 Animated Musicals," *Film Daily*, June 3, 1933.
48. Glenn McNeil, "It's in the Air," *Knoxville* (TN) *News-Sentinel*, March 31, 1938.
49. "'That's My Boy' Makes TV Debut April 10 Starring Eddie Mayehoff," *Boston Daily Globe*, April 6, 1954.
50. Donald Freeman, "'My Boy' Proves Headache to Dad," *San Pedro News-Pilot*, April 23, 1954.

51. "CBS Slates Re-Runs of Comedies," *Victoria* (TX) *Advocate*, June 21, 1959.
52. Ed Keath, "Mayehoff May Have a Winner with 'That's My Boy' Entry," *St. Louis Globe-Democrat*, April 25, 1954.
53. Bob Foster, "'Cinderella' to Get Two TV Airings," *San Mateo Times*, February 28, 1957.
54. *TV Guide*, April 16, 1954.
55. *Daily Independent* (Kannapolis, NC), May 9, 1954.
56. *Boston Globe*, May 8, 1954.
57. *Windsor Star* (Ontario, Canada), May 15, 1954.
58. *TV Guide*, May 21, 1954.
59. *Latrobe* (PA) *Bulletin*, May 29, 1954.
60. *TV Guide*, June 4, 1954.
61. *Boston Globe*, June 12, 1954.
62. *Evening Sun* (Baltimore, MD), June 19, 1954.
63. *Tucson Citizen*, June 26, 1954.
64. *Capital Journal* (Salem, OR), July 3, 1954.
65. *Latrobe* (PA) *Bulletin*, July 10, 1954.
66. *San Mateo* (CA) *Times*, July 17, 1954.
67. *Fort Worth Star-Telegram*, July 14, 1954.
68. *Ventura County Star-Free Press*, July 31, 1954.
69. *TV Guide*, August 7, 1954.
70. *Boston Globe*, August 14, 1954.
71. *TV Guide*, August 21, 1954.
72. *Boston Globe*, August 28, 1954.
73. *Detroit Free Press*, September 4, 1954.
74. *TV Guide*, September 18, 1954.
75. *Rock Island* (IL) *Argus*, September 25, 1954.
76. *TV Guide*, October 2, 1954.
77. *TV Guide*, October 9, 1954.
78. *Long Beach Independent*, October 16, 1954.
79. *Fort Worth Star-Telegram*, October 23, 1954.
80. *Waco* (TX) *News-Tribune*, October 23, 1954.
81. *TV Guide*, November 6, 1954.
82. *Times-Mail* (Bedford, IN), November 13, 1954.
83. *Latrobe* (PA) *Bulletin*, November 20, 1954.
84. *TV Guide*, November 27, 1954.
85. *Times-Mail* (Bedford, IN), November 27, 1954.
86. *Times-Mail* (Bedford, IN), December 4, 1954.
87. *Times-Mail* (Bedford, IN), December 11, 1954.
88. *TV Guide*, January 1, 1955.

Guest Performances
89. *Broadcasting*, October 22, 1951.
90. "Bob Lanigan's TV Review," *Brooklyn Daily Eagle*, March 5, 1952.
91. *Daily Times* (Davenport, IA), October 10, 1952.
92. Horace Newcomb, *Encyclopedia of Television*, 2d ed. (New York: Fitzroy Dearborn, 2004), p. 81.
93. Patrick McGilligan, *Robert Altman, Jumping Off the Cliff* (New York: St. Martin's Press, 1991), p. 104.
94. *TV Guide*, September 13, 1955.
95. *Star-Gazette* (Elmira, NY), March 27, 1965.
96. "Door-to-Door Selling Via TV Commercials," *Broadcasting*, November 28, 1955.

Bibliography

Alexander, Linda. *I Am Mister Ed: Allan "Rocky" Lane Revealed.* Duncan, OK: BearManor Media, 2014.
Arce, Hector. *The Secret Life of Tyrone Power.* New York: Morrow, 1979.
Barrier, Michael. *Hollywood Cartoons: American Animation in Its Golden Age.* New York: Oxford University Press, 1999.
Black, Shirley Temple. *Child Star: An Autobiography.* New York: McGraw-Hill, 1988.
Castle, William. *Step Right Up! I'm Gonna Scare the Pants Off America.* New York: Pharos Books, 1992.
Crivello, Kirk. "Rochelle Hudson." *Film Fan Monthly* #166, April 1975.
Curtis, James. *W.C. Fields: A Biography.* New York: Knopf, 2003.
Custen, George F. *Twentieth Century's Fox: Darryl F. Zanuck and the Culture of Hollywood.* New York: BasicBooks, 1997.
Davis, Ronald L. *Mary Martin, Broadway Legend.* Norman: University of Oklahoma Press, 2014.
Eyman, Scott. *Print the Legend: The Life and Times of John Ford.* New York: Simon & Schuster, 1999.
_____. *20th Century-Fox: Darryl F. Zanuck and the Creation of the Modern Film Studio.* Philadelphia: Running Press, 2021.
Ford, Peter. *Glenn Ford: A Life.* Madison: University of Wisconsin Press, 2001.
Fowler, Gene, and Bess Meredyth. *The Mighty Barnum.* New York: Garland, 1978.
Frascella, Lawrence, and Al Weisel. *Live Fast, Die Young: The Wild Ride of Making Rebel Without a Cause.* New York: Simon & Schuster, 2005.
Gussow, Mel. *Don't Say Yes Until I Finish Talking: A Biography of Darryl F. Zanuck.* Garden City, NY: Doubleday, 1971.
Hanke, Ken. *Charlie Chan at the Movies: History, Filmography, and Criticism.* Jefferson, NC: McFarland, 1989.
Hoey, Michael A. *Elvis' Favorite Director: The Amazing 52-Year Career of Norman Taurog.* Duncan, OK: BearManor Media, 2014.
"The Hottest Typewriter in Football: The 'Drop Kick' Who Lived the American Dream." https:oztypewriter.blogspot.com/2015/10/the-hottest-typewriter-in-football-drop.html, accessed December 20, 2021.
Hyatt, Wesley. *Short-Lived Television Series, 1948–1978: Thirty Years of More Than 1,000 Flops.* Jefferson, NC: McFarland, 2003.
Irvin, Richard. *George Burns Television Productions.* Jefferson, NC: McFarland, 2014.
Kaufman, David. *Some Enchanted Evenings: The Glittering Life and Times of Mary Martin.* New York: St. Martin's Press, 2016.
Knowlden, Marilyn. *Little Girl in Big Pictures.* Albany, GA: BearManor Media, 2011.
Kroeger, Brooke. *Fannie: The Amazing Rise to Fame of Author Fannie Hurst.* New York: Times Books, 1999.
Lamparski, Richard. *Whatever Became of: Third Series.* New York: Crown, 1970.
Lemmo, David. *Tarzan, Jungle King of Popular Culture.* Jefferson, NC: McFarland, 2017.
Maltin, Leonard. *The Great Movie Comedians: From Charlie Chaplin to Woody Allen.* New York: Harmony Books, 1982.
_____. *Hooked on Hollywood: Discoveries from a Lifetime of Film Fandom.* Pittsburgh: GoodKnight Books, 2014.
Newcomb, Horace. *Encyclopedia of Television.* 2d ed. New York: Fitzroy Dearborn, 2004.
Norris, Kathleen. *Walls of Gold.* New York: Triangle Books, 1941.
Roberts, Barrie. "Rochelle Hudson: Square Peg in a Round Hole." *Classic Images,* #272, February 1998.
Rollins, Peter C. *Will Rogers: A Bio-Bibliography.* Westport, CT: Greenwood Press, 1984.
Staggs, Sam. *Born to Be Hurt: The Untold Story of Imitation of Life.* New York: St. Martin's Press, 2009.
Terrace, Vincent. *Encyclopedia of Television Shows, 1925 through 2010.* 2d ed. Jefferson, NC: McFarland, 2011.
Van Neste, Dan. *They Coulda Been Contenders: Twelve Actors Who Should Have Become Cinematic Superstars.* Orlando: BearManor Media, 2019.

Vermilye, Jerry. *Buster Crabbe: A Biofilmography*. Jefferson, NC: McFarland, 2014.
Weaver, Tom. *Eye on Science Fiction: 20 Interviews with Classic SF and Horror Filmmakers*. Jefferson, NC: McFarland, 2007.
Weldon, Michael, with Charles Beesley, Bob Martin, and Akira Fitton. *The Psychotronic Encyclopedia of Film*. New York: Ballantine Books, 1983.
Wellman, William, Jr. *Wild Bill Wellman, Hollywood Rebel*. New York: Pantheon Books, 2015.
Youngkin, Stephen D. *The Lost One: A Life of Peter Lorre*. Lexington: University Press of Kentucky, 2005.

Archival Materials

Hudson, Rochelle, and Leonora Mae Hudson. *Papers, 1916–1972*. Accession #6792. American Heritage Center, University of Wyoming, Laramie, WY.

Websites

The AFI Film Catalog, https://catalog.afi.com.
www.findagrave.com.
The Internet Movie Database, www.imdb.com.
Media History Digital Library, https://mediahistoryproject.org/.
www.newspapers.com.

Index

Numbers in ***bold italic*** indicate pages with photographs

The Addams Family 179
Alexander, Katharine 126
"Alibi Ike" 187
Alice Adams 137
Allen, Fred 55, 56
Allen, Vera 67
Allwyn, Astrid 99, 116
Altman, Robert 195
Ames, Rosemary 76
Anderson, Eddie 104
Angel's Holiday 125
Are These Our Children 14, 52–54
Arledge, John 15
Arlen, Richard 134
Armand, Joseph S. 34
"Armored Taxi" 120
Asmussen, Julia 35
Atwater, Edith 177
Auer, John H. 136

Babies for Sale 29, 149–***151***
Bachelor Bait 18, 77–79
Backus, Jim 175
Baker, Diane 177
Bakewell, Billy 25
Baldwin, Bill 188
Ballard, W.C. 9
Baly, Henry William 32
Barbier, George 91, 137
Bari, Lynn 96
Barker, Lillian Kenton 155
Barnum, Phineas T. 86–87
Barnum and Bailey Circus 86
Barrett, Claudia 188
Barrie, Mona 76
Barrymore, Diana 125
Barthelmess, Richard 97
Bartlett, Michael 104
Barton, Charles 148, 150
Baxter, Warner 76, 77
Beal, John 94
Beavers, Louise 18, 56, 65, 83–84
Beck, Thomas 117
Beecher, Janet 87
Beery, Wallace 87
Belcher, Ernest 10
Bennett, Bruce 150
Bennett, Constance 183
Bennett, Joan 183
Bennett, Marjorie 180

Berke, William 171
Beyond the Rockies 14, 54–56
Bing, Herman 104
Blackmer, Sidney 160
Blake, Larry 188
Blake, Pamela 172
Blandick, Clara 75
Blane, Sally 125
Bloch, Robert 177, 179
The Blood Suckers see *Gallery of Horror*
Blue, Monte 183
Bogart, Humphrey 134
Boles, John 23, 96
Boleslawski, Richard 94
Boone, Pat 196
Borden, Olive 108
Born Reckless 119–121
Borzage, Frank 12
Bosko 185–186
Branded 46, ***197***, 198
Brasno, George 87
Brasno, Olive 87
Breck, Peter 198
Bright Eyes 124
Bromberg, J. Edward 118, 128
Brown, Helen 150
Brown, Joe E. 183, 187
Brown, Marie 23
Brown, Melville ***13***
Brown, Tom 23, 26, 56, 81
Bruce, Virginia 87
Brust, Charles Kenneth, Jr. 43–44
Bryar, Paul ***164***
"Buck the Wonder Dog" 108
Burke's Law 132
Burlesque 36–37
Burnap, Sidney 26
Burroughs, Edgar Rice 29
Burroughs, Florence 29
Bush Pilot 2, 35, 166–168, ***167***
Byington, Spring 99
Byron, Walter 60

Cabot, Bruce ***101***–102, 153, 184
Caine, Georgia 150, ***151***
Calvert, John 168–169
Campbell, Sterling 167
Carey, Harry 121

Carrillo, Leo 23
Cartwright, Charles 33
"The Case of Captain Denning" 195
Castle, William 45, 177
Chambers, Stan 196
Chandler, Chick 75, 121, 128
Chesterfield Pictures 16, 62–63, 64
A Christmas Carol 136
Christmas Lane Parade 196
Chrysler Corporation 190, 195–196
Churchill, Berton 81
Cimarron 52, 54
Claremore, Oklahoma 3, 20
Clark, Daniel B. 114
Clute, Chester 126
Cobb, Irvin S. 23, 81–82, 107
Cohn, Harry 27
Colbert, Claudette 18, 83, ***84***
Coleman, C.C., Jr. 134
Columbia Pictures 27
Comingore, Dorothy 144
"Communications" 45
Compson, Betty 65
Conkey, Louie 5
Convicted Woman 29
Cook, Jenny 49
Coonan, Dorothy 68–69
Corday, Mara 197
Corey, Wendell ***197***, 198
The Corn Is Green 153
The Corpse Vanishes 173
Cortez, Ricardo ***162***
The Country Beyond 24, 108–***109***
The Country Doctor 115
"The Cowboy and the Blind Man Story" 195
Crawford, Joan 2, 14, 45–46, 177
Cromwell, Richard 91, 112, 129
Crosman, Henrietta 77
Curly Top 21, 94–96, ***95***, 125
Curwood, James Oliver 108

Dafoe, Allan R. 114
Dale, Esther 144
Dancing in the Streets 34
Dane, Bonnie Irma 158
Darling, W. Scott 168

207

208   Index

Darro, Frankie 68
Darwell, Jane 91, 96
A Date with Judy 159
Daughters of Today see *Convicted Woman*
Davis, Bette 134, 184
The Dawn Patrol 167
Day in Court 45, **196**, 197–198
Dean, James 43, 48, 174
The Dean Martin Show 48
de Cordova, Fred 25
Dee, Sandra 85
Deere and Company 172–173
Desert Symphony Auxiliary 49
Desmond, Florence 71, 72
Devil's Cargo 168–170
Devine, Andy 67, 99
The Diary of a Line Smasher: Adventures of a College Football Player 37
Dillaway, Donald 65
Dillon, Josephine 32, 33
Dinehart, Alan 109
Dionne Quintuplets 114–115
"The Director" 196
Dix, Richard 56, **58**
Doc Corkle 188
Doctor Bull 17, 20, 65–67, 81
Dr. Terror's Gallery of Horror see *Gallery of Horror*
Dominion Productions 167
Donlevy, Brian 120–121
Doucet, Catherine 112
Downs, Johnny **106,** 107, 194
Dratler, Jay 155
Duna, Steffi 125
Dunbar, Dixie 27
Dunn, James 131
Dunne, Irene 195
Dwan, Allan 116, 118

Earhart, Amelia 128
Eburne, Maude 113
Edwards, Cliff 136
Eichelberger, Buddy 21
Eilers, Sally 44
Eldridge, Florence 93
Ellis, Dellie *see* Lorring, Joan
"Entertainment on Wheels" 195–196
Erickson, Leif 177
Erwin, Stuart 18, 78
Everybody's Old Man 23, 70, 105–108, **106,** 184, 194
Everything's Rosie 183

Fanny Foley Herself 14, 51–52, 183
Faye, Alice 184
Fetchit, Stepin 81
Fidler, Jimmie 184
Field, Mary 144
Fields, W.C. 48, **111**–112
Finkel, Bob 188
Fiske, Richard **138**
The Fleet's In 104
Florey, Robert 155
Fonda, Henry 19, **98**
Forbes, Brenda 194

Ford, Francis 81
Ford, Glenn 144, 145
Ford, John 81
Forde, Eugene 108
Foster, Norman 70
Foulger, Byron 156, 158
Fowler, Gene 87
Fox, Wallace 173
Fox Studios 11–12, 15, 16–21, 23–27
Foxy & Roxy 187
Francis, Kay 70
Frascella, Lawrence 174–175
Freedley, Vincent 34
Freeman, Everett 188

Gallagher, "Skeets" 78–79
Gallery of Horror 47, 180–182, **181**
Gaynor, Janet 12, 19, 23, 184
Gemora, Charles 60
The George Gobel Show 190
The Ghost and Mr. Chicken 179
Gilligan's Island 163
Girardot, Etienne 96
Girl Crazy 183
Girls Under 21 151–154, **153**
Gish, Lillian 97
Glasmon, Kubec 102
Gobel, George 42, 190
Goddard, Homer Clinton 9, **10, 30, 40**
Goddard, Homer Deane **40,** 47, 50
Goddard, John 20
Goddard, Rachel Elizabeth Coppinger 5, 6
Goddard, Rochelle 9, **40,** 47–48, 50
Gone with the Wind 158
Goodman, Dody 44
Graham, Sheilah 42
Grant, Cary 61
Gray, Coleen 198
The Great American Harem see *Bachelor Bait*
The Greatest Show on Earth 9
Green, Harry 72
Green Acres 179
Griffith, D.W. 97, 98
Grindé, Nick 141, 142, 145
Gurie, Sigrid 185

Haden, Sara 99, 184
Hadley, Reed 194
Hale, Alan, Jr. 163
Haley, Jack 122–123
Hamilton, Margaret 99
Hanke, Ken 127
Happy Harmonies 185
Harlow, Jean 183
Harman, Hugh 185
"The Harmonica Rascals" 125
Harold Teen 50, 73–75
Hart, Eddie 56
Hathcock, Luther 49
Haydon, Julie 184
Hayworth, Vinton 158
Hell's Angels 167

Hell's Highway 56–59, **58**
Helm, Anne 177
Henie, Sonja 116
Henry, Bill 162
Here's Lucy 102
Hersholt, Jean 114–115
Heydt, Louis Jean 194
Hollywood Hotel 107
Hollywood Open House 34, 187
"Hollywood Starlit" 31
Honey, I Shrunk the Kids 182
Hoover, J. Edgar 100
Hopper, Hedda 38
Hopper, William 175
How Do I Know It's Sunday 187
Howard, Cy 41, 188, 190
Hudson, Leonora Mae Goddard 1, 5–15, **10,** 17, 20, **22,** 24, 27–29, 32, **40,** 48, 49–50
Hudson, Ollie Lee 5–14, 15, 44, 48
Hugo, Victor 93
Humberstone, H. Bruce 126
Hurst, Fannie 82
Hyland, Dick 37–39
"The Hyland Fling" 37

I Am a Fugitive from a Chain Gang 56
I Dream of Jeannie 158, 180
I Married Joan 175
I'm the Law 195
Imitation of Life (1934) 2, 18, 50, 82–85, **84**
Imitation of Life (1959) 85
In Old Arizona 76
Is My Face Red? 183
Ising, Rudolf 185
Island in the Sky 121
Island of Doomed Men 146–149, **147**
It's a Great Life 131
I've Been Around 88–89

Jane Wyman Presents the Fireside Theatre 196
Jessel, George 31
Jewell, Isabel 89, 134, 150, **151**
Jones, Edgar Allan, Jr. 198
Jones, Russ 182
Jory, Victor **157,** 158
Journey to the Center of Time 182
Judge, Arline 53–54, 185
Judge Priest 79–81
Jukebox Jury 194

Kalloch, Robert 148
Karns, Roscoe 170
The Kate Smith Hour 187
Keaton, Buster 183
Keene, Tom 14, 55
Kelly, Paul **153**
Kelton, Pert 79
Kennedy, Florence 168
Kennedy, Tom 160
Kent, Robert 108, 115, 128
King, Henry 98
Kirkland, Fairy 7–8, 49
Kleeb, Helen 188

Kline, Benjamin 148
Knowlden, Marilyn 85, 93
Knowles, Patric 129
Konga the Wild Stallion 137–*138*
Krasna, Norman 26
Kruger, Otto 141

A Lady's Morals 87
Lahr, Bert 2, 35–37
Lally, Howard 67
Lambert, David 118
Lamont, Charles 131
Lane, Allan 25
Lane, Charles 121
Lane, Lola 144
Lane, Richard 155–156
Lang, June 115, *143,* 144
La Rue, Jack 118, *167*
Laugh and Get Rich 14, 52, 183
Laughton, Charles 93, 94
LeBaron, William 13, 54
Lee, Jessie 11
"The Legend of Leckonby" 196–197
Le Roy, Harold 74–75
Leslie, Aleen 158–159
Levien, Sonya 114
Lewis, Jerry 188
Life Begins at 40 89–91
Lind, Jenny 86, 87
Linden, Eric 14, 53
Lippert, Robert L. 171
Litel, John 145
The Little Professor see *Girls Under 21*
Lloyd, Harold 46
Lockhart, Gene 89
Long, Richard 197
Look Out, Mr. Moto see *Mr. Moto Takes a Chance*
Looney Tunes 185
Lorre, Peter 127, *147,* 148
Lorring, Joan 153
Louise, Anita 14, 81
Love Is Dangerous 62–63
Love Is Like That see *Love Is Dangerous*
Loy, Myrna 184
Luciano, Lucky 134
Lucky Devils 184
The Lux Radio Theater 187
Lydell, Al 99
Lynn, Emmett *164*

MacDonald, Kenneth 148
MacKay, Barry *136*
MacKenna, Kenneth 70
MacLane, Barton 121
MacMurray, Fred 184
Madame X 140
Majors, Lee 177
Mallory, Boots 17
Malone, Dorothy 144
Maltin, Leonard 98
Man Without a Country see *Men Without Souls*
Mander, Miles 150
March, Fredric 18, *92,* 93–94

Mark, Michael 170
Marked Woman 133–134
Marquand, J.P. 127
Marsh, Marian 64, 185
Marsha, the Erotic Housewife 182
Marshall, George 102
Marshall, Herbert 194
Martin, Dean 188
Martin, Mary 34
Maxwell, John 188
Maxwell, Max 185
Mayehoff, Eddie 41–*42,* 188–191, *189,* 196
Mayo, Donald 165
McCadden Productions 189
McCrea, Joel 184
McCullough, Rusty 165
McDaniel, Hattie 81, 84, 115
McGilligan, Patrick 195
McKay, George 158
McKeen, Marion 27
McKenzie, Fay 36
McMahon, Horace 131, 158
McNear, Rochelle Goddard see Goddard, Rochelle
McQuarrie, Haven 187
Medford, Kay 48
Meek, Donald 107
Meet Boston Blackie 154–156
Melchior, L.C. 46–47, 48
Men Without Souls 144–146
Menjou, Adolphe 87
Mercer, Beryl 141
Meredyth, Bess 87
Merrie Melodies 187
Methot, Mayo *140,* 141
Middleton, Charles 56, 148
The Mighty Barnum 85–88
Miller, Virgil 128
Mindell, Robert Lewis 45, 47, 48, 49
Mineo, Sal 174
Minevitch, Borrah *125*–126
Les Misérables 2, 18, 91–94, *92*
Missing Daughters 28, 65, 133–134
Mister Ed 25
Mr. Moto Takes a Chance 126–128
Mr. Skitch 17, 66, 70–73, *72*
Mizzy, Vic 179
Moore, Juanita 85
Morgan, Ralph 89, 137
Morris, Chester 89, 155
Motion Picture and Television Fund 50
Motion Picture Mothers, Inc. 23
Mummert, Danny 158
The Music Goes 'Round 103–105
"The Music Goes 'Round and Around" 104–105
Myers, Harry C. 60

Nagel, John 16
Naish, J. Carrol 65
National Film Registry 50, 69, 85, 175
Naval Aid Auxiliary 34

The Night Walker 178–180
Nine Million Women see *Such Women Are Dangerous*
Nixon, Marian 67
Noah Webster Says 34, 187
Norris, Edward 19, 25, *101*-102
Norris, Kathleen 70
Notorious But Nice 63–65, 140

The Officer and the Lady 138, 150, 159–161
Oliver, Edna May 14, 15, 52, 183
Oliver, Gordon 131, 141
Ottiano, Rafaela 96
Overman, Lynne 112

Pallette, Eugene 72, 121
Palm Desert Country Club 47, 49
Pangborn, Franklin 123
Parker, Jean 31, 36, 69
Parker, Lottie Blair 97
Parsons, Louella O. 18, 19–20, 21, 23, 27, 29, 34, 35
The Past of Mary Holmes 184
Peach Edition see *Woman-Wise*
The Penguin Pool Murder 15, 183
Perry Mason 148, 175
Phillips, Edwin 68
Picture People 185
Pierlot, Francis 189
Pinocchio 136
Pirates of the Skies 132–133
Pitkin, Walter B. 90
Pitts, ZaSu 71–72
Plan 9 from Outer Space 55, 172
Poppy 110–113, *111*
Potter, Peter 194
Powell, Dick 107
Power, Tyrone 26
Poynter, Beulah 62
PRC see Producers Releasing Corporation
Price, Walter 47, 48
The Pride of the Family 175
Pride of the Navy 130–132
Prince (dog) 108
The Private Life of Don Juan 136
Private Secretary 41
Producers Releasing Corporation 2
Professional Father 190
Pryor, Roger 160
The Public Defender 18, 183
Pulse of the City 195
Puttin' on the Ritz 104

Qualen, John 115, 150
Queen of Broadway 2, 3, 32, 163–166, *164*

Racket Squad 40, 188, 194
Raft, George 195
Ralston, Esther 115
Ramona 23, 24
Ramsay, Quen see Smith, Quentin
Randolph, Roy 34
Rascals 123–126

Ray, Nicholas 174
Rebel Without a Cause 2, 43, 44, 50, 173–175
Reed, Tobe 187
Republic Studios 27
Return from the Past see *Gallery of Horror*
The Return of Boston Blackie see *Meet Boston Blackie*
Reunion 113–116
Rice, Florence 125
Richman, Harry 104
Ring 194
Rivero, Julian 56
RKO Radio Pictures 12–14, 15–16
Robb, Cleora 72
Robb, Glorea 72
Roberts, Allene 189
Robinson, Ray 172
"The Rochelle Hudson Tango" 44
Rocky King, Detective 170
Rogers, Will 17, 18, 20, 23, 31, 66–67, 71, 73, 81–82, 90, 107, 138
Rollin' Along see *The Music Goes 'Round*
Romero, Cesar **101**–102
Roots in the Soil 39, 75, 172–173
Rorke, Hayden 180
Rosenbloom, "Slapsie" Maxie **157**, 158
Rubber Racketeers 161–163, **162**
Ruggles, Wesley 53, 54

St. Clair, Malcolm 122
St. John, Howard 177
St. Johns, Adela Rogers 38–39
Sally of the Sawdust 112
The Savage Girl 16, 59
Sawtelle Veterans' Administration Hospital 40
Sayre, George Wallace 165
Scarlet River 184
Scheinost, Adriane 47, 50
Schertzinger, Victor 104
Schlesinger, Leon 185
Schlitz Playhouse of Stars 194, 195
Screen Snapshots 183, 184, 185
Secrets of the French Police 184
Seiler, Lewis 118
77 Sunset Strip 45, 196–197
She Done Him Wrong 16, 61–62
She Had to Eat 121–123
Sheehan, Winfield 12, 18, 21, 23
Shoestring '57 44
Show Them No Mercy! 20, 26, 99–102, **101**
Shower of Stars 195–196
Shurlock, Geoffrey 101
Shurr, Louis 36
"The Simple Things in Life" 96
Simpson, Russell 99
Sinkin' in the Bathtub 185
Sirk, Douglas 85
Sky Liner 39, 170–172
Slaughter, Anna May 172

Smith, John 189
Smith, Lucile Rawling 32
Smith, Quentin 32, 33
Smuggled Cargo 134–137, **136**
Snatched see *Show Them No Mercy!*
Sothern, Ann 41, 184
Stahl, John M. 82, 85
Stander, Lionel 104
Stanwyck, Barbara 179
Starrett, Charles **72**
Stern, Stewart 174
Stevens, George 18, 79
Stone, Fred 137, **138**
Stone, George E. 148, 156
The Stork Pays Off 156–159, **157**
Storm Over Bengal 128–130
Strait-Jacket 2, 45–**46,** 176–178
Stratton, Gil, Jr. 41–43, 188–190, **189,** 196
The Stu Erwin Show see *The Trouble with Father*
Such Women Are Dangerous 3, 75–77
"Sugar House" 82
Sullivan, Ed 3, 20, 25, 27, 33, 34, 125
Summerville, Slim 99, 115
The Sun Shines Bright 82
Sutherland, A. Edward 112
Sutton, Grady 79

Tainted Money see *Show Them No Mercy!*
Talbot, Lyle 170, 194
Tamiroff, Akim 194, 195
Tarzan the Ape Man 59
Taylor, Kent 132
Taylor, Robert 179
Temple, Shirley 21, 95, 124
That I May Live 116, 117–**119**
That's My Boy 41, **42,** 44, 188–193, **189**
The Thing with Two Heads 182
Thompson, Harold Edward Mexia (Hal) 2, 27–**28,** 29, **30,** 31–32, 34, 43
Thorpe, Richard 62
The Three Stooges 184, 185
The Three Wishes 10
Tong, Kam 163
The Tonight Show 25
Too Many Women see *Such Women Are Dangerous*
Toomey, Regis 132
Toones, Fred "Snowflake" 84
Trans World Airlines 171–172
Travis, Richard 172
Treacher, Arthur 96, 121
Treasure Quest 194
A Tree Grows in Brooklyn 131
Treen, Mary 131
"Trouble on Pier Twelve" 195
The Trouble with Father 78
Trowbridge, Charles 131

Turner, Lana 85
20th Century-Fox 21–27, 43, 45, 102, 127

The Unexpected 194
United States Coast Guard Band 34
Universal Pictures 18, 27
The Unwritten Law see *Devil's Cargo*

Vallée, Rudy 34
Van Nuys High School 9
Verdugo, Elena 194, 195
Verner, Lois 154
Visit to a Small Planet 190
Vohs, Joan 198
The Voice of Hollywood 183

Wagenheim, Charles 156
Walls of Gold 16, 44, 69–70
Walter Winchell's Jergens Journal 187
Walthall, Henry B. 81
WAMPAS Baby Stars 2, 14–15, 64, 183, 187
Warburton, John 62
Warner, Jack 69
Washington, Fredi 84
Way Down East 19, 21, 24, 96–99, **98**
Wayne, Patrick 198
Weeks, Barbara 14
Weigel, John 194
Weissmuller, Johnny 184
Wellman, William 17, 68–69
Wellman, William, Jr. 69
Wells, Marie 56
West, Mae 16, 61–62
West, Vera 84–85
Whalen, Michael 115, 116
White, Sam 160
Wilcox, Robert **125**
Wild Boys of the Road 17, 50, 67–69
William, Warren 18, **84**
Willis, Austin 168
Willow 182
Winchell, Walter 20, 27, 35, 134, 187
Wissman, Josephine 8
Withers, Jane 124–125
Wolfe, Bill 112–113
A Woman Is the Judge 139–141
Woman-Wise 116–117
Wood, Edward D., Jr. 55, 172
Wood, Natalie 174, 175
Worth, Constance 156
Wurtzel, Sol M. 27

Young, Loretta 23–24
Youngkin, Stephen D. 127, 148

Zanuck, Darryl F. 18, 21, 24, 25, 87, 101, 114

www.ingramcontent.com/pod-product-compliance
Lightning Source LLC
Chambersburg PA
CBHW060343010526
44117CB00017B/2941